A Farthing for the Ferryman

The Surprising Story of a Norfolk Village

Richard L. Coates

Published by Harpsden Press 2019

ISBN:
978-1-9998236-2-7 - paperback
978-1-9998236-7-2 - ebook

Contents

Introduction

Stoke Ferry – Market Town or Hamlet?

Stoke Ferry has an amazing history. The Iceni, Romans, Angles and Vikings all left their mark before the Normans arrived. From the Middle Ages, it was a bustling market town, with a busy inland port on the River Wissey. It was a centre of trade by river and road, a lively hub for drovers and a staging post for changing horses and refreshing passengers in the extensive stage coach traffic of the late eighteenth and early nineteenth centuries. Later that century, the railway produced a further economic boost.

When the first edition of this book was written by my mother in 1980 under the title *Stoke Ferry – The Story of a Norfolk Village*, it clearly qualified for the title of 'Village'. There was a school, several shops including a chemist, a doctor's surgery, at least four public houses, a chapel and, most importantly for the definition, an Anglican Church.

Today, Stoke Ferry, despite its recent growth in population, could be described as a hamlet, if the definition depends on the presence of an active parish church. All Saints Church was closed in 2002 and Anglican worship, christenings, marriages and funerals for Stoke Ferry's residents have since then been conducted in Wretton Church. Now, there is no church, chapel or doctor's surgery; there is only one shop, two takeaways and an occasional pub. The port and railway closed long ago.

Fortunately, perhaps, the Charter for the market and the fair has not been revoked, so technically at least Stoke Ferry can still claim the title of 'market town'.

This book describes how, long before Stoke Ferry existed as a recognisable community, humans lived in this part of Norfolk. For hundreds of thousands of years they were semi-nomadic, but when eventually they began to form settlements, their siting usually depended on the topography of the location. In the case of the settlement that came to be Stoke Ferry, two features were of paramount importance. Firstly, the land was slightly higher than the nearby fenland and free from flooding. And secondly, the river could be relatively easily crossed at that point, allowing for an embryonic roadway running north and south, skirting the fens.

It seems that the river was, however, too deep simply to ford (or its name may have ended up as Stokeford). The ferry was critical to the development of the community until replaced by a bridge, initially in the thirteenth century. Later, it is likely that the bridge and the ferry co-existed for periods of time.

Undoubtedly, the man who owned the boat would need payment for this vital service. While it is relatively clear *who pays the ferryman?* – the passengers for themselves, their freight and their animals – there is no record of how much they had to pay.

So why the title for this book? If one assumes that today a reasonable fare for a similar passenger ferry could be one pound[1], the equivalent fare in the thirteenth century would be a farthing[2].

A Farthing for the Ferryman traces the history of a relatively small but important piece of East Anglia from prehistoric times to the present day. It examines what created and shaped Stoke Ferry, how it came to be so wealthy, and how it is thriving or surviving into the twenty-first century. It is a truly surprising and fascinating story.

---

1   See Walberswick Ferry in Suffolk, for example

2   A farthing was one quarter of an old penny (240d in £1). Hence a farthing is £0.001

The First Part

In which is revealed
Ye Anciente Historie
from time immemorial of this place
known *as* STOCHES
in the time of Domesday

Chapter One

Prehistoric Times – Before the Romans

Nine hundred thousand years ago – yes, that's 900,000 – the area of land that we know as Norfolk was part of a very different geographic environment. To begin with, 'Britain' was truly part of Europe – there was no English Channel separating it from the rest of the continent. The coast of the 'North Sea' bordered the current Norfolk coast, and extended across to what is now the mouth of the Rhine in the Netherlands.

The great European rivers flowed into this sea – the Rhine much further north than today, whilst the mouth of the Thames was on the north-east 'Norfolk' coast at Happisburgh. At that time, another great river – the Bytham - crossed the peninsula of Britain, rising in 'the East Midlands', and joining the Thames somewhere near the 'Norfolk-Suffolk border'.

Recent discoveries – some the result of painstaking archaeological research over many decades and others the result of fortuitous conditions – provide proof that humans lived in this part of the world as long as 900,000 years ago.

At Happisburgh on the Norfolk coast, Pakefield on the Suffolk coast and across the Breckland area of south-west Norfolk, significant finds show that prehistoric people lived here. There is clear evidence that the River Bytham at one stage flowed through Tottenhill, Shouldham Thorpe and Feltwell, strongly suggesting that its course passed through, or very close to where Stoke Ferry is today.

It is thought that the climate in that era was similar to southern Scandinavia today, with mean winter temperatures ranging from 0° and -3°C, and summer temperatures between 16° and 18°C. This has largely been determined by analysis of the skeletons of numerous species of beetles whose tolerance for certain temperature bands is known and is further supported by the types of plant material and seeds found particularly at Happisburgh.

Animals at that time are likely to have included both herbivores and predators, living on the plains alongside the great rivers. They are thought to include mammoths, rhinos and horses as well as hyenas and sabre-toothed cats.

The Happisburgh Footprints

In May 2013 the oldest human footprints found anywhere outside Africa appeared on the beach at Happisburgh, exposed by the tide and the ongoing erosion of this part of the coast. Within two weeks they had been washed away by the same marine forces. Amazingly, before that happened, scientists using a technique known as photogrammetry to create 3D images were able to confirm that they were, indeed, human footprints.

The prints have been dated to the period 850,000 – 950,000 years ago, predating any others found in Europe by about 500,000 years. They appear to be from a group of about five individuals, pottering about on what would then have been the muddy bank of the Thames estuary, probably looking for food, most likely plants or shellfish. The group included children, the smallest of whom was about 0.9m tall (about 3ft). The clearest prints are about a UK 8 shoe-size – suggesting a man of about 1.7m (about 5ft 6in) in height.

The footprints support earlier finds by the Happisburgh project of fossilised animal bones and flint implements, which suggest that this bank of the Thames was one of the most northerly settlements in Europe in that era. They were dated from the overlying sedimentary layers and glacial deposits, as well as fossilised bones from a number of animals – a mammoth, a type of horse and a vole, all now extinct.

Unfortunately, as yet, no human remains have been found at Happisburgh, but on the evidence of the footprints, fossils, tools and animals found there, scientists[1] are fairly confident in their time estimate. They describe the humans of this era as *Homo Antecessor* or 'Pioneer Man' but will only be able to confirm this estimate as and when human fossils are discovered. What is clear, however, is that these finds substantially pre-date the Anglian Ice Age of about 450,000 years ago.

Breckland Paleolithic Discoveries

Meanwhile, fifty miles to the south-west, and much closer to Stoke Ferry, ongoing research over the past 150 years has confirmed that there were

---

1 Scientists working on this site were from the British Museum, The Natural History Museum and Queen Mary University of London. Information for this section is drawn from the British Museum website www.britishmuseum.org.

inhabitants of the Breckland area 600,000 years ago[2]. The studies of the Bytham river banks, in particular those at Maidscross Hill near Lakenheath and Frimstone's Pit near Feltwell date the findings at about 550,000 years ago, and certainly, again, before the Anglian Ice Age.

From these two sites and from Brandon Fields, a number of Acheulean[3] hand-axes, and scrapers have been discovered. Acheulean hand-axes are large chipped stone objects - the oldest, most common, and longest-used formally-shaped working tool ever made by humans. The sites provide some of the earliest evidence for use of these tools in north-west Europe.

Archaeologists have identified three types of axe of different degrees of development – crude thick hand-axes probably created by a hard-stone hammer, more refined egg-shaped or heart-shaped hand-axes, which may have been created using a softer hammer (antler or bone) and the third a series of elaborate scrapers. It is thought that these may have been made by independent groups of humans, probably originating from different areas of 'mainland Europe'. They are also quite dissimilar to simpler tools found at Happisburgh or at the Pakefield, site where discoveries of tools were dated to about 700,000 years ago.

The Anglian Ice Age

All the habitation which existed in Norfolk in the era described above was gradually pushed to the south by an encroaching ice cap over a period of around 50,000 years starting about 475,000 years ago.

The ice itself was up to one kilometre thick and seasonally produced an increase of water into the river systems, as well as changing the course of many of them. During this period, the Thames was pushed southwards, creating an outflow into an expanding North Sea and the Bytham was completely buried by the ice.

Towards the end of this period, the origins of English Channel were formed, starting the process of creating the island of Britain and separating it from the rest of the European landmass. This happened as a massive glacial

---

2   Information for this section is drawn from an article by Robert J. Davis, Simon G. Lewis, Nick M. Ashton, Simon A. Parfitt, Marcus T. Hatch and Peter G. Hoare, *The early Paleolithic archaeology of the Breckland: current understanding and directions for research.* The Journal of Breckland Studies, Vol 1. 2017.

3   Acheulean refers to stone tool manufacture characterised by distinctive oval and pear-shaped "hand-axes". It is thought that this technology was first developed in Africa as far back as 1.76 million years. Named after a site at Saint-Acheul in France where artifacts were found, Acheulean tools have been the dominant technology for the vast majority of human history.

lake that had been building up in the North Sea for thousands of years from the waters of the Rhine and the Thames broke through a natural dam and flowed towards the west. It created the valley which ultimately (after several more global warmings and coolings) became the English Channel - or La Manche – and in the process, provided a natural outlet for the River Seine.

The Hoxnian Period

Following the Anglian Ice Age, a warmer era, known as the Hoxnian period[4], lasting around 30,000 years from 420,000 to 390,000 years ago, saw populations returning to Norfolk, now significantly changed in its geographic structure since the River Bytham had disappeared. In its place, shallow lakes and new river-systems had been formed and provided the beginnings of recognisable modern topography. In this period the climate was broadly in line with current temperatures.

Excavations at Elveden and Barnham, west and south of Thetford respectively have discovered tools and cut-marked bones, which provide evidence of human presence. Hand-axes and tools of the Acheulean design were also found, similar to those from the pre-glacial era and suggesting that similar human populations returned to the area as the ice receded. Sediments in the lakes have preserved both flora and fauna from this period.

What is particularly interesting from Elveden and Barnham is evidence of the use of fire, with the remains of what were probably hearths at these sites. Were these used for cooking? Most probably - this is the oldest evidence for human use of fire anywhere in Europe.

A later less extensive ice age known as the Devensian ended a mere 27,000 years ago. The ice cap covered 'Scotland' and parts of 'northern England', but did not reach as far south as Norfolk, although the climate there would have been significantly cooler again. Between these two major glaciations, human groups returned.

Neolithic Age

The Neolithic Age is characterised by the use of stone implements and lasted from the Anglian Ice Age all the way through to the Bronze Age which began in Britain in around 2,000 BC. This vast stretch of time is divided into three distinct eras:

---

4   Named after the village of Hoxne, near Diss, where extensive finds from this period were found.

- Paleolithic Period – up to around 10,000 BC
- Mesolithic Period – 10,000 – 8,000 BC
- Neolithic Period   – 8,000 – 2,000 BC

These are differentiated by the relative sophistication of the tools used. As we have seen, much of Norfolk had been inhabited from the time when the Anglian Ice retreated, and it is reasonable to assume that Breckland and the area around Stoke Ferry were home to a number of semi-nomadic people in that period, given the number of finds in the area.

There have been individual finds of arrowheads in Feltwell and Methwold Hythe dating from the late Neolithic period, but perhaps the most significant is the site of Grime's Graves, in what is now Thetford Chase, less than ten miles away. This is a Neolithic flint mine, thought to have been in active use for two to three hundred years between 2,500 and 2,200 BC[5].

The site comprises some 350 pits, which mark the location of ancient mine shafts some as deep as ten metres. Many of the shafts have lateral galleries where veins of stone were excavated, before moving on when these were exhausted. They produced flint for making axes which were traded from this site over a wide area. Miners would have used only antler picks and other bones so it is remarkable how extensive the workings are. To provide light for their work they had lamps burning animal fat. Soot marks are still visible on the ceilings of some of the galleries.

The earliest archaeological finds in the immediate vicinity of Stoke Ferry date from this era. Flints and 'pot boilers' - stones used for heating food - have been found in significant numbers, particularly to the north of Methwold Hythe.

The Bronze Age

The Bronze Age period, from about 2,500 BC to 800 BC in Britain, came about with the start of tin and copper mining, enabling the manufacture of bronze. Despite having no reserves of either metal, the inhabitants of Norfolk somehow imported them, most likely from Cornwall and North Wales respectively, suggesting a sophisticated trade and distribution system across the country[6]. A major benefit of working in metal is that items could be melted down and recycled as designs developed over the period.

---

5   Information for this section drawn from Norfolk Heritage Guide.

6   The ancient roadway known as Icknield Way stretched from the south-west of England all the way to Norfolk and this is the likely route for tin imports to the area. Other roadways linked North Wales to this route. See Chapter 6.

It is thought that Bronze Age families were relatively settled, living in wooden and thatched farmsteads, with surrounding managed fields for grazing animals and arable farming. Horses were used as well as wheeled vehicles (essential for the shipment of large quantities of tin and copper as well as local agricultural needs). This period saw the transition to a somewhat more structured and hierarchical society with resources relatively less evenly distributed than previously.

The relatively recent find, known as 'Seahenge', of a wooden circle surrounding a massive upturned tree root, at Holme-next-the-Sea[7] is specifically dated to the year 2049 BC, known from analysis of the tree rings. Research suggests that the various timbers were worked by at least 50 bronze axes. The effort involved in creating this site supports the view that it was constructed by a settled population most probably for ritual or funeral purposes.

Also in this period a new pottery style known as the Beaker style was seen for the first time. It is not clear whether pottery-making skills and designs came to Britain with migrants from the continent of Europe, or through transference of knowledge (and if so, how did that happen?). Most likely it was from migration, and it has been suggested that the origins of 'Beaker culture' could be traced to the Iberian Peninsula, or possibly central European regions near modern Switzerland.

Stoke Ferry and its immediate vicinity were obviously populated during this period, as can be seen from the numerous significant archaeological finds in the area[8]:

- A spearhead and a hoard of Bronze Age treasure found between Stoke Ferry and Boughton
- A spearhead found near Stoke Ferry Bridge
- A palstave (a type of chisel) and axe found between Oxborough Road and the River Wissey
- Numerous finds including a bronze bowl, rapier, spearheads, palstaves, axes, a mace-head, an awl, various finds of pottery and a skeleton found south of Stoke Ferry and Wretton, near Wissington
- Another Bronze Age hoard of treasure, an axe, spearhead and more pottery found between Boughton and Barton Bendish.

---

7   This was dubbed 'Seahenge' by the press given the visual similarity to Stonehenge, but there is no archaeological evidence that they are linked, or indeed served the same purpose.

8   Finds recorded by www.archiuk.com - a comprehensive website of British archaeological sites.

The Iron Age

The final period of development before the arrival of the Romans was the Iron Age dating from the end of the Bronze Age - about 800 BC - through to the first century AD, ending with the Romanisation of Britain. For the later part of this period, at least, the Iceni Tribe occupied and ruled a territory which encompassed the whole of modern-day Norfolk, along with parts of northeast Cambridgeshire and north Suffolk.

Progressively through the period and particularly from 500 BC onwards, artefacts and weapons were made of iron, replacing the bronze used previously. Iron ore was in much greater supply than copper and tin and the technology for smelting and working iron was developed in that era.

Throughout this period, the development of farming and villages continued. In addition to agriculture, villages produced their own pottery and made cloth, using looms. In the later Iron Age, the first towns, generally known as 'oppida', were built and these would have had much better defences than villages. The nearest to Stoke Ferry were at Saham Toney and Thetford. In these new towns, the structure of society changed, with specialist jobs or crafts emerging and currency being used for trade. Different parts of the town were dedicated to particular activities, and also formal places of worship were built.

People lived in family groups and networks of families developed into tribes with similar cultures, religions, languages and beliefs. It is thought that three to four million people lived in Britain by the first century BC. The population grew rapidly during this period, mainly by immigration from the nearer parts of Europe. When Julius Caesar mounted brief expeditions to Britain in both 55 and 54 BC, he described a country populated by a relatively small number of tribes, each with quite extensive territories.

The Iceni tribe was one of these. Its territory was bounded to the north and east by the sea and to the west by the Fens – an area of water and marsh that formed a natural and reasonably secure barrier. To the south, in modern Suffolk and Essex, lived the Trinovantes Tribe[9].

The Iceni, the Celtic tribe best remembered today, had most likely originated from the North Sea or Baltic areas of Europe. They formed part of the waves of migrants from Europe who came to Britain during the Iron Age, probably arriving around 100 BC. They quickly came to dominate the

---

9   As well as the Trinovantes, other tribal groups in southern England included the Iceni's main rivals the Catevellani who occupied most of modern Cambridgeshire, Bedfordshire, Hertfordshire, Buckinghamshire and parts of Essex, the Cantiaci, who occupied Kent and East Sussex, and the Regnenses who lived in what is now West Sussex and Surrey.

previous population, most probably because of their greater technical skills and cultural development.

The Iceni's early dealings with the Romans were as allies, siding with Caesar's armies in their battles with the Catavellani, the Iceni's neighbours across the fens. Caesar described them as the Cenimagni (great Iceni). Because of this collaboration, they were allowed a much greater degree of self-rule than most of the other tribes in the long period between Caesar's expeditions and the full Roman military occupation of Britain in 43 AD.

What was the status of Stoke Ferry during this era, and particularly during the Iceni period? A number of finds[10] show the presence of a local population suggesting that the area continued much as in the Bronze Age, without gaining any greater significance:

- Iron Age pottery near the river at Stoke Ferry, as well as in Wretton and Wereham
- A gold ring shaped like a torc[11], found in Stoke Ferry
- A possible burial-site between Whittington and Foulden
- A series of pottery finds in the area of Methwold Hythe
- An Iceni coin with a Boarhorse design found at Methwold Hythe

The final part of the story of the Iceni, and Britain's famous warrior-queen Boudicca (Boadicea or Boudica) forms part of the history of Roman Britain and is described in the following chapter.

Stoke Ferry in Prehistoric Times

While having no particular prominence of its own, it is clear that the land where Stoke Ferry now stands was home to humans from the very earliest periods of history.

Before the Anglian Ice Age, the River Bytham flowed through the area and people lived along its banks. After the ice age had completely changed the geography, obliterating the Bytham and creating the marshy fenlands, human groups returned to the area. In the late Neolithic Age, nearby Grime's Graves signifies a sizeable local population devoted to mining, in addition to the various agrarian settlements around the area.

Although numerous, archaeological finds in and near Stoke Ferry do not

---

10 Finds recorded by ArchiUK.

11 Sometimes spelled torq or torque, is a large metal neck ring made either as a single piece or from strands twisted together.

suggest that it was an important centre of population or give any indication that there was a ferry across the river at that time. However, it is clear that it was an inhabited agricultural area from at least the Bronze Age.

One assumes that these people had some way of naming or describing locations, but in the absence of any written evidence[12] it is impossible to know what Stoke Ferry might have been called during the Neolithic Age, Bronze Age or Iceni period. It would be several more centuries before the name 'Stoke' or 'Stoches' came to be used.

---

12 Although the Iceni had symbols which were probably letters on their coins, there is no other evidence of literacy before the Romans arrived. This is, in fact, the definition of 'prehistoric' - before the existence of any written records - and hence the date of prehistory varies for each civilisation. Britain was relatively late in becoming literate.

Chapter Two

From Rome to Normandy – an Era of Conquests

The Iceni Rebellions

As we have seen, the Iceni tribe inhabited Norfolk and adjacent parts of Cambridgeshire and Suffolk from about 100 BC. They had co-operated with Julius Caesar's Roman invasion in 55 BC, taking advantage of Roman strength in their ongoing rivalry with the neighbouring Catavellani tribe to the south-west.

However, this was to change radically following the Roman occupation of Britain in 43 AD[1]. The Iceni King, Antedios, welcomed the Romans as allies, though it is apparent that this was not fully supported by all Iceni groups, with at least two other 'nobles' (probably named Aesunos and Saenuvax[2]) vying for leadership at that time.

Relations with the Roman occupiers deteriorated rapidly in 47 AD when the Roman Governor of Britannia, Publius Ostorius Scapula, sought to disarm the Iceni (and the other Celtic tribes) following uprisings in the north of the country and fearing similar rebellions elsewhere. The result was a serious uprising by the Iceni, which was put down by the highly effective Roman army at Stonea Camp near March in Cambridgeshire. Following this defeat, the Iceni became a 'client kingdom' and a new Iceni King, Prasutagus, installed (it is thought that the three previous contenders – Antedios, Aesunos and Saenuvax - were all executed).

---

1 Information for this section is largely drawn from *The History Files www.historyfiles.co.uk - Celtic Kingdoms of the British Isles.*

2 All three 'rulers' had coins issued in their names, suggesting some power, or at least aspiration to power. These names are most probably Latinised versions of Celtic names used by the chronicler.

Peace prevailed for a dozen years until Prasutagus died in 59 AD, when the occupiers appropriated all Iceni land and sought to disarm the tribe (contrary to the King's will leaving only half of the Kingdom to Rome, and retaining the other half for his family – surely rather optimistic on his part!). His widow, Boudicca (Boadicea) protested, but was publicly flogged by the Roman soldiers, and her daughters raped.

Understandably incensed by this, Boudicca raised an army from her own tribe as well as the neighbouring Trinivantes and possibly others. It is reported that there were about 100,000 tribal forces which inflicted great damage while the Roman Governor was absent fighting uprisings in North Wales. The rebels attacked and burned down the cities of Camuludunum (Colchester), Londinium (London) and Verulamium (St. Albans) and 70 - 80,000 people were killed in the process.

Cassius Dio, the Roman historian, described Boudicca:

> *In stature she was very tall, in appearance most terrifying, in the glance of her eye most fierce, and her voice was harsh; a great mass of the tawniest hair fell to her hips; around her neck was a large golden necklace; and she wore a tunic of divers colours over which a thick mantle was fastened with a brooch. This was her invariable attire*[3].

Eventually the Romans regrouped and confronted Boudicca's forces somewhere along the ancient Watling Street[4], although the precise location is unknown. The smaller but better disciplined and equipped Roman army routed the rebels and Boudicca is thought to have committed suicide, rather than face capture by the Romans. Again, the reports are of massive casualties, with tens of thousands of rebels killed, but only 400 Roman soldiers.

Thus ended one of the most famous events of early British history. Boudicca's statue adorns the bank of the Thames next to parliament and she is hailed as a heroine, standing up against the invaders, however ultimately futile. The inevitable failure of the uprising, however, cemented Roman rule for the next 350 years.

As before, there are no records confirming participation in these events from 'Stoke Ferry', but it would seem highly likely that a force the size of Boudicca's

---

3   Cassius Dio, *Roman History* Harvard University Press, Cambridge MA, 1987.

4   Watling Street was one of the main Roman roads, running from Dover, through London and St. Albans and northwest to Chester.

contained men and women from all parts of her kingdom, including the western areas bordering the fens.

The Roman Occupation

Following the defeat of Boudicca's uprising, the Roman occupying forces moved to secure their dominance over the local tribes. In the ten years following the rebellion, they built a new town of Venta Icenorum (sometimes known as Caister St Edmund) to the south of modern Norwich as an administrative centre for the Iceni people. They did not build any fortified castles or towns in the region until much later and these were coastal defences against European invaders, rather than garrisons to control the local population (at Caister, Burgh Castle and Brancaster, for example).

Britannia was both geographically and politically at the fringes of the Roman Empire, which stretched, at the time of the invasion, from modern-day Iran to the Atlantic coast of Spain and France, and from North Africa to Germany. It reached its greatest extent at the end of the first century AD.

The original invasion in 43 AD had been an opportunity for a newly elected Emperor, Claudius, to demonstrate his power by invading and capturing new territories. The Iceni were not the only tribe to resist. The Romans faced long-term rebellions in Wales, and were never able to conquer much of present-day Scotland, despite a number of expeditions to do so. They finally settled for building a wall to control the border with the 'barbarian' northern British tribes during the reign of Hadrian, in the years 122-128 AD.

Over the 350 years between Boudicca's rebellion, and the final Roman withdrawal in about 425 AD, Britannia was converted into a Roman colony. However, apart from the necessary garrisons to maintain their power (mostly stationed in the north and west), the country was never much of a destination for immigration from Rome or elsewhere in the Empire. Rather the local population, particularly those higher in society, became 'Romanised' and managed the colony on behalf of the invaders.

There was, of course, constant contact with Rome through trade, governance and military rotations, enabling an inflow of ideas, culture, science and architecture. This lead to former Celtic settlements being rebuilt as modern Roman towns, with formal street-grids, markets, basilicas, temples, theatres, bathhouses, amphitheatres, shopping streets and inns. These often became the administrative centres for their regions. Elite groups from the former tribes saw their opportunity for advancement and became colonial administrators, collecting taxes for Rome and keeping the peace in the surrounding country. This was a highly effective system of ruling a far-flung Empire.

The level of development of the Roman Empire was far in advance of the Celtic tribal nations found in Britain at the time of the conquest. There are many descriptions of the benefits brought to the colony by the Romans. *English Heritage*[5] *lists ten, though other lists may include many more*[6]:

- Architecture
- Towns built across the country
- Roads to link them
- Plumbing and sanitation including aqueducts, running water, baths, and toilets
- The Latin language, root of much of modern English (and literacy in general)
- The Julian twelve-month calendar
- Currency and the wide-spread use of money
- Advertising and trademarks
- Fast food stalls and the introduction of apples, pears and peas
- Administrative systems

The impact of many of these can still be felt in the twenty-first century.

Although the region of the Iceni was something of a backwater in Roman Britain, hemmed in by the sea and the fens, there is extensive evidence of Roman habitation in all parts of Norfolk. In and around Stoke Ferry, finds include[7]:

- A Roman settlement by the River Wissey, south of the current bridge
- A Roman site and two wells near the bypass
- A number of Roman villas in the nearby villages of Gooderstone, Beachamwell, Fincham, West Dereham and Barton Bendish
- A building with a hypocaust (a system of underfloor heating) between Methwold and Brookville
- Hoards of Roman treasure in Fincham and Southery
- Numerous coins, tiles, pottery, bricks and other Roman artefacts

---

5   English Heritage website www.english-heritage.org.uk posted in August 2016.

6   In Monty Python's *Life of Brian* in response to the question "What have the Romans ever done for us?" the following answers are given by the masked activists – the aqueduct, sanitation, roads, irrigation, medicine, education, health, the wine, public baths, it's safe to walk the streets at night and peace!

7   Finds recorded by ArchiUK.

In total, nearly 200 Roman finds have been registered within 10 km of Stoke Ferry. Nearby is Peddars Way, thought to be a Roman road, built on the track of a much older highway going to the north Norfolk coast.

It is unclear what 'Stoke Ferry' was called in Roman times. There is some supposition that the road from Thetford to King's Lynn existed, but few finds to fully support this theory. Local roads and byways would have been in place for many years, linking the farms and the villas. It seems likely that there was a means of crossing the river at that time, probably a ferry. Given that the Latin for 'ferry' is 'pendentes' this may have featured in the name – but there is, unfortunately, no evidence to support this view.

The Roman occupation was a period of relative peace lasting 350 years. As early as the first century, Christianity was one amongst several Roman and local pagan religions and was officially allowed from 313 AD by Emperor Constantine. However, the Roman Empire eventually declined under continued military threat from the Goths (from Germany), leading to an increase in military expenditure and resultant taxation.

Locally, over some decades, marauding groups from across the North Sea attacked the coast, not with the intent to conquer, but to plunder. With the heart of the Empire under pressure, garrisons were gradually withdrawn or demobilised locally (many of the soldiers would have been local recruits), and the occupation gradually came to a rather messy conclusion in about 425 AD.

This provided the opportunity and the catalyst for the next conquest of East Anglia.

The Kingdom of East Anglia

The period following the Roman withdrawal is usually described as 'sub-Roman', chronicled at the time by Gildas[8], and later by Bede[9], though their accounts differ in a number of respects. After the effective decolonisation of Britain, the country reverted to a fragmented set of provinces or tribal areas, similar to pre-Roman times. The provinces were well able to fend for themselves without the burden of Roman taxation, while Romanesque building, education and culture continued. However, Gildas, writing in the early 500s, criticised an era of excess and sinfulness; over time the momentum of development slowed.

---

8 Gildas, *De Excidio et Conquestu Brittaniae,* Date uncertain, c 530 - 540 AD.

9 Bede, Historia ecclesiastica gentis Anglorum, c 731 AD.

The next major transition in British history was already under way. Early Germanic settlers (mainly Saxons) had been brought to Roman Britain as 'foederati' – former mercenaries whose reward had been a gift of land and permission to settle in the Empire. Germans were also used as mercenaries by the post-Roman provinces and there were a number of migrations or invasions of the country in the century and a half after Roman rule. The invaders / settlers came across the North Sea by boat, landing on the east coast, or penetrating inland by river, including the fenland rivers Ouse, Nene and Cam.

The settlers in the east were the Angles, while Picts and Saxons went to other parts of the country. These immigrants were all from what is now northern Germany and southern Denmark. The Angles came from a small region on the Baltic coast of the Danish peninsular in Schleswig Holstein between the towns of Flensburg and Schleswig. They were, in modern parlance, economic migrants.

Recognisable place names begin to appear in this period. The Angles settled in the east and the midlands, giving their name to East Anglia, and were generally divided into a northern group – the North Folk, and a southern group – the South Folk. Elsewhere in the country, the Saxons settled in the west in Wessex (the West Saxons), in the east near the Thames estuary – Essex (the East Saxons), along the south coast – Sussex (the South Saxons) and in an area to the west of London, between these other groups – Middlesex (the Middle Saxons)[10].

Progressively, as more and more Angles arrived in East Anglia they began to take over and then dominate civic society. By the end of the fifth century, the town of Venta Icenorum was abandoned and the previous local government collapsed. In the first half of the sixth century, the Angles continued to build settlements and gradually took over the region, which was already ruled at the time by Anglian princes. By 571 AD, they had established a Kingdom of East Anglia, the first monarch being Wehha, establishing a dynasty known as the Wuffingas which lasted until King Edmund was killed by the Danes in 869 AD.

The area around Stoke Ferry continued to be populated in this period, although it was not an important centre at that time. A significant number of Anglo-Saxon finds[11] have been made in the area, including:

---

10 For the development of the name 'Stoke Ferry' see the insert *What's in a Name?* at the end of this chapter.

11 Finds recorded by ArchiUK.

- Two burial sites between Stoke Ferry and Wereham, and a Saxon cemetery between Gooderstone and Cockley Cley
- Three further burial sites near Foulden, Little London and Mundford
- A Saxon church at Cranwich
- A spearhead near the River Wissey
- A gold coin near the River Wissey
- Finds of pottery near Wretton
- Jewellery, coins and ornaments near Northwold

The time of the Kingdom of East Anglia was a turbulent period of history. For three separate periods the Kingdom was annexed by Mercia[12]. Firstly, in 654 – 655: after defeat in battle in 654, East Anglia joined forces with Mercia against Northumbria, but they were defeated. Following this, the East Anglians took the opportunity to install a new king, Aethelwold and reclaim their independence.

After a period of relative peace and prosperity, Mercia, led by Offa, again conquered the area in about 792, stripping the nobility of their lands and treating the Kingdom as a vassal state. A rebellion in 796 regained independence, but briefly. From 799 - 829, East Anglia was again ruled by Mercia. During this period, the port of Dunwich was built, becoming the third largest in the country after London and Bristol. Mercian rule was finally broken with the help of Wessex, but independent East Anglia under Athelstan, Aethelweard, Beorhtric and finally Edmund was cut short by the arrival of the Danes in 869.

Danish Conquest and Rule

From early in the 9th Century, Danish or Viking raids took place along the east coast of England, from Northumbria, to Lindsey (Lincolnshire), East Anglia and Kent. The raids were conducted by bands of marauders and initially targeted monasteries or abbeys and churches which had a wealth of valuable objects. The local populations seemed powerless to prevent this plunder, perhaps because the Vikings were better equipped and more ruthless.

In about 865, possibly to avenge the capture, mistreatment and execution of a Viking chief, Ragnar Lodbrok, the Vikings assembled a *Great Heathen*

---

12 Mercia was the largest of the Anglo-Saxon Kingdoms in this period, bordering East Anglia to the west and occupying the whole of the middle of England as far as the Welsh border. The best-known King of Mercia was Offa (ruled 757 – 796 AD) who built Offa's Dyke to defend his kingdom against the Welsh.

Army under the leadership of the unlikely-named Ivarr the Boneless which landed in East Anglia with a view to conquest, rather than mere thievery. After a reign of terror in the area for a year, the army marched north, captured York and Northumbria, and eventually returned to East Anglia to do battle with Edmund in 869 at Hoxne. Edmund may have been killed in battle, but legend has it that he was captured by the Danes and tortured before being slain and dismembered.

Edmund was subsequently canonised for his refusal to forsake Christianity and laid to rest at Beadoriceworth, later known as Bury St Edmunds.

This marked the end of the East Anglian Kingdom, to be replaced by Danish rule. The Danes were much more militaristic than the Angles and did not share their Christian beliefs. By 878, they had captured most of the Anglo-Saxon kingdoms which constituted England at that time. The one exception was Wessex which defeated the Danes at the battle of Edington in that year. The Peace of Wedmore (Somerset), which followed, divided the country between Wessex, where Alfred the Great continued to rule, and the rest of England which was given over to the Danes whose King Guthrum agreed to be baptised and ruled under his Christian name as Aethelston.

The peace allowed members of the invading army to return to East Anglia, divide the land between them and live as masters of the conquered Angles. But it was not to last. After a turbulent period of war, Wessex re-conquered East Anglia in 918. The Saxons continued to rule the country under a series of kings until 1013, when the Danes invaded yet again under Sweyne Forkbeard and his son, Cnut (who at that time was also King of Denmark and Norway. The English king at the time was Aethelread, known in history as 'the Unready', despite having had evidence of Viking hostile intent over many years. He was exiled to France after the defeat.

Forkbeard died very soon after the conquest, and Aethelread quickly returned from exile for two further years of reign. On his death, he was succeeded by Cnut. His name is known to all for attempting to stop the waves (a more recent explanation is that he was trying to illustrate to his followers that even a king as great as himself could *not* overcome the power of the sea).

Cnut is generally regarded as an effective leader during his twenty years on the throne, improving civic administration and increasing the power of the church, but at a huge cost to the population.

There are few finds from this period. A Viking ring was discovered near Boughton but, unlike previous eras, there is little evidence of widespread settlement by the Danes. They may have taken overall control of the land, but their rule can be characterised as leaving little whilst taking a lot from the conquered territories. This was in the form of widespread taxes, perhaps more accurately described as 'protection money'.

During the time of the Viking occupation, they systematically extracted vast sums of money from the local populations, levying payments relative to the wealth of each town and village. In this period, these payments were called 'gafol', later known as 'Danegeld'. To illustrate their rapaciousness, it is catalogued that the following 'transfers' were made to the Danes[13]:

- 991   10,000   Roman pounds[14] (weight) of silver, after the Battle of Malden
- 1002   24,000   Roman pounds of silver to Forkbeard
- 1007   36,000   Roman pounds of silver to buy two years of peace
- 1012   48,000   Roman pounds of silver
- 1016   72,000   Roman pounds of silver to pay for Cnut's navy

Each town and village had to pay what was, in effect, a land tax. Unsurprisingly, after the Danes had established this highly effective way of collecting money, later rulers from the House of Wessex and the Normans continued to use it for similar purposes.

Stoke Ferry had to pay its share of these levies, which must have been progressively more financially crippling. Interestingly, the levy on Stoke Ferry was significantly higher than that of Downham Market. It is recorded that for the first of the above payments, Downham Market contributed 4½ pence, and 'Stoches' 6½ pence.

Following Cnut's death in 1035 his two sons briefly ruled in succession, before, in 1042, the House of Wessex was restored with Edward the Confessor as king. He ruled for nearly 24 years, built Westminster Abbey, and died in 1066, childless, and without an heir. The stage was set for the last invasion and conquest of England, by William the Bastard of Normandy.

---

13 Dowell, Stephen, *History of Taxation and Taxes in England, Volume 1*, First published by Longmans Green, 1884, Republished in Digital Edition, Routledge 2006.

14 A Roman pound weight is equivalent to approximately 0.329 kilograms or 0.725 Imperial Pounds. The silver consisted of coins and religious artifacts.

STOKE FERRY
What's in a name?

Stoke and Stock are amongst the most frequently used place names in England, either as a prefix (as in Stoke Ferry, Stoke Mandeville, Stoke Newington – there are at least 75 of these) or as part of a longer name (Stockton, Basingstoke, Stokenchurch – with nearly as many examples).

Whereas people must have had ways of identifying locations for thousands of years, many English place names as we know them today only have their origins in Latin, from the Roman era (43 – 410 AD), Old English from the Anglo-Saxon period (from 410 – 1066) or French following the Norman invasion in 1066. Wales, Scotland and Ireland also had many derivations from their own native languages and a few pre-Roman Celtic forms survive in England as well – particularly in the names of rivers. Stoke Ferry's name had its origin in Old English from the Anglo-Saxon period and, like most of its namesakes elsewhere in the country, was originally known as 'Stoches' as recorded in the Domesday Book of 1086. However, for such a common name, there seem to be several different explanations of the meaning:

- Eilert Ekwall,[15] the noted scholar of English place names suggests that in certain circumstances it could be
  - a place or perhaps holy place
  - a monastery cell
  - an outlying settlement or farm dependent on a larger village nearby
  - a cattle-farm or dairy farm
- Blomefield[16], writing in 1781 says that 'In the book of Doomsday (sic) it is wrote Stoches, not taking its name (as thought by some) from stock, that is, some wood; but from stow, a dwelling, or habitation and Ches, by the water'
- Rye[17], states that Stoke has three possible meanings – place, religious place and dependent farm, agreeing with Ekwall and with no reference to Blomefield's explanation
- Gelling[18] emphasises the woodland conotations of the element 'Stock'. She believes that the element *stoches, or stoces* could have have been applied to recently cleared woodland where only stumps or stubs remain

---

15 Ekwall, Eilert, *The Concise Oxford Dictionary of English Place-names*, OUP, First edition 1935, Fourth Edition 1960

16 Blomefield, Revd. Francis, *History and Antiquities of the County of Norfolk*, Booth Bookseller, 1781

17 Rye, James, *A popular Guide to Norfolk Place-names*, The Larks Press, 1991

18 Gelling, Margaret, *Place-names in the Landscape*, Dent 1993

The first edition of this book referred solely to the Blomefield version, drawing feedback from the then secretary of Heritage Norfolk that the author should not solely rely on 'Blomefield's Water on the Brain derivation'.

But at least the word Ferry should be unambiguous. This was where the River Wissey could be crossed by a ferry on the road between London and King's Lynn. The name Wissey itself is probably of earlier, Celtic, origin and, like 'Ouse' the river into which it now flows near Hilgay, may just mean 'water' or 'muddy water'[19].

By 1248, when a Charter was granted, the village was already known as Stokeferie, and it is easy to see how this migrated into its current form.

---

19 Ooosthuizen, Susan, *The Anglo-Saxon Fenland*, Windgather Press, 2017

Chapter Three

Catastrophe and Domesday

The Norman Conquest

1066 is probably the best-remembered date in English history – the death of Edward the Confessor, succeeded as king by Harold Godwinson; the Battle of Hastings where he was shot in the eye (and killed!); and the successful takeover of England by William the Conqueror. It was the last conquest of England by a foreign power. While most of the bare bones of this story are correct, the detail is much more interesting.

When he became king, Harold was the Earl of Wessex, an Anglo-Saxon with family ties to Cnut. His father, Godwin, had been intimately involved in the royal succession following Cnut's death and was instrumental in Edward the Confessor becoming king in 1042. Edward married Godwin's daughter (Harold's sister) Edith, in 1045. In the same year, Harold himself became the Earl of East Anglia, probably to bolster its defences against an invasion threat from Norway. On his father's death in 1053, he became the Earl of Wessex and in 1058 added the Earldom of Hereford to his portfolio.

The saintly[1] Edward the Confessor was childless and therefore had no obvious heir. It appears that he promised the kingship after his death to at least three different people – Harold (Earl of Wessex), William of Normandy (a relative of his mother's) and also, some years previously, to Edward Aetheling, son of Edmund Ironside, a former king who had died in 1057. In addition, Aetheling's young son, Edgar Aetheling who had been brought up in the Court, Harold's brother, Tostig, and King Harald Hardrada of Norway all believed they had some claim to the vacant throne.

---

1   He was actually canonised nearly 100 years after his death in 1161.

As a leading modern historian has written:

> *Edward's handling of the succession issue was dangerously indecisive, and contributed to one of the greatest catastrophes to which the English have ever succumbed[2].*

Indecisive or keeping all his options open, knowing in any case that the succession would not be his to decide? That was the responsibility of the *Witanagemot,* a Saxon council of the nobility, usually referred to as the 'Witan'. Edward died on 5th January 1066, and the Witan promptly appointed Harold Godwinson King; he was crowned the following day (in undue haste, it was thought).

William of Normandy (illegitimate son but heir of Duke Robert I of Normandy - hence his sometime title 'the Bastard') was not impressed. Two years earlier Harold had landed in France, perhaps to swear loyalty to William as King Edward's designated heir, although there are a number of other potential reasons for his visit, among them that he was merely blown off-course during a fishing trip. William strongly believed, however, that he was the designated heir and immediately began preparations for an invasion of England to secure the throne. He assembled a mighty army and built a sizeable fleet to transport them across the Channel. They were ready to sail from Normandy by August 1066, but were held in port due to storms until September.

Meanwhile, King Harald Hardrada of Norway and Tostig Godwinson (Harold's brother) formed an alliance and invaded Northumbria, where they defeated the local forces at the Battle of Fulford near York on 20th September. On hearing this, King Harold rapidly marched north with his army and defeated the invaders at the Battle of Stamford Bridge nearby, a mere five days later on the 25th.

Fortuitously, or as a result of accurate intelligence, William's fleet sailed on the 27th, landing the next day at Pevensey in Sussex with about 7,000 men. Harold's army had to march back the 240 miles to the south coast to intercept them. On 14th October, the armies clashed near Hastings, Harold was killed (most probably by the swords of four knights, rather than an arrow in the eye) along with his two loyal brothers and many of his troops.

---

2   Stephen Baxter, *Edward the Confessor and the Succession Question*, in Mortimer ed., *Edward the Confessor – The Man and the Legend*, Boydell Press 2009.

Immediately, the Witan was again called into action, naming Edgar Aetheling as king in succession to Harold. However, English resistance to the invasion was divided and ineffectual. Edgar was never crowned and William continued forcefully to press his claim. By December Edgar Aetheling and all the surviving nobility had submitted to Norman rule and William became king.

William had triumphed, and Harold's death at Hastings after only nine months on the throne effectively brought an end to the Anglo-Saxon and Viking eras of English history. The whole story of the invasion, battle and conquest (from the winner's perspective) is told in nearly seventy metres of embroidered linen in the magnificent Bayeux tapestry. It was commissioned by William's half-brother, Bishop Odo, and most probably created in England in the decade following the Battle of Hastings.

Though far from these great events of 1066, Stoke Ferry, along with every other part of England, must have been affected, providing men on demand and possibly supplies to the English army, but probably unaware of imminent upheaval. What is certain is that during the reign of the William I the whole country felt the impact of the new era.

Norman Occupation

It was not altogether straightforward, however. For the first ten years after the Battle of Hastings a series of uprisings in various parts of the country threatened the stability of the new regime. These were not only by the previous Anglo-Saxon aristocracy, but also in some cases, by recently-installed Normans jockeying for position in the new kingdom. Meanwhile, William himself spent more time in Normandy than in England, often dealing with uprisings and rebellion there as well, whilst England was left under the supervision of his trusted followers.

Throughout this period, the Danes, under King Swayne II, were perpetual trouble-makers, harrying the coastline and providing armed support to various rebel-groups in eastern England. In 1070, Swayne personally came with his navy to support Hereward the Wake[3], who was at that time based in Ely. Hereward was an Anglo-Saxon nobleman and one of the leaders of resistance to Norman rule. He is known to have operated throughout the fens and surrounding areas, no doubt passing through or staying in Stoke Ferry at times. Hereward and the Danes fought a battle with the Normans at Ely and ransacked Peterborough Cathedral, but lost a subsequent battle

---

3   Wake probably has the obvious meaning of 'watchful'. He was also known at times as 'The Exile' or 'The Outlaw'.

with the Normans at Ely. It is not clear what happened to Hereward. Some stories suggest that he was pardoned eventually by William, others that he was killed or went into exile, like many other Anglo-Saxon nobles at the time. His legend, however, lives on.

Another insurrection involving Norfolk took place a few years later in 1075. In the 'Revolt of the Earls', Ralph de Gael, Earl of Norfolk together with Roger de Bretieul, Earl of Hereford, conspired to overthrow the king. The plot was hatched at Ralph's wedding to a relative of Roger's at Exning, near Newmarket. It was a short-lived revolt, not least because Roger was unable to bring his forces to Norfolk to join up with Ralph's. Ralph himself was besieged in Norwich by the combined forces of Odo of Bayeux and other loyalist knights. The city surrendered and Ralph went into exile. William was not even in the country for these events.

This largely brought the threats to the Norman monarchy to an end, and the process of settlement and domination could be stepped up. From the conquest onwards, the Normans confiscated property from the English nobility, with William himself claiming ultimate ownership of all land for the Crown. This process of confiscation and redistribution continued following each of the uprisings, so that within a dozen years the Norman invaders had seized ownership of most of the country. This is particularly remarkable as it is thought that no more than 8,000 Normans ever settled in England.

A massive programme of castle-building was undertaken during this period to ensure that the threat of force was enough to subjugate the whole population. Initially the castles were pre-fabricated wooden structures, brought over from France; later they were converted into massive, stone-built, fortified structures, many of which still stand today. Locally, castles at Thetford, Castle Acre and Norwich were started within a couple of years of 1066 while the Tower of London was also begun in the immediate aftermath of the Battle of Hastings.

William systematically and comprehensively replaced all of the previous aristocracy with his own followers, and by 1075 all Earls were Normans. In local government, a few English Sheriffs remained, but all ecclesiastical appointments as bishops or abbots were in the hands of the Normans over the next few years.

Domesday Book

Just how successful William and the Normans had been in taking possession and settling the whole country is shown in the Domesday Book. Complied in just over one year, Domesday catalogued the country in varying degrees of detail, describing the value and size of all land-holdings in each 'hundred' or district, their proprietors, tenure and value, the quantity of meadow, pasture, wood and arable they contained, and in some counties the number of cottages, tenants and vassals of all denominations who lived in them.

It was a remarkable undertaking, the first attempt anywhere in the post-Roman world to create a comprehensive record[4]. Why did William authorise this survey to be conducted? At one level, he wished to understand the make-up of England twenty years after his invasion, but, more significantly, he wanted a structured way of raising taxation, as shown in the following quotation:

[In the winter of 1085] *the king (had) a large meeting and very deep consultation with his council, about this land; how it was occupied, and by what sort of men. Then sent he his men over all England into each shire; commissioning them to find out "How many hundreds of hides were in the shire, what land the king himself had, and what stock upon the land; or, what dues he ought to have by the year from the shire*[5].

Domesday is, in fact, two separate records – the Little Domesday, which covers Norfolk, Suffolk and Essex in considerable detail, and the Great Domesday which documents the rest of the country in somewhat less detail. The originals did not have a title, but came to be known as *Liber Wintona* (the Book of Winchester), where they were kept.

The 'Domesday' title was colloquially coined later. The records were deemed to be totally accurate, with no right of appeal. The outcome - the amount of taxation due - was like 'The Book of Doom' or Judgement Day.

Stoke Ferry (Stoches) in Domesday Book

So here, in Little Domesday, Stoke Ferry, or Stoches, is recorded for the first time. Happily, this was the more detailed of the two books and documents in comprehensive detail the holdings in the village.

Firstly it records the 'Tenant-in-Chief' - the primary feudal tenant of the king - and the Lord(s) of the Manor in 1086, who were, in effect, his tenants.

---

4   It is known that over a thousand years earlier, the Romans had conducted a census of the whole Empire, again aimed at effective tax-gathering.

5   The *Anglo-Saxon Chronicle*, Translated by Giles, J. A. and Ingram, J., Project Gutenberg 1996.

It also shows who had been Lord of the Manor or owned the land in 1066.

Four separate entries cover Stoches. These show Rainald fitz (son of) Ivo as Tenant-in-Chief of one, Ralph Barnard two more and Count Alan of Brittany the fourth. These were highly important allies of the king, and had been amply rewarded in the redistribution of land:

- Count Alan of Brittany – Tenant-in-Chief of about 100 villages and Lord of nearly 60 of them
- Rainald fitz Ivo – Tenant-in-Chief of about 58 villages in Norfolk alone, and Lord for 36 of them
- Ralph Barnard (two entries) – Both Tenant-in-Chief and Lord for 5 villages

The Stoke Ferry records are as follows:

Lands of Count Alan:

In Stoke (Ferry), *the same* (Ribald, brother of Count Alan) *holds 3 free men with 7 acres TRE*[6] *and it is worth 12d.*[7]

This land was held by the three free men in 1066.

Lands of Rainald fitz Ivo

In Stoke (Ferry) [there are] *4 free men in commendation and every customary due at 12 acres. And* [there is] *1 free man at 2 acres. In the same* [vill] *Roger and Hugh hold 2 sokemen and 74 acres.* [There have] *always been 1½* [ploughs]. *And* [there are] *10 acres of meadow. The whole of this is worth 20s*[8].

This land was most probably held in 1066 by 'Toli' a Danish Sherriff of East Anglia during Edward the Confessor's reign. Ivo, and probably his son Rainald came with William on his conquest, though their names do not appear on the roll of the Battle of Hastings.

Lands of Ralph Baynard

In Stoke [Ferry] [there are] *13 free men in soke.* [There have] *always* [been] *6 bordars. And* [there is] *1 fishery and 2 ploughs. And it is worth 60s.* [There is] *a quarter part of a church, 5 acres* [and it is worth] *27d.*

---

6   For glossary of Domesday terms, see below.

7   *Domesday Book – A Complete Translation*, Penguin Books 1992, p1080.

8   *Ibid*, p1147.

This he (ie Ralph] *claims by exchange*[9].

The appropriation of Baynard

In Stoke [Ferry] *Ulfkil held 100 acres TRE.* [There have] *always* [been] *4 villans and 4 bordars.* [There is] *1 plough, 10 acres of meadow. It is worth 40s. He claims this through exchange*[10].

It is likely that both parts of Baynard's land were held in 1066 by Ufkil, who is listed in Domesday as having a large number of Lordships in both 1066 and 1086, though not necessarily in the same villages in each year. He appears to be a relatively rare example of a pre-conquest landowner who had somehow transferred allegiance to the Normans and been well rewarded for doing so. Baynard held the majority of the land of Stoke Ferry, with Rainald and Count Alan having comparatively smaller holdings.

At last, Stoke Ferry, or Stoches, was firmly on the map (or in the book). The four Domesday entries cover the whole land area of the settlement and include the total economically active population (numbering 37). This suggests a total population of around 200 and shows that Ralph Baynard was then the dominant (though certainly absent) figure in the community.

In many locations throughout West Norfolk during the early medieval period, these were not necessarily compact settlements as we would understand by a 'village' today. Inhabitants moved out from the areas around the church and manor to settle along the edge of common grazing grounds, resulting in a dispersed settlement pattern. Locally, farmsteads were established well beyond the centre of Stoke Ferry, along the present day Oxborough Road, Wretton Road, School Road and Low Road, Wretton as well as along tracks and footpaths. Most of these dwellings no longer exist but can be traced by scatters of pottery and building material in cultivated fields. The homes of the people mentioned in the Domesday Survey of Stoke may well have been spread over a wide area, including parts of what is now Wretton[11].

In this era, people lived in wooden or adobe dwellings with thatched rooves, probably with adjoining shelters for horses and other farm animals during winter. They would have been largely self-sufficient. Water came from wells, as the river was likely to be tidal and therefore saline. Tracks lead between the

---

9   *Ibid,* p 1162.

10   *Ibid,* p1181.

11   I am indebted to Dr. Patsy Dallas for this insight, which is based on her extensive study of East Anglian landscape history.

dwellings and the land, and there would have been a community meeting place in the middle of the settlement, though probably no community buildings other than a simple church.

Importantly, however, there was a 'road' through the village and occasional travellers from Thetford or Lynn or even further afield would have passed through, using the ferry to cross the river. Though Stoches was in many ways a quiet rural community, it was not isolated, and as we will see in the following chapter, would have been affected by events and movements taking place in Norfolk and the wider country.

Domesday Glossary

Domesday entries require some explanation, and translation –

- Acre – this was a measure of length as well as area, and comes from the Latin word *ager*, meaning 'field'. Generally, a medieval acre was the equivalent of 160 perches, 1 perch being 30.25 square yards

- Free men – non-noble landowners

- Sokemen – a free man who owed service to a lord, known as soccage

- Vill – the lowest administrative entity after a Shire and a Hundred. It is generally an area of land, rather than necessarily a settlement

- Villan (sometimes Villein) – a peasant, living in a Vill. They held land of the manorial lord and provided labour services to him, but did not necessarily live in a settlement

- Bordars – a peasant, of lower status than a villan, who had a small amount of land from a manorial lord, in return for labour services to him

- Plough – an assessment of the arable capacity of an estate in terms of the number of eight-ox ploughs needed to work it

- Fishery and meadow have the same meanings as today

- TRE – *Tempore Regis Edwardi*, or 'in the time of King Edward' This abbreviation appears throughout the book to identify the status quo prior to 1066

Chapter Four

Normans, Tudors and Stuarts

The End of The Middle Ages

William of Normandy died in 1087, shortly after Domesday had been completed. He was succeeded by his unpopular son, William II, who reigned for twelve years before dying in a hunting incident (accident or not?). This event triggered a power struggle between two of William II's brothers Robert (then Duke of Normandy) and Henry who eventually prevailed. He was the youngest son of William the Conqueror and subsequently ruled for thirty-five years.

William Lord Baynard (grandson of Ralph Baynard[1]) backed Robert in this conflict. When Henry was established on the throne he seized all of Baynard's lands and passed them to the Earl of Clare[2]. As a direct consequence of a contended succession, the ownership of Stoke Ferry changed hands. Whether this had much impact on day-to-day life or on how the land was managed is not known.

A hundred years later his descendent, Roger, Earl of Clare made an endowment to the Priory at Shouldham and gave his interest in Stoke Ferry to the Priory[3]. By this deed the Prior of Shouldham became Tenant-in-Chief of the whole district. In 1239, King Henry III granted the Prior a Charter for a fair and a market in Stoke Ferry, from which he would make considerable profit and conferred the status of 'town' (see box on Charters and Fairs later in this chapter).

---

1 See Chapter 3. According to Domesday, Ralph Baynard was Tenant-in-Chief of much of Stoches (Stoke Ferry) in 1087. He was an ally of William of Normandy, Sheriff of Essex and built Baynard's Castle on the banks of the Thames not far from the Tower of London.

2 This is Gilbert fitz Richard de Clare who was already a very extensive landowner before being given Baynard's land. There is a suggestion that he might have somehow been involved in the death of William II, but no proof exists to support this.

3 Shouldham Priory was originally founded in the reign of Richard I (1189 – 99) by Jeffrey fitz Piers, Earl of Essex, and later received additional endowments from a number of wealthy patrons, including Roger, Earl of Clare in the reign of Henry III..

The Prior also had control of the ferry, the only way of crossing the Wissey, which lead to a notable dispute with the locals in 1275[4].

The Peasants Revolt

In 1381, when Richard II when was still only fourteen, a major insurrection took place known as the Peasants Revolt. Led by Walter (Wat) Tyler, this was triggered by the imposition of a poll tax and was initially focused on London, with peasant armies descending on the capital from Essex and Kent. The rebellion rapidly spread across the country. In Norfolk, it began on 14th June, when groups of rebels from Suffolk travelled via Thetford to west Norfolk and the fens on to the north-east of the county around Norwich and Yarmouth. Property and legal records (particularly those associated with the tax) were destroyed in Swaffham and Lynn amongst other places, and it seems very likely that the furore also reached Stoke Ferry.

The rebellion was short-lived. Already by mid-June the attacks on London had been repelled, Wat Tyler was dead, and the king reneged on the promises made to the rebels. In Norfolk, the action was centred on Norwich and the north-east of the county, where a decisive 'battle' was fought near North Walsham on 25th June. The army of the establishment, lead by the Bishop of Norwich, Henry Le Despenser, either routed the rebels or they surrendered without much of a fight, depending which account is believed. However, their leader, Geoffrey Lister, was captured then hung, drawn and quartered. A fifteenth century historian wrote:

> *The traitor was sought and found; he was captured and beheaded; and, divided into four parts, he was sent through the country to Norwich, Yarmouth, and Lynn, and to the site of his mansion; that rebels and insurgents against the peace might learn by what end they will finish their career[5].*

Whatever the truth of the Battle of North Walsham, it was the last action of the Peasants Revolt anywhere in the country. It can be imagined that in defeat the peasants' resentment deepened and they became even more antagonistic to the monarchy and nobility.

---

4   See Chapter 6.

5   John Capgrave, *The Book of Illustrious Henries* Translated from the Latin by Francis Charles Hingiston, 1838. Capgrave lived from 1393 – 1464, and probably wrote this in the 1420s.

A Royal Visit

The Bedingfelds, owners of Oxburgh Hall just three miles from Stoke Ferry, must have had considerable influence in the area. They are said to descend from Ogerlis, a Norman who as early as 1100 owned land at Bedingfeld in Suffolk. His descendent Edmund Bedingfeld married Margaret Tuddenham, so acquiring the manor of Oxburgh where he built the Hall – a magnificent moated manor house – completed in 1482.

In 1487, soon after the Hall was completed, Henry VII (having recently seized the throne by defeating Richard III at Bosworth field) made a Royal Progress and pilgrimage to Walsingham. On the way, he paid a visit to Sir Edmund at Oxburgh. With him were his queen, Elizabeth of York, the Bishops of London and Bath and a large retinue of nobles and servants. This vast entourage probably crossed the River Wissey at Stoke Ferry, and no doubt the local people would have been involved in providing and serving the vast quantity of food needed to entertain them royally for several days.

Apart from such excitements Stoke Ferry must have remained a relatively quiet agricultural community. However, unlike many small towns and villages, it had its own mill and alehouse, shoemaker, carpenter, blacksmith, other tradesmen and small shopkeepers, a weekly market and frequent travellers passing through. The Prior of Shouldham and the Lord of the Manor (who had taken the name of Stoke as his family name) owned most of the land. Thus we read of Robert de Stoke in Henry III's reign (1216 - 72), Roger de Stoke in Edward I's reign (1272 - 1307), and the heirs of John de Stoke succeeding in Edward II's reign (1307 - 27).

Dissolution of the Monasteries

The influence of the Prior and his monks would have been very strong in everyday affairs, as well as in the Church. This came to an abrupt end when Henry VIII quarreled with the Pope and declared himself Head of the Church in England. The Dissolution of the Monasteries soon followed, and Shouldham Priory was closed in 1538. It had first been endowed in the twelfth century by St Gilbert and included two establishments, a nunnery of the Order of St Benedict, and a Priory for Canons of the Augustine Order.

Charters and Fairs

The first Royal Charter for Stoke Ferry was granted by King Henry III to the Prior of Shouldham (then Lord of the Manor) on 6th April 1248[6]. At that time the grant was for a Market to be held every Friday and an annual Fair on St. Nicholas Day (6th December). Both were to be held at The Manor.

By the fifteenth century these seem to have fallen into abeyance because a second Royal Charter was granted in 1426 by Henry VI to the town of Stoke Ferry. This too stipulated a weekly Market and an annual Fair on 6th December. This Charter was never revoked, so Stoke Ferry technically still has the status of a town.

The market continued to the end of the nineteenth century, and Directories of that period list Stoke Ferry as a market town, together with nearby Swaffham, Downham Market and Diss (all significantly larger centres of population).

The character of the market may have changed over time but would usually have included sales of sheep, cattle, poultry, eggs and vegetable produce. By this time two new sites were being used. The earlier was on The Hill, the open ground in front of the church[7]. The second site was on a field opposite the turning into Furlong Road. This is marked *Market Field* on an auctioneer's plan as late as 1912.

The annual Fairs were also held on these sites. In different forms they have been celebrated from the fifteenth century onwards to relatively modern times. Kelly's Directory of 1888 states:

A fair for horses and cattle is held on December 6th and one for hiring servants on the Thursday before Old Michaelmas Day (29th September)

Hiring Fairs were normal in an age when employment in both domestic and farm work was ill-paid and scarce. Workers seeking jobs or wishing to change their masters would attend the Fair, often sporting symbols of their trade in their caps - a wisp of wool for a shepherd, a whip-lash for a carter or a piece of straw for a ploughman. Prospective employers would choose men they thought suitable and bargain with them for a year's work. Maids were generally engaged using the same system.

Both the Cattle Fair and the Hiring Fair were holidays and great occasions for junketting and merry-making, often the main highlights of the year.. Travelling pedlers and quacks would set up their stalls with ribbons and trinkets, 'cure-alls', toffees and brandy-snaps. There would be drinking, wrestling and dancing, cock-fighting, and possibly bear-baiting in earlier times. As late as the 1980s, travelling fair-grounds set up annually on the Market Field, offering a tenuous link with the Fairs of the past.

---

6   Taken from *The Gazetteer of Markets and Fairs in England and Wales to 1516*, Centre for Metropolitan History. Last updated 2013.

7   The Hill has nothing to do with altitude, but it is thought that *Hill* in this case is a corruption of the Saxon word *Hal* or market.

According to Blomefield[8]:

In the reign of Henry VIII on the 15ᵗʰ October 1534, Robert Swift, the Prior, with nine Canons and seven nuns, surrendered this house into the King's hands. At which time the King was pleased to grant pensions to them for their annual subsistence.

The Priory had immense landholdings and great privileges but also a mixed record. By the time of the dissolution, Shouldham, like many other religious establishments, was tainted by corruption.

After the dissolution, the Prior's estates in Stoke Ferry were granted to Sir Edmund Bedingfeld of Oxburgh Hall. During the religious upheavals and persecutions of Tudor times the lives of the people would be linked with the fortunes of the traditionally Catholic Bedingfeld family. When Mary, daughter of Henry VIII and Catharine of Aragon, came to the throne in 1553, Sir Henry Bedingfeld provided one hundred and forty armed men to support her. It is likely that some Stoke Ferry men were among them.

A Royal Scandal

The marital arrangements of Henry VIII and the affairs and intrigues at his court were at a considerable distance from west Norfolk. However, events there during 1540 and 1541 had very local connections, and would, at the very least, have been a source of local gossip.

Following his brief marriage and prompt divorce from Anne of Cleves (wife number four), Henry's wandering eye was drawn to one of her ladies-in-waiting, a familiar route for recruiting his wives (both Anne Boleyn and Jane Seymour had been ladies in waiting before becoming queen). Catherine Howard was brought up by her step-grandmother in a very easy-going and sexually tolerant environment. She was allegedly molested by her music-teacher and later 'courted' by her step-grandmother's private secretary Francis Derham with whom she undoubtedly had an affair. Indeed, it is thought that they intended to marry and had, informally at least, become 'engaged'.

None of this was known by the King when he courted Catherine and married her (still only 16 or 17 years old) in 1540. He was besotted – Catherine's youth, prettiness and vivacity were captivating to Henry, then aged 49. He called her his 'rose without a thorn' and the 'very jewel of womanhood'.

---

8   Francis Blomefield, *History and Antiquities of the County of Norfolk*, Norwich 1781.

When, a few months later he learnt of her prior relationship with Derham and a more recent one with Thomas Culpeper, one of his courtiers, the King was understandably furious.

The outcome was inevitable. Derham and Culpeper were executed in December 1541, and Catherine a few months later, still not yet 20.

The connection is that Francis Derham was a local boy - born in Crimplesham, four miles from Stoke Ferry. Following his execution, as was customary, his head was displayed on a pike on London Bridge. It is believed that his headless body was returned to Norfolk for burial at West Dereham Abbey. Superstition has it that a headless ghost still haunts the grounds of the ruined abbey, seeking to be reunited with its severed head.

Ketts Rebellion

In 1549 (during Edward VI's reign) there was another short-lived rebellion in Norfolk, this time mainly in Wymondham and Norwich.

The critical issue was enclosure (appropriation and fencing of land) by wealthy landowners to the very serious detriment of the peasants who had, for centuries, farmed their smallholdings and grazed the common land. The demand for wool greatly increased in this period, making sheep farming highly profitable especially on large farms. As described below, it takes far fewer men to tend large flocks of sheep than to conduct the type of farming which it replaced, thus depriving large numbers of peasants of both land and means of livelihood.

The process of enclosure had been under way since the turn of the 16th century in some parts of the country. Thomas More wrote[9] as early as 1516:

> *For look in what parts of the realm doth grow the finest and therefore dearest wool, there noblemen and gentlemen, yea, and certain abbots, holy men no doubt, not contenting themselves with the yearly revenues and profits that were wont to grow to their forefathers and predecessors of their lands, nor being content that they live in rest and pleasure—nothing profiting, yea, much annoying the public weal—leave no ground for tillage, they inclose all into pastures; they throw down houses; they pluck down towns and leave nothing standing but only the church to be made into a sheep fold. . . .*

---

9   Thomas More *Utopia Part 1*, 1516.

They turn all dwelling-places and all glebe land into desolation and wilderness. Therefore, that one covetous and insatiable cormorant may compass about and inclose many thousand acres of ground together within one pale or hedge, the husbandmen be thrust out of their own, or else either by cunning and fraud, or by violent oppression, or by wrongs and injuries they be so wearied, that they be compelled to sell all. By one means therefore or another, either by hook or by crook they must needs depart away, men, women, husbands, wives, fatherless children, widows, mothers with their babies, and their whole household small in substance and large in number, as husbandry requireth many hands. Away they trudge, I say, out of their known and accustomed houses, finding no place to rest in. . . .

And when they have wandered abroad till the little they have be spent, what can they then else do but steal, and then justly be hanged, or else go about a begging. And yet then also they be cast in prison as vagabonds, because they go about and work not: whom no man will set a work, though they never so willingly proffer themselves thereto. For one shepherd or herdsman is enough to eat up that ground with cattle, to the occupying whereof about husbandry many hands were requisite.

This superbly detailed description of the impact of enclosure on society as a whole provides the context for unrest across the country in the first half of the sixteenth century, exacerbated by the dissolution of the monasteries.

In Stoke Ferry, this type of enclosure did not take place until the beginning of the nineteenth century, although some common land had been taken in connection with early attempts to drain the fens[10]. However, there appears to have been support for the rebellion in neighbouring Roxham and Ryston and rumours of these tumultuous events would undoubtedly have reached Stoke Ferry.

The Puritans

In the early part of the seventeenth century one religious movement had a significant impact on Norfolk in particular. The Puritans, who were essentially Calvinists, were at odds with the established church, the Church of England. In particular, they were opposed to the ritual nature of the Church, since in reality little had changed since Henry VIII's breakaway from Rome. They

---

10 See Chapter 5.

disliked the Church's formal structure and the role of bishops, preferring to emphasise preaching and the sanctity of the Sabbath each Sunday.

King James I made some efforts to reconcile the Puritan clergy within the Church, but after his death in 1625 religious conflict worsened. Even before this the first Puritans left England on board the *Mayflower* in September 1620, setting sail from Plymouth. Sixty-six days later, following a hazardous transatlantic crossing in autumn storms, 102 migrants made landfall at Cape Cod, Massachusetts and became known as the Pilgrim Fathers – founders of the colony of Plymouth. Not all were Puritans; some were adventurers looking for a new life or seeking a fortune. However, the predominant ethos in the colony was Puritanism.

Of the passengers who can be identified, one of the largest groups was from Norfolk. These included:

- Edward Fuller, from Redenhall, his wife, son Samuel and brother (also Samuel)
- Thomas Tinker, his wife and baby son (who died in the terrible first winter in 1620)
- John Turner and his two sons (both of whom died in the first winter)
- John Hooke, a servant (died in the first winter)
- Desire Winter, a servant

The *Mayflower* was the first of many ships that made the crossing to and from the New World and other, nearer destinations. Between 1620 and 1640 some 80,000 people left England (known as the Great Migration), with around 20,000 migrating to New England and the rest in approximately equal numbers making for Ireland, the Netherlands and the West Indies. Up to 10% of these returned during the Civil War to support Cromwell.

The frequency of old English place names in New England illustrates the widespread nature of the migration. Several states contain a county or a town called Norfolk, and there are examples of Norwich, Yarmouth, Lynn, Windham and Hingham, amongst many others. Perhaps the most important descendent of Norfolk stock was Abraham Lincoln, 16th President of the United States, a direct descendent of an apprentice weaver who emigrated from Hingham in 1637.

There is no specific evidence of individual emigrants from Stoke Ferry itself. However, given that many departed to the New World from the port of King's Lynn it is very likely that people from the village would have been among them. What is certain however, is that the Puritan movement would have strongly influenced the whole county, leading to its widespread support for Cromwell in the Civil War.

The Civil War and Another Royal visitor

After decades of simmering unrest, when Civil War actually broke out against Charles I in 1642, supporters of both sides could be found across the country. In villages and even households, loyalties were split.

Locally, the Bedingfeld family at Oxburgh Hall raised and equipped a regiment of foot soldiers to fight for the King. Local men from the estate and surrounding villages, including Stoke Ferry, were enlisted.

In the main however, Norfolk supported the Parliamentarians, raising a makeshift citizen army to fight against the King. As a result, soldiers on both sides must have come from every village and the area around Stoke Ferry had its share of skirmishes. As the number of Cromwell's supporters grew, they besieged Oxburgh Hall and set fire to it. The contents were destroyed but most of the structure survived. The Hall was surrendered to the Parliamentary forces, and the estate was confiscated.

This was not the only fighting close to Stoke Ferry. On 13th August 1643, the town of King's Lynn declared its support for the King, encouraged by the success of royalists in Lincolnshire, led by the Earl of Newcastle. Cromwell's troops, led by the Earl of Manchester, blockaded the town. Their ships cruised in the Wash and intercepted supplies. A military headquarters was set up at Setch Bridge and reinforcements were requested from across the Eastern Counties. A citizen army from Essex and Suffolk, together with locally conscripted men, marched or rode on horseback through Stoke Ferry. It is believed that some of these 'Roundhead' troops were quartered in Wretton Church. Eventually they were strong enough to take West Lynn and bombard King's Lynn and on 16th September 1643 it was forced to capitulate.

Amazingly, King Charles himself rode through Stoke Ferry during the last weeks of the Civil War, but this was no Royal Progress and probably no-one recognised him as he passed through the narrow streets and market place. By this time, he was losing the war, and had decided to escape from Oxford which was on the brink of being captured by the Roundheads. He fled the city in disguise with his two most trusted personal attendants, John Ashburnham and Dr. Michael Hudson. Their initial destination was King's Lynn, where they hoped either to rally support or take a boat to safety on the continent.

It is from Ashburnham and Hudson's evidence at their trial that the details of the journey are known. They disguised the King as a servant, and Ashburnham roughly cut his hair and beard. The other two dressed as gentlemen, carrying pistols and swords. The three rode out secretly from Oxford at three o'clock in the morning on 26th April 1646.

At Baldock, Hudson left the others, travelling on his own to Downham Market to arrange accommodation at The White Swan and make contact with Ralph Skipworth, a loyal supporter, at Snore Hall.

The King and Ashburnham stayed the night of 28th April at The Cherry Tree, a common ale-house at Mundford. The next day they rode through Whittington, along the causeway to cross the River Wissey and through Stoke Ferry to another 'blind ale-house' at Crimplesham, the King now disguised as a parson.

Here Ralph Skipworth met them with fresh horses and a new grey coat for the King, and together they went on to Downham Market. The King's disguise had been successful until then, but when a barber in Downham Market looked at him suspiciously and remarked that his hair and beard must have been cut with a knife, he feared discovery and hastily returned to Mundford. Here he learned that his hoped-for support would not be forthcoming and decided to surrender himself to the Presbyterian Scottish Army at Newark who, though opposing the King, appeared to be offering better protection than some of his other enemies.

It did not work out well for him. In time, the Scots passed Charles back to the English army - Cromwell and the Parliamentarians had won. Charles was brought to trial for treason in January 1649, presided over by Judge John Bradshaw (my ancestor)[11]. He was sentenced to death and executed in Whitehall on 30th January. Cromwell ruled as Lord Protector for only five years before his death in 1858, followed, ironically for a Republican, by his son Richard. In 1660 the monarchy was restored with Charles II as king.

Stoke Ferry through Turbulent Times

As described, even a remote corner of England could not escape involvement in the great events and issues affecting the country at large. Changes of dynasty, uprisings and rebellions, overseas wars, changing religious practices, even the changing face of agriculture all affected every part of the country, including Norfolk and always, to a greater or lesser extent, Stoke Ferry.

---

11 See Doris E Coates, *Tunes on a Penny Whistle – a Derbyshire Childhood*, 2nd Edition, The Harpsden Press, 2018.

While there are few specific historic references to the village in this period, by 1700 Stoke Ferry was a thriving commercial centre. For the next two hundred years it continued to grow in size and wealth, benefitting from its markets, road, ferry and subsequent trade. Finds of coins in and around the village attest to its importance as a trading hub throughout many reigns:

- Henry III shilling divided into quarters. Date appears to be 1220
- Elizabeth I shilling, 1571
- Charles II half-crown, 1676 or 1677 - 28th year of his reign[12]
- King's Lynn farthing, 1669, found in the Manor House, Wretton Road in a wall between the original building and a later wing
- Queen Anne two-penny piece with a hole in the centre possibly used as a medallion, 1707
- George III halfpenny, 1773
- One guinea-weight, stamped with a crown, presumably used to test whether guinea-coins were genuine, 1775
- George III large coin of yellow metal, 1817
- George IV penny, 1825

Further evidence of wealth is that many prominent houses, still standing, were being built in this period. Later chapters examine the village as it was in the 1700s and 1800s and look at important institutions such as the church, schools, inns, and other public buildings. Stoke Ferry's golden age was beginning.

---

12 Dated from the death of his father.

The Happisburgh Footprints, thought to be about 900,000 years old

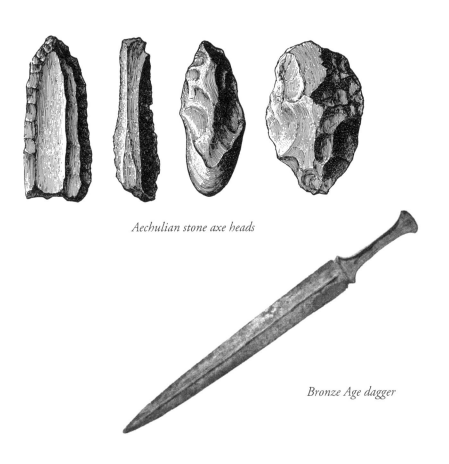

Aechulian stone axe heads

Bronze Age dagger

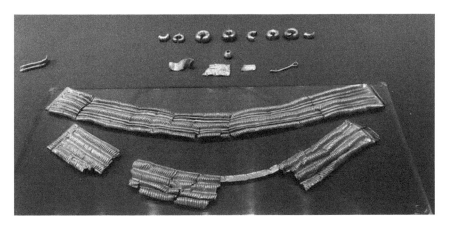

Bronze Age artifacts – Norwich Museum

Seahenge, discovered at Holme-next-the-Sea carbon-dated from 2049 BC

Grime's Graves – a Neolithic flint mine near Mundford, active between 2500 and 2200 BC

Boudicca (Boadicea), Queen of the Iceni – statue on the Embankment in London

Roman coins

Map of Roman Britain, showing the route of Icknield Way

William the Conqueror

Typical Norman longhouse

Commemorative stamps – Issued 1986, 900 years after Domesday

Castle Acre Priory, founded in 1089 in the reign of William II, showing typical round-arched Norman architecture - dissolved in 1537 by Henry VIII

Oxburgh Hall – late medieval style, completed c.1482, the last year of Edward IV's reign

Henry III
Granted Charter to Stoke Ferry in 1248

Henry VII
Visited Oxburgh Hall in 1487

Catherine Howard
5th wife of Henry VIII, executed for affair
with Thomas Derham of Crimplesham

Charles I
Travelled through Stoke Ferry in
1646 trying to avoid capture

The Second Part

In which is explained
the vital importance of several forms
of transport to the creation of great
wealth in Stoke Ferry

Chapter Five

Waterways - the Fens and the Wissey

Long before the advent of any road networks, boats of every description were the primary means of transporting people and goods. As described in earlier chapters, family groups, marauding raiding parties, settlers and whole armies came to our shores by boat from across the Channel or the North Sea. The Danes (Vikings) were renowned sailors, most probably 'discovering' the American continent long before Christopher Columbus' and Amerigo Vespucci's expeditions at the end of the fifteenth century[1]. In Chapter 3 it was noted that the Vikings not only landed on the coast of East Anglia when invading but sailed up the rivers of the Fens.

Stoke Ferry, as the name asserts, owes its very existence to the river crossing. The ferry, and later the bridge, is its defining feature. This, and the village's location on the first 'high ground'[2] at the edge of the fens has been highly significant to the wealth and development of the village, both when the whole area was mostly covered by water and in more recent times when it has become an extensive and abundant agricultural centre.

The Fens

The fens were formed following the retreat of the Anglian Ice Age, leaving an extensive area of marshy ground and wetlands in what is now Cambridgeshire, south Lincolnshire and west Norfolk. While there is evidence of settlements around the fringes of this area, the fens themselves were mainly unpopulated, except for a few islands appearing above

---

1 There were extensive Viking settlements in Greenland from the tenth century and strong evidence that they also settled parts of the North American continent after landing in Newfoundland in 985 AD.

2 Stoke Ferry is 65ft (19m) above sea level, while the lowest elevation in the fens is about 10ft (3m) below sea level.

the water line. These include the religious centres of Ely, Peterborough, Crowland, Ramsey and Thorney which had priories, cathedrals or both. The Romans built a causeway across the marshes, linking Denver in Norfolk to Peterborough but the whole area remained isolated and virtually impassable for many centuries.

However, although sparsely populated, the undrained fens were of immense economic value to those living on their fringes, including communities such as Stoke Ferry, Whittington, Wretton and West Dereham. Locals could navigate the wetlands using punts and other shallow-draught vessels allowing them to harvest wildfowl and fish in vast numbers, including industrial quantities of eels. Plant material, particularly reeds and willows also played an important role in the fenland economy. Additionally, lush seasonal grazing grounds were available for dairy herds supplying produce to Ely, Cambridge and further afield as well as for fattening livestock.

Nowadays the picture is completely different - the fens form the most productive area of arable farmland in the country, with its rich black soil producing a wide array of crops. There are estimated to be about 4,000 farms in the fens involved in agriculture and horticulture including vast bulb-fields in Lincolnshire. As a consequence, many food and drink manufacturers have based their operations in the region.

The drainage of the fens has had a progressive impact on the surrounding areas, including Stoke Ferry. As far back as Roman times, attempts were made to drain parts of the western fens and there is further evidence of schemes in the Middle Ages.

The first widespread attempt to drain the area was in the 1630s, when the Fourth Earl of Bedford, with the support of Charles I, commissioned a Dutch expert, Cornelius Vermuyden, to undertake the work. Two large cuts or drainage channels were made across the Cambridgeshire fen joining the River Ouse to the sea. These were known as the Old Bedford Level and the New Bedford Level after their sponsor.

Initially successful, the work was interrupted by the Civil War and hampered by fierce local resistance and even sabotage, a recurring theme. To the communities bordering the wetlands the fens were a vital and very profitable resource. Drainage schemes were, in effect, a form of enclosure creating a more manageable agricultural environment for the landlords, while depriving the commoners of their previous means of livelihood.

Following these early projects and due to the shrinkage of the land after it had been drained, the area was still constantly at the mercy of the tides. By the end of the seventeenth century the land was again under water.

Longer-term results were achieved by new drainage projects in the eighteenth and nineteenth centuries, again not without local opposition. These schemes were more effective when steam pumps replaced wind-driven versions in the 1830s, enabling constant pumping from the land, by then mostly below the level of the rivers and the sea.

Work continued well into the twentieth century, since fenland areas were still vulnerable to disastrous floods. In 1949 and 1953 the effect of exceptionally high winds backed tides up the rivers of the fens and caused numerous breeches of riverbanks and widespread inundation of the surrounding land.

With the aim of finally eliminating the risk of flooding, a major three-part project was implemented between 1954 and 1964. The first two phases of the project consisted of straightening and deepening the River Ouse between Denver and Ely and construction of a Relief Channel parallel to the Ouse from Denver to Wiggenhall, just south of King's Lynn, intended to regulate the flow of the river during high tides.

The third stage was known as the Cut-off Channel, a new drainage channel from Barton Mills in Suffolk to Denver, passing through the parish of Stoke Ferry and, during construction, providing endless fascination to local residents, young and old. The original concept and plan for this waterway had been proposed by Vermuyden in the 1630s; three hundred and thirty years later, in 1964, it was finally put into effect.

The eventual success of fenland drainage transformed the agricultural economy of East Anglia but saw the demise of a form of land management that had supported the fen-edge communities for centuries.

The River Wissey

Until the end of the nineteenth century when the railway arrived in the village, the river was of vital importance of Stoke Ferry. The Wissey rises near Bradenham in mid-Norfolk and flows a total of thirty-one miles (nearly fifty km) to join the Ouse near Hilgay. The last eleven miles (seventeen km) are still navigable.

It is perhaps surprising that such a small river should generate any literary attention, but Roger Deakin[3] wrote this about a stretch of water a few miles upstream from Stoke Ferry, after taking a swim along its course for about a mile:

It was full of fish and wild flowers, and, for all I knew, crayfish and naiads, wonderfully remote from any sort of civilisation. The banks were thick with purple water-mint, forget-me-not, hawkbit, and clouds of yellow brimstones and cabbage whites browsing on the purple loosestrife along the banks. The water was polished, deep green and gold, shining from its velvet bed of crowfoot and fine gravel; it seemed quite out of time, flowing as sweetly as the river in Millais' painting of the drowned Ophelia, decked with wild flowers.

Five hundred years ago the Great Ouse was tidal for forty-nine miles up-river from King's Lynn, and the Wissey for at least six miles from its confluence with the Ouse. Because of this, navigation has always been possible at least as far as Stoke Ferry, and in early times the upper limit was Oxborough Hythe where there was a landing stage and granaries until 1800.

King's Lynn was already a considerable port in the fifteenth century. It had extensive coastal traffic, and its sailing ships ventured to the Baltic and France to trade. A list of imports to Lynn at that time includes wax, Spanish iron, nails, mace, frankincense, figs, raisins, ginger, nuts and sugar. It is recorded that boats carrying forty tons could sail thirty-six miles up the Ouse at neap tide[4]. Some of the imports must have found their way up the Wissey to Stoke Ferry.

Corn was a major commodity handled by King's Lynn at that period, collected from the fertile regions of the area, taken there by boat and bought by merchants. It was then dispatched either by coastal routes or through a network of waterways to other parts of the country. This early trade was only possible by boat, since there were no roads suitable for carrying goods for more than a few miles. For hundreds of years boats sailed up and down the Wissey, carrying a variety of goods, and using some form of wharf or landing stage near the bridge or ferry.

In medieval times, sailing barges had been used for river transport, but they

---

3   Deakin, Roger and Holmes, David, *Waterlog – A Swimmer's Journey through Britain*, Vintage, 1999. This section is about the river near Didlington.

4   Neap tide is the average high tide occurring twice per lunar month, midway between full moon and no moon.

were too dependent on winds and currents. In the seventeenth century, 'fen lighters', built of oak or elm were introduced and remained in use until the nineteenth century when they were replaced by iron barges. Fen lighters were 'haled' or towed by horses led by boys or men, and wherever possible 'haling paths' were constructed on the riverbank. Accounts from the eighteenth century tell of boys and horses often wading waist-deep in water. When the mouth of a dyke had to be crossed they often boarded both boy and horse onto the barge, sometimes with disastrous results.

Cargoes of wheat must have been common, since by the mid-seventeenth century, the Ouse basin was the leading wheat and barley area in England, and the chief source of corn exports. The size of the Lynn Cornmarket gives some idea of the importance of this trade.

Transport of goods remained difficult and expensive, even when turnpike roads[5] made it easier for people to travel. Carters with their horses and waggons could only travel short distances but improved roads provided better access to the wharf, so the effect was actually to increase water-borne freight.

It was between 1750 and 1880 that Stoke Ferry enjoyed the greatest prosperity as an inland port. Several factors led to increased traffic: movement of cargo was easier after the second Denver Sluice opened in 1748 improving control of tides and water levels; demand for coal continued to grow; and merchants took advantage of the improved roads to collect and deliver goods to and from riverside stores. From 1800 onwards the malting industry added to the tonnage. Above all, transport of freight by water was cheap. It was said that a waterman with one horse pulling a barge could carry as much as a carter with forty horses[6].

By 1800 the wharf near the bridge had been developed, providing granaries, warehouses and coal-stores for storage. A little later, a maltings was added to process barley for the brewing industry. In addition there was a staithe (a smaller landing dock) at Whittington to serve the maltings there, and further storage facilities at Oxborough Hythe. Throughout the 1700s a thriving merchant class became more and more influential. Farmers and traders became inter-dependent and made considerable financial gains. Barley, wheat, wool, seeds, locally brewed ales, hides and later, malt were sent by

---

5   Stoke Ferry Turnpike was opened in 1770 – see Chapter 6.

6   Until the motor age, bulk transport of goods by water was cheaper than any form of land transport. The price was per journey, not per mile, and additional fees were paid at each sluice or lock. Charges for most goods were by the 'load', a measure which varied with each commodity, e.g. 40 cwt. of salt, 54 bushels of barley or potatoes, 1,000 bricks, tiles or slates. The cost of carrying coal was calculated by the 'chaldron', sometimes called the 'Lynn Measure' and equivalent to 53 cwt. Actual charges are not easy to verify, but in 1750 a load from King's Lynn to St Neots – about 60 miles (96 km) - cost four shillings (equivalent to £42 in 2018).

barge to Lynn via the Wissey and the Great Ouse. Returning barges brought coal, wine, salt, barrels of fish, pots, timber, bricks, slates and tiles to be sold in the surrounding neighbourhood.

The trade in coal is particularly interesting. Without water transport Norfolk would have had little opportunity to obtain coal until the coming of the railway. In fact, coal had been brought to Stoke Ferry since about 1700. These early supplies arrived at Lynn in coastal ships from Newcastle, trans-shipped in barges up-river towards Ely and Cambridge and then brought up the Wissey in smaller loads.

In the early nineteenth century, coal came from another source and direction. The opening of the Grand Junction Canal from London to Birmingham in 1805 made it possible for strings of barges to carry coal from the Midlands to Bedford, and thence to Cambridge and Ely. This became the main distribution centre from which Stoke Ferry coal merchants were supplied. The returning barges carried farm produce which could then be sold in the rapidly developing industrial towns of the Midlands.

Stoke Ferry's status as a port considerably enhanced the community's prosperity in the eighteenth and nineteenth centuries, by far the most prosperous era for the village[7]. Farmers took advantage of an extended market for their products and even remote farms had access to the river on the numerous drainage lodes on their land. To them the barge traffic made all the difference between poverty and relative economic security. Merchants grew rich and spent their wealth constructing new houses or giving a face-lift to existing ones. Most of the larger houses in the area date from the period 1720 to 1800, the true Golden Age for Stoke Ferry.

Two major local industries, malt and sugar manufacture, depended on the river in the early days of their development. At Whittington, the maltings with their own staithe appear in the details of the sale of the Partridge estate in 1809. In pre-railway days the barley arrived by barge and the processed malt left the same way.

The maltings buildings could still be seen on the wharf until the late twentieth century. For several generations these were owned by the Winfield family. White's Directory for 1845 lists 'Frederick William Winfield and Henry William Winfield, corn and coal merchants and maltsters, doing considerable business at the wharf'. Kelly's 1888 Directory shows 'Frederick

---

7   See Chapter 8.

Charles Winfield, maltster, corn, coal and coke merchant and wharfinger[8] and agent for the Life Association of Scotland'.

When the sugar factory was first built at Wissington it had no road access and all supplies in and out of the plant had to be transported by either water or rail. This continued after 1936 when British Sugar Manufacturers were absorbed by the British Sugar Corporation. The first hard road to the factory was built during 1939 - 45 by Italian prisoners of war.

On the river, they operated at least three tugs, named 'Wissington', 'Stoke Ferry' and 'Littleport', and a fleet of barges. Sugar beet was collected from a wide area of fen. There were many staithes along the waterway to which the farmers brought their beet, either by horse and tumbril or by small boats along their own lodes and dykes. The tugs would tow strings of empty 'lighters' (barges) and leave them at the staithes, picking up others loaded with beet. From some places (including Stoke Ferry wharf) horses were used to 'hale' or tow the lighters.

In summer the lighters were used to bring coal from Lynn Docks to stockpile for the following season. They also carried quantities of limestone, essential in the processing of sugar.

By the 1920s the river traffic had virtually disappeared and the Wissey reverted to a quiet and peaceful waterway, teeming with fish, including pike, roach, bream, perch, tench and occasionally seatrout. In the early summer the stretch between Stoke Ferry and Whittington was ideal for 'babbing'[9] for eels, an excellent source of supplementary nutrition or income.

Today the river is a quiet backwater. No commercial traffic operates but riverboats and canal narrow boats can still be seen chugging quietly along, sometimes mooring along the banks near Stoke Ferry bridge. The buildings by the wharf, lying disused in the 1980s, have been demolished and replaced by a small housing development which tastefully reflects their earlier usage. Where once there was a teeming commercial wharf, now there is an idyllic and quiet residential and leisure area.

---

8 The owner of a wharf.

9 Babbing is fishing without a hook.

Chapter Six

Roads, Turnpikes and Droves

From earliest times human populations have migrated vast distances across open country, but it was not until the growth of commerce and trade that 'roads' were needed and constructed, firstly in areas of difficult terrain, such as marshy or hilly ground. The earliest road in England is at Glastonbury in Somerset, which, according to highly precise carbon dating of the trees used, was made in 3807 or 3806 BC.

Of more importance to East Anglia is the Icknield Way, a road named after the Iceni, but thought to be in use for some centuries before their appearance. Ordnance Survey[1] shows the track running from the north Norfolk coast near Thornham, south and southwest passing close to Stoke Ferry, on past Cambridge to Dunstable and the Chiltern hills, crossing the Thames between Dorchester and Reading and on to Salisbury. From there, it may have continued to the Dorset coast and linked up with other ancient tracks from Cornwall. This road must have been used during the Bronze Age to transport tin from Cornwall and copper from Wales to Norfolk.

Also nearby is Peddars Way, thought to be a Roman road, built on the track of a much older highway running up to the north Norfolk coast. While this could have been used to bring troops to the Iceni region, it was more likely an alternative route to the north, by sea from a port at Holme-next-the Sea. Interestingly, the road does not go to the Roman settlement at Brancaster, which would have been easy to achieve across the relatively flat countryside if that had been the aim. There is also evidence of an east-west Roman road from Caister, passing very close to the village before crossing the fens and linking up with the main Roman Road highway from London to Lincoln.

---

1   *Map of Roman Britain*, Third Edition, Ordnance Survey 1956.

Local Roads near Stoke Ferry

As has been described in previous chapters, the village developed from early settlements on a narrow belt of firm land on the edge of a large region of fens. Its exact siting was the river crossing, enabling communication between King's Lynn northwards and Thetford, Brandon and London to the south. Furthermore, since the river was navigable to Stoke Ferry, the wharf constituted the main point for onward distribution by road for the whole district. Thus this was not an isolated agricultural community but a place well connected to the rest of East Anglia and beyond.

This road from Whittington to Stoke Ferry over or across the Wissey has existed in some form for many centuries. There are records of a dispute in 1275 between the villagers of Stoke Ferry and the Prior of Shouldham, then the Lord of the Manor about the ferry, which he controlled. Inhabitants resented the crippling tolls charged for this crossing and, showing considerable independence, built a bridge. Angry at the loss of revenue from his ferry, the Prior destroyed the bridge. Not to be deterred, the people had the Prior summoned before the 'Hundred Court' where a jury found him guilty of 'breaking down the bridge and disturbing the passage, to the great injury of the neighbourhood and travellers', and ordered him to rebuild it.

It may be assumed, therefore, that there was a bridge over the Wissey at Stoke Ferry from the last quarter of the thirteenth century.

Another reference to the road in medieval times is a record, dated 1482, stating that Richard Constable of Wretton *left by will 4 or 5 acres of land for the reparation of a Causey (causeway) which extended from Whittington to Stoke Ferry.* A much later Whittington record states *The land left by Richard Constable for the reparation of the Causey was vested in the Trustees of the Turnpike by the Act passed in 1770.*

The Stoke Ferry Turnpike[2]

In this period roads throughout England were very basic, mere dirt tracks, muddy and impassable after heavy rains. They were constantly rutted with the mud churned up by coaches, farm wagons, trains of packhorses, relays of post horses, great droves of cattle and herds of sheep, geese and turkeys. Most were so narrow that two trains of packhorses could not pass each other. There are reports that travellers actually drowned in some potholes in East Anglia.

---

2   Additional material for this chapter drawn from J.F. Fone, *The Stoke Ferry Turnpike*, Norfolk Archaeology, October 1981.

The roads received very little maintenance until an Act of 1555 in the reign of Queen Mary (in force until 1835), made each parish responsible for the roads within its boundary. Owners or occupiers of land valued at £50 per year were obliged to provide a cart, horses and two men, and each parishioner was expected to contribute four days' work a year to road-mending (later increased to six days). This usually entailed nothing more than filling the worst holes with piles of large stones. Since each village was virtually self-sufficient there was no great enthusiasm for improving communications with nearby towns. In fact, a tidy profit could sometimes be made by helping to dig out travellers bogged down in the mud. It is no wonder that travel was hazardous and slow.

By the late seventeenth century the increase in traffic, particularly between the larger towns, had made this system unsustainable. To deal with the problem Turnpike Trusts were established to repair and improve particular stretches of road. This was essentially a seventeenth century form of privatisation. 'Trusts' were set up by landowners or businessmen who, in return for shares in the venture and the ability to charge tolls, undertook to keep the road in good repair.

Each Turnpike Trust required a separate Act of Parliament, but Norfolk was very tardy in setting them up. The first Trust in the county was established in 1695, but it was not until the whole of the Norwich to London road had been 'turnpiked', that other areas of the county started to develop their own trusts. Only in the late 1760s were proposals made for turnpikes radiating from King's Lynn to Gayton, Grimston, Babingley and Hillington. A further decade later - in 1770 - the King's Lynn to Brandon and the Stoke Ferry Trusts were established.

There is some controversy over the ownership and establishment of the Stoke Ferry Trust. It was intended that the turnpike roads should serve the wider community not just the needs of the local aristocracy. The ideal principle was that the turnpikes should link up with others so that travel across the county and the country as a whole could be more joined up. The Stoke Ferry Trust seems to have widely ignored this. Moreover, the branch roads from Stoke Ferry were particularly favourably routed to serve the estates of Sir Hanson Berney at Barton Bendish, Sir Richard Bedingfeld at Oxburgh and John Richard Dashwood at Cockley Cley and, further south towards Brandon, to the Earl of Mountrath's estate at Weeting (unsurprisingly, these noble gentlemen were Trustees).

The approval of the Stoke Ferry Trust was 'fast-tracked' through parliament in 1770, most probably because its four noble promoters managed to obtain 157 Trustees from a wide area of the county, including four MPs, four mayors of Lynn, the Recorder of Lynn and 25 clergy. Only seven appear to be from Stoke Ferry itself, but one was Roger Micklefield, the local solicitor. Paid-up capital of £1,500 was required for the trust, but there isn't a complete record of shareholders[3].

Tollgates were erected so that money for the roads could be collected. The income enabled road surfaces to be improved, making travel in wheeled vehicles faster and encouraging more traffic, and therefore more profits for the Trustees. The cost and inconvenience of stopping every few miles to pay the toll and wait for the gates to be opened was therefore offset by the greater speed and comfort for travellers.

At first, whatever local material was available was used for surfacing the Turnpike Road. In Stoke Ferry area this would be pebbles, flints and limestone, dug from the numerous pits that are still a feature of the area.

The 'pike-man' or gatehouse keeper who collected the tolls was housed in a small, often one-storey cottage, circular or octagonal in shape, with windows facing in all directions so that approaching traffic could be seen. He typically wore a uniform of black glazed hat, corduroy breeches, white stockings and a white linen apron. He was a most unpopular man.

At Stoke Ferry the toll-gate cottage stood at the junction of Oxborough Road and Bridge Road (remaining in use as a dwelling until demolished in 1970). Tolls were collected from traffic from all three directions. Villagers from Stoke Ferry, Wretton, West Dereham, Wereham and Boughton were exempt from the tolls if they were only travelling as far as the river to collect supplies from the staithe[4].

Toll charges varied from place to place and from one period to another. The only remaining local list of charges is on the wall of The Jenyn's Arms pub at Denver Sluice. These tolls were still applied until 1963, although most of them had remained virtually unchanged since the construction of the second Denver Sluice in 1748.

Following the 1830 Trust Renewal, Stoke Ferry Trust introduced rates for new-fangled vehicles drawn by steam and gas for the first time: these were the same as at Denver - 2s 6d - whereas the highest toll for an animal-drawn vehicle was only 4d. Interestingly, charges for wheeled vehicles varied with the width of the wheel, in the belief that wider wheels were less harmful to the road surface than narrow ones –

3 The only evidence we have is from the will of Dr. William Harvey (see Chapter 15), made in 1801, two years before his death which included a bequest of '*Two several Turnpike Securities of £100, secured by way of a mortgage of the Tolls arising and becoming payable on the Turnpike Road from Stoke Ferry to Brandon and Thetford*'.

4 A landing stage for loading or unloading boats.

Carts with wheels over 6 inches wide - three pence
Carts with wheels over 4½ inches wide - three pence, three farthings
Carts with wheels under 4½ inches wide - four pence

Charges at Denver Sluice Bridge
(The Jenyn's Arms)

	s	d
Every person on foot on Easter Monday		1
Every horse, mare, gelding or ass, ox, cow or large cattle		1
Every sheep, lamb, pig or calf		½
Every cycle with three or less wheels		1
Every cart or carriage with two wheels, including one horse, mare, gelding, or ass if drawn by same		6
Every additional horse etc. drawing cart or carriage		1
Every wagon, road trolley, van, implement, thrashing or other machine, vehicle or carriage with four wheels if unladen	1	0
As above, if laden	2	0
Thrashing or traction engine or steam roller whose weight does not exceed 5 tons	2	6

Vehicles over 5 tons prohibited

EXEMPTIONS Members of the Board, Officers, Servants and workmen when engaged in the business of the Board. Inhabitants on the West Side of the Sluice when going or returning to Divine Service on Sunday.

Note: Some of these descriptions would not have appeared on earlier lists and reflect the development in transport and agricultural equipment in the late nineteenth and early twentieth centuries.

The Stoke Ferry Trust did not result in increasing the wealth of its Trustees. The original Act expired in 1791 and was renewed, as it was again in 1811 and 1830. This last Act states that great improvements had been made in the roads with the money borrowed, but it could not be paid off, requiring a further renewal of the Act. The accounts submitted with this application make poor reading.

Accounts of the Stoke Ferry Turnpike Trust

Income (£)	1823 - 4	1824 - 5	1825 - 6	1826 - 7	1827 - 8
Tolls	380	384	384	384	386
Contributions from parishes	85	96	116	102	101
Total Income	**465**	**480**	**500**	**486**	**487**

Expenditure (£)	1823 - 4	1824 - 5	1825 - 6	1826 - 7	1827 - 8
Repairs	225	273	250	326	369
Administration	106	87	71	100	118
Interest	236	198	105	156	135
Total Expenditure	**567**	**558**	**426**	**582**	**622**
Profit / Loss	**-102**	**-78**	**76**	**-96**	**-135**

The 1832 Act was the last private act obtained by the Stoke Ferry Trust, and it finally ceased operating on 1st November 1870, exactly 100 years after it had been set up. In 1870, The Highways and Locomotive Act provided that 'disturnpiked' roads should become 'main roads' and revert to the parish with the County Council bearing 50% of the costs. With the exception of a small number of bridges and tunnels, the era of private enterprise road building was at an end for the next 100 years.

Droving - Impact on Stoke Ferry

On most turnpikes there were special rates for animals in large numbers. In 1839 the general charge for cattle was 1s 6d a score (20), and for sheep 1s 0d a score. Local residents and farmers who needed to move animals from one pasture to another generally opposed these tolls. Where possible, alternative routes were devised so that carriages and stock could avoid the tollgate.

Among the bitterest opponents of the new turnpike roads were the drovers. For over two hundred years droving had been an essential feature of a vast logistics system supplying London and other centres of population with beef and lamb. By 1864 over two hundred thousand cattle and one and a half million sheep arrived annually at Smithfield Market. These all arrived 'on the hoof' giving an indication of the continuous traffic along the droving routes. Sheep, turkeys and geese were also walked long distances to market, but it was the cattle trade which was most important to the Stoke Ferry area.

Cattle breeding was largely centred in Scotland and Wales. However, animals could not be fattened up there, so large numbers were wintered in the south on the way to London. Scottish drovers would travel down the eastern side of England to East Anglia with herds of about two hundred cattle each. They travelled at two miles an hour covering fourteen to sixteen miles in a day. At night they grazed the cattle in fields rented to them by farmers, taking care that the beasts did not trespass on other private land. Stray animals were put in the village 'pound' or 'pinfold', where they were kept under the care of the 'pinder' until the offending drover had paid a fine to the village constable.

The drovers slept at nearby inns, rising early to get their herds on the way before other traffic. Where possible, they avoided direct roads and travelled on drove-roads, lokes or drifts[5]. On arrival in Norfolk, the cattle were sold to local farmers at Cattle Fairs, especially those at St Faith's near Norwich and Setchey near King's Lynn. Many cattle also found their way to smaller fairs and markets including Stoke Ferry. Once fattened up on local farms they set off on weekly droves[6] to London to be sold at Smithfield.

This continuous movement of livestock began to decrease after 1830. Better feeding methods made it easier for the Scottish breeders to fatten them up for market in Scotland. The Industrial Revolution opened the possibility of sending stock by rail or sea, instead of walking them hundreds of miles overland. By the 1840s, railways were taking over the traffic on a large scale. Cattle from Scotland could be transported directly to London and were also needed locally to feed the ever increasing urban population of Glasgow and the central belt. This was not only a loss to Norfolk farmers; it also reduced the importance of cattle fairs and markets like those of Stoke Ferry.

Road Improvements

When the Trustees of the Turnpikes made more profits, they started to employ engineers to improve methods of road construction. The most famous, John McAdam (1756 - 1836) invented the method used today of packing together

---

5 Various terms for minor roads not subject to tolls. Here, 'drove' is the road or lane, and is still used for identifying a number of small roads in Stoke Ferry, such as Furlong Drove, Limehouse Drove and River Drove.

6 In this context, a drove is the movement of large groups of cattle from one place to another, managed by a 'drover'.

small broken stones above the level of the surrounding land. This was rolled tight by passing traffic (later by steam-rollers). Roads were cambered with drains on each side, solving many of the previous problems of mud and ruts. This method was adopted on the local turnpike and Stoke Ferry was opened to the outside world (in a north-south direction, at any rate; there was no direct route to Norwich or the east coast, and only very limited access across the fens).

By the early 1800s, stagecoaches (now able to travel at up to ten miles an hour on the new roads) and carriages of all kinds were commonplace. Traffic through Stoke Ferry was heavy and The Hill saw great activity, with three inns - The Crown, The Duke and The King's Head - catering for travellers and their horses[7]. People could move more easily to neighbouring towns and buy things formerly made at home (e.g. clothes and shoes), impacting local shops and artisans.

All this increased traffic put a great strain on the roads, which had changed very little over the centuries. In 1894 the Local Government Act set up County Councils, which assumed control over roads, but did little to improve them.

Stoke Ferry suffered one unfortunate change with the demolition of its beautiful bridge with wrought-iron railings. This was because it was deemed unsafe for the steam traction engines which were becoming widely used at that time. The old bridge was demolished in 1899 to be replaced by the ugly flat steel construction still in use today.

Traffic increased even more with the advent of motor transport in the first two decades of the twentieth century. By this time, roads had to be surfaced with tar, a costly process, partly funded by taxes on motor vehicles. Stoke Ferry gained an improved road surface, but its route and structure remained as it had been in the days of horse transport.

The Bypass

As time went on the main road through Stoke Ferry became grossly inadequate for the volume and size of traffic passing through the village, generating pollution and posing a serious danger to pedestrians.

For many years the Parish Council petitioned the County for a bypass without success. There were multiple half-promises and postponements and only after a number of fatal road accidents was approval finally given. Work started in 1983 and on 8th August 1985 the bypass was officially opened. The programme that day stated:

---

7   See Chapter 9.

Lifting the Siege

Many of those attending today's opening ceremony will have horror stories to tell of the traffic through Stoke Ferry; stories of pedestrians knocked down, walls demolished, and buildings so scraped and blackened by traffic that the residents either abandoned them or shut up their front rooms to live only at the rear. Stoke Ferry, created and made prosperous by trade from river and railway, has been under siege from the traffic of the A134 road.

When Sir Paul Hawkins cuts the tape today he will not only open a new bypass but also initiate a renaissance of the town.

It was the beginning of a new era for Stoke Ferry[8].

---

8   For a review of how that renaissance worked out in practice, see Chapter 19.

Chapter Seven

The Coming of the Railway

The Railway Age began with the opening of a line between Stockton and Darlington in 1825. For the next decade and a half numerous relatively short lines were built, but it was not until the 1840s that railway-building mania fully took hold. Private companies were set up, believing that fortunes could be made from this new means of passenger and freight transport. While some did indeed make fortunes, many faced financial difficulties from the outset.

The railways first came to Norfolk as part of the 1840s boom. By 1845, two principal routes linked Norwich to London - one through Colchester and Ipswich and the other through Cambridge and Brandon. From Cambridge (linked to London in 1844) the west Norfolk line extended to Ely by 1845, finally linking to King's Lynn in 1847.

The development of these lines brought considerable benefits to East Anglian farmers and traders. Freight trains carried vast quantities of wheat, malt, barley, oats, flour, thousands of live-stock and huge supplies of meat, poultry, milk and other products to London and other markets. In the opposite direction coal, fertilisers, animal food and other supplies became more easily available in East Anglia, often at a lower cost than previously.

Agriculture was transformed. The introduction of rail transport eliminated the practice of droving cattle from Scotland to the London markets. As a result, the business of fattening Scottish cattle in Norfolk, described in Chapter 6, was no longer necessary. Many Norfolk landowners switched to arable farming and breeding cattle locally. Farming in Norfolk enjoyed its greatest prosperity in the 1850s and 1860s when rail-borne trade with London was booming.

The Stoke Ferry Branch Line

In November 1864 it was proposed to build a railway linking Downham Market to Brandon, through Stoke Ferry (known as The Downham, Stoke and Brandon Railway). Railway 1 was to run from Downham to a point just north of Stoke Ferry, with a tramway linking to Stoke Ferry Wharf. Railway 2 would continue on an arched 50ft bridge over the Wissey north of Whittington, through Methwold and on to Brandon. For some reason this proposal was never implemented. In 1877 a further proposal by a company called The Norfolk Central Railway to build a line linking March and Wymondham via Downham Market and Stoke Ferry was vetoed by the Great Eastern Railway (GER).

Consequently, as late as the 1870s, Stoke Ferry's nearest point on the railway was Downham Market, seven miles away. Local farmers were disadvantaged and recognised that there would be considerable benefits in having a rail link to the village. Permission to build a branch line was sought from Parliament and granted on 21st July 1879.

The Downham and Stoke Ferry Company was formed by local businessmen with a share capital of £60,000[1]. A single-track line, measuring 7 miles 1 furlong was built, with stations at Stoke Ferry, Abbey (for West Dereham), Ryston and Denver, where it joined the main line to Downham Market. It was opened for freight only on 1st August 1882 as a private line under Great Eastern Railway (GER) operation, providing speedy and efficient transit of goods at economic rates. This led to a steep decline in water-borne traffic, as maltings, grain and coal merchants switched from lighters to railway trucks.

Freight Charges – Great Eastern Railway (GER) October 1880

As an indication, the charges on GER from 1880 for 'Brewers and Distillers Grains' were as follows:

Scale of rates for the conveyance of the above traffic, in truck loads, of 5 tons and upwards, at the owners risk, Station to Station, distant 50 miles or more apart, on the Great Eastern Railway (per ton):

---

1   Equivalent to nearly £7m in 2018.

	s.	d.
up to 50 miles	4	2
51 to 60 miles	4	7
61 to 70 miles	5	0
71 to 85 miles	5	5
86 to 100 miles	5	10
101 to 120 miles	6	3
121 and above	6	8 [2]

This table shows that the maximum charge was only one penny per ton per mile, and for longer distances considerably less than this. While this is still likely to be much higher than an equivalent load by canal, the advantage of speed to market clearly outweighed the additional cost, resulting in the rapid demise of the canals in this period.

Passenger Traffic

After operating independently for over fifteen years, the Downham and Stoke Ferry Company was acquired by GER on 1st January 1898 and the branch line absorbed into its operations. From then until 1930 there was, in addition to the freight, a frequent passenger service between Stoke Ferry and Downham Market, with connections to King's Lynn, Hunstanton and Wells and to Cambridge and London.

For most of this period up to six trains ran each way per day, with additional trains for King's Lynn market on Tuesdays and Saturdays, as seen in the timetable for 1899 below. The same pattern, with small variations in timings was still operating in the 1911 timetable. The passenger service was slightly reduced after World War I, but the September 1929 timetable still shows four weekday trains in each direction, with an extra passenger train on Saturday. Most of these trains had two coaches and a parcels van.

---

2 Between £25 for 50 miles and £40 for 121 miles and above at 2018 values.

1899 Timetable

	morn	morn	morn	aft	aft	aft
Stoke Ferry	8 10	9 18	1115	1 58	5 15	6 55
Downham Market	8 35	9 43	1140	2 23	5 40	7 20
	a					b
Liverpool St. (connection)	1110	1235	2 50	6 10	8 25	9 50

	morn	morn	morn	morn	aft	aft	aft	aft
Liverpool St. (connection)		5 45	9 10	1150		2 30	4 30	5 15
Downham Market	8 48	1025	1215	2 40	4 30	6 00	6 43	7 50
Stoke Ferry	9 13	1055	1240	3 05	4 55	6 25	7 08	8 15
	a				c	d	a	b

a. Monday only, b. Except Monday and Tuesday, c. Tuesday only, d. Except Monday
No trains on Sundays
All trains stop at Abbey, Ryston and Denver

Fares[3]

		s	d
Stoke Ferry to Liverpool Street	1st Class Single	15	3
	3rd Class Single	8	0
Stoke Ferry to King's Lynn	1st Class Single	2	1
	3rd Class Single	1	7½
	3rd Class Return	2	8

September 1929 Timetable

	am	am	pm	pm	pm
Stoke Ferry	8 25	1015	1 34	5 15	5 25
Downham Market	8 50	1040	2 06	5 40	5 50
				a	b
Liverpool St. (connection)	1127	2 07	6 10	8 35	8 33

---

3   1st class single to Liverpool Street was an expensive £95 in 2018 equivalence and 3rd class c. £37. Fares to Lynn were c. £13 for a 1st class single, £10 for 3rd class single and £16.50 for 3rd class return.

	am	am	am	pm	pm	pm
Liverpool St. (connection)	5 50	8 30	1150		2 34	2 34
Downham Market	9 22	1107	2 23	4 20	5 57	6 12
Stoke Ferry	9 52	1132	2 48	4 47	6 22	6 37
				c	a d	b

a. Saturdays excepted, b. Saturdays only, c. Tuesdays only, d. Tuesdays arrives Stoke Ferry at 6 27pm
No trains on Sundays

In addition, cheap excursion trains ran to Hunstanton - very popular for children's treats and club outings. The excursion fare to Hunstanton from Stoke Ferry was 4s 8d return between 1920 - 30[4]. Mr. F. T. Bush[5] remembered paying one shilling for a return trip to Hunstanton when he was a child in about 1900. Meanwhile Mr. G. A. Jolly[6] of Tilney St. Lawrence, remembered the range of goods carried to and from Stoke Ferry between 1920 and 1930 when he was employed as porter and guard at the station:

> *Daily trains of many wagons of coal arrived to serve four merchants with extensive local trade. Churns of milk were picked up from Stoke Ferry and Abbey to connect with London trains. The maltings at Stoke Ferry and Whittington did considerable business, receiving loads of barley and dispatching processed malt. Grain, seeds and wool fleeces were carried in considerable quantities.*

Mr. Jolly often acted as guard on an extra train of cattle trucks, loaded with stock for King's Lynn Market every Tuesday. The return run back to Stoke Ferry brought sheep, pigs and other livestock. Trainloads of Irish cattle arrived at Stoke Ferry for dealers in the area. Timber was regularly carried, chiefly from woodlands in the Brecklands area. At Ryston they often picked up a load of willow to be sent to factories manufacturing cricket bats.

Parcel traffic was also very important at Stoke Ferry station. Each of the six daily passenger trains had a parcels van and one clerk was employed full time at the

---

4 Equivalent to c £13 in 2018.

5 'Freddy' Bush grew up in Whittington and was a frequent correspondent of Doris Coates. His writings and pictures have been a useful first-hand source. One shilling in 1900 would be worth c. £6 in 2018.

6 Another of Doris Coates's correspondents.

Stoke Ferry parcels office to deal with them. This included a daily consignment of eggs. There was an egg-packing depot actually on the station which received eggs from poultry keepers throughout the district for packing and dispatch.

At Keeble Sidings at Wissington trains picked up large quantities of agricultural produce of all kinds: celery, mushrooms, strawberries and other fruit, lettuce and a wide range of vegetables for the London markets. The produce had been collected by the Light Railway which served fenland farms (see below). This system ensured the profitability of intensive farming of nursery crops on the fertile black soil.

The construction of a sugar factory at Wissington, sited next to the railway line, was begun in 1925 at a time when there was no road access to the site. Hundreds of train-loads of soil left Stoke Ferry to be used in the foundations of the factory. When it was operational about 60 per cent of beet supplies arrived at the factory by rail (including from Stoke Ferry) and the final product - processed sugar - left by rail. Lighters and barges carried beet from farms more easily reached by water.

By the late 1920s passenger transport on the railways was declining as motor transport, particularly cheaper local motor-buses, increased. The passenger service from Stoke Ferry to Downham was withdrawn on 22nd September 1930, but freight traffic continued for more than thirty years after that.

Throughout the 1930s the line (now part of the L.N.E.R.) continued to carry a large quantity of goods. Kelly's Directory of Norfolk for 1929 says that at the station: *Considerable business is done in corn, coal, lime, malt and timber*[7].

Farmers still used the railway for sugar beet and other agricultural products. Whitbread's Maltings in Whittington used the service, and there were several firms of merchants in Stoke Ferry which continued to depend on rail transport. The 1933 directory lists:

Favor Parker & Son - Seed merchants
Wilson Longmuir & Co. - Saw-millers, timber merchants & builders
Harry Darkins – Coal dealer
W. A. Buckenham & Son - corn, cake, seed, coal & coke, salt and manure merchants, millers, game and poultry specialists
W. H. Tuck & Son - corn, cake, seed, coal and coke, salt and manure merchants

---

7   *Kelly's Directory of Norfolk* 1929.

In addition, many village shops used the parcel service, and the Egg Depot still dispatched eggs to market or wholesalers by train.

It was not until after 1945 that road transport seriously competed with the railway for freight business. From that time, the volume of goods to and from Stoke Ferry station slowly declined. By the late 1950s only one small train used the route each day. Usually consisting of an engine, brake and a couple of goods vans, it chugged slowly down the line, whistling at the un-gated level crossings. It was affectionately (but unfathomably) known as 'The Crab and Winkle Express' and could be seen and heard chugging along the line (including from the nearby Stoke Ferry School). Until 1961, this was hauled by steam and in its last few years by diesel.

The last freight train ran on 19th April 1965, the track from Abbey to Stoke Ferry was removed and the land reverted to farming. Abbey station and the line from Abbey to Denver continued to be used by the sugar factory for a few more years before it was finally closed in January 1983.

At Stoke Ferry the station buildings and stationmaster's house were abandoned and after years of neglect are now derelict. Planning permission was eventually granted to build a number of houses on the station site more than fifty years since the last train left the station. Construction has yet to start.

The Wissington Light Railway[8]

The Wissington Light Railway was an extensive set of branch lines linking farms in the agricultural fenland to the Stoke Ferry to Denver branch line near the river crossing at Wissington. It contributed considerably to the development of the surrounding district and the volume of freight carried on the Stoke Ferry line.

Following the agricultural boom of the 1860s the years between 1880 and 1900 saw a disastrous decline in English agriculture. Improved techniques in canning and refrigeration led to massive competition in meat, dairy produce and corn from America, Australia and New Zealand. Many farmers faced ruin. Land values fell 40 per cent on average throughout the country and even more on farms with poor transport links. The only answer was a switch in land use to growing other crops, and this was dependent upon getting the new produce to buyers quickly.

One man to spot an opportunity in this recession was Mr. Arthur J. Keeble. Originally from Peterborough, Keeble had made a fortune, along

---

8   Material for this section is drawn from Roger Darsley, *The Wissington Light Railway – A Fenland Enterprise*, Industrial Railway Society 1984.

with his elder brother George, in a corn and hay merchants business and manufacturing bricks, with factories all over the country. Although not clear why, at the age of 47 he ceased to play an active part in his other businesses and took up farming, buying up fen land from the Duchy of Lancaster, extending to over 7,000 acres south of the River Wissey. He moved from Peterborough, firstly to Denver and later resided at Wereham Hall.

An historian of the fenland wrote:

> ...in one of the most isolated spots in the Norfolk Fens was a place called Five Mile, just a few scattered cottages close to the bank of the River Wissey. This river, choked with weeds, carried no traffic to spoil the carpet of yellow and white lilies that stretched from bank to bank...but change was at hand. Already, looking northward, one could see gangs laying down a railway track to cross the river and snake across the Fen. The new landlord [Keeble]... made plans whereby he hoped to extract much wealth from the water-locked Fens he had purchased[9].

To do this, Keeble initially built a ten-mile network of standard-gauge light railways from Abbey Station to the fenland near Southery, Feltwell, Methwold Hythe and Wissington. The terminus was at Poppylot on the bank of Sam's Cut. The line wandered through the area which was singularly devoid of roads, serving most farms. The steam locomotive with its train of trucks stopped frequently to allow farmers to load their potatoes, carrots, celery and market garden produce at their farm gates. There were numerous sidings at such interestingly-named places as Decoy, Poppylot, Severals, Four Scores, White Dyke and Six Oaks. Back at Keeble Sidings (later Wissington Sidings) the trucks were transferred to the GER branch line and from there to the Downham-Ely line. Produce could be in London by next morning in time for Covent Garden Market. The line was intended for freight only, but a passenger coach was provided on Tuesdays to enable farmers and their families to go to King's Lynn market.

For ten years the light railway did much to re-vitalise local agriculture. There were plans to build a factory beside the line to extract ammonia from the peat, but this ran into financial difficulties. Serious flooding in the area caused Keeble to close the line in 1917. Later it was taken over by Mr. W. A. Towler, a farmer, who repaired the flood damage and reopened the line.

---

9 W. H. Barrett, *Tales from the Fens*, Routledge & Kegan Paul Ltd., 1964.

In 1925, (influenced by Mr. Towler) the original sugar factory at Wissington was built. Somewhat surprisingly the site had no road access, so all construction materials had to arrive by rail or water. Once operational, British Sugar Manufacturers (the factory owners) leased the line and extended it to eighteen miles to ensure supplies of sugar beet from an extensive area, as well as collecting other farm produce.

British Sugar Corporation, BSC as it became, took over operation of the line in 1936 on a five-year lease. When this expired in 1941, growers feared that the railways would be sold for scrap and made urgent representation to Parliament. Using war-time powers the Ministry of Agriculture requisitioned the line to keep it running and later bought it. In war-time, food production was vital and the retention of the line, together with better drainage and concrete roads, enabled increased food production in this fertile land. The Minister of Agriculture (then R.S. Hudson) showed his encouragement by travelling on an engine over the entire length of the track, with the train bearing the placard 'Bread and Butter Express'. The Ministry of Agriculture owned the railway throughout the war, with BSC responsible for its management.

After the war the Ministry wanted to return the property to private hands. The growers appealed against the sale, pointing out that the line was still necessary for the delivery of produce under Government cropping directions. So, as a temporary measure, the Ministry agreed to continue running the enterprise.

By 1956 cropping direction[10] had ceased and the Minister of Agriculture decided to withdraw from the only railway owned by his department. He offered local farms first opportunity of buying it if they wanted to keep it open. By this time road transport had penetrated the fens and there were no buyers for the 18 miles of track, one locomotive (1924 vintage) and 80 - 100 trucks.

Still, there were voices of dissent. In an article in *Sugar Topic* (BSC's house magazine) several users summarised the effect of the closure would have on their business:

- Mr. L. C. Fletcher of Duchy Farm, Feltwell, said that he loaded a quarter of the output of his 500 acres at Poppylot. He thought that closure would encourage farmers to turn to more grass and cattle. He argued that this would not be the best use of soil which at that time would grow 15-16 tons of onions per acre, 12 - 14 tons of potatoes, 10 - 15 tons of sugar beet and 15 - 20 tons of carrots.

---

10 Throughout the war and for some years following, the Ministry of Agriculture directed farmers on the type and quantity of crops they had to produce, rather than leaving it to market forces.

- Mr. C. F. Langley of Bourne Farm, Southery, said the closure would be a severe blow. Some of his fields were two miles from a hard road. For twelve to sixteen weeks each winter the drove to his farm was impassable. In 1947 it was under five foot of flood water and in 'normal' years he had seen water in the mud-holes reach the bottom of the horses' collars. He loaded all his produce at Bourne siding, and the light railway was vital to his survival.
- Also badly affected was the F. & S. Farming and Supply Co., farming 800 acres at Methwold Hythe. They used the railway to load 1,500 tons of beet a year, and 50 per cent of their other produce.

However, economic facts made line closure inevitable, as the following figures show:

Freight carried

1942 - 43	59,000 tons of produce
1950 - 51	29,683 tons (including 17,542 tons of sugar beet)
1954 - 55	19,512 tons (including 14,966 tons of sugar beet)

Profitability

1943 - 44	Deficit	£2,640
1945 - 46	Surplus	£1,594
1949 - 50	Deficit	£ 287
1950 - 51	Deficit	£ 192
1952 - 53	Deficit	£ 429
1953 - 54	Surplus	£ 617
1954 - 55	Surplus	£ 496

These figures included the administrator's fee of £500 annually, but no allowances for depreciation or interest on capital. The Minister of Agriculture said that the operation of the line by a Government department at the cost to the Exchequer for the benefit of a limited number of customers was no longer justified.

So in June 1957 all of the line south of the sugar factory was closed and the sight of an engine and wagons chugging though beet fields became a thing of the past. The BSC continued to use the remaining line to Abbey station as sidings for a number of years.

By 1972 the only remaining steam engine on the Light Railway was the

Wissington, a 0-6-0 saddle-tank engine, built in 1938 by Hudswell Clarke at Leeds and used for many years to haul trucks. The engine continued to be used in the sidings at the factory until the acquisition of a new diesel made it redundant. In 1972, when the diesel broke down, the *Wissington* was brought back briefly once again steamed.

Now the *Wissington* is in honourable retirement. Early in 1978 it was donated to the Midland and Great Northern Joint Railway Society by the BSC. It is based at the Sheringham headquarters of the steam-operated North Norfolk Railway where it is still occasionally used for passengers.

***

The Railway Age, so important to Stoke Ferry and the Fens for nearly 100 years, was over. Almost every trace of the Stoke Ferry Branch Line and the Wissington Light Railway has disappeared. The main line to London now exists in diminished form: reduced to a single line in parts (between Littleport and Downham Market, for instance), and closed altogether north of King's Lynn. Even so, some current residents of Stoke Ferry and district commute to London on a regular basis – though not, as would have been possible a century ago, from Stoke Ferry's own station.

Old bridge over the river demolished in 1899

Approaching the bridge from Stoke Ferry.
The original Bull Inn on the left and granary buildings on the right
(early 1900s)

*Granary and wharf
buildings (1970s)*

River Wissey today

The Bull Inn in the 1920s, (top) 1950s (middle) and as a private house today (bottom)

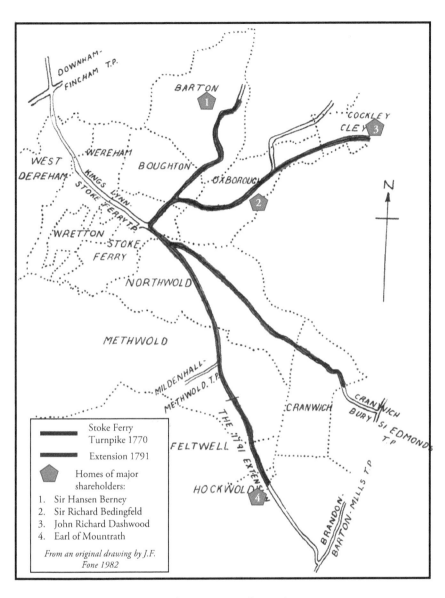

Within the map:

DOWNHAM-FINCHAM T.P.

BARTON
1

COCKLEY CLEY
3

WEST DEREHAM

WEREHAM

BOUGHTON

KINGS LYNN

STOKE FERRY T.P.

OXBOROUGH
2

N

WRETTON

STOKE FERRY

NORTHWOLD

METHWOLD

MILDENHALL-METHWOLD T.P.

CRANWICH

CRANWICH BURY S! EDMONDS T.P.

THE 1791 EXTENSION

FELTWELL

HOCKWOLD
4

BRANDON-BARTON-MILLS T.P.

Legend:

— Stoke Ferry Turnpike 1770

= Extension 1791

⬠ Homes of major shareholders:
1. Sir Hansen Berney
2. Sir Richard Bedingfeld
3. John Richard Dashwood
4. Earl of Mountrath

From an original drawing by J.F. Fone 1982

Stoke Ferry Turnpike Road

The High Street in the 1920s, showing the old tollhouse in the distance

Tollhouse and Bridge Road

Example of tolls charged –
at the Jenyns Arms at
Denver Sluice

STOKE FERRY STATION.

*Stoke Ferry Station
in its heyday during
the early part of the
twentieth century
and as it is today*

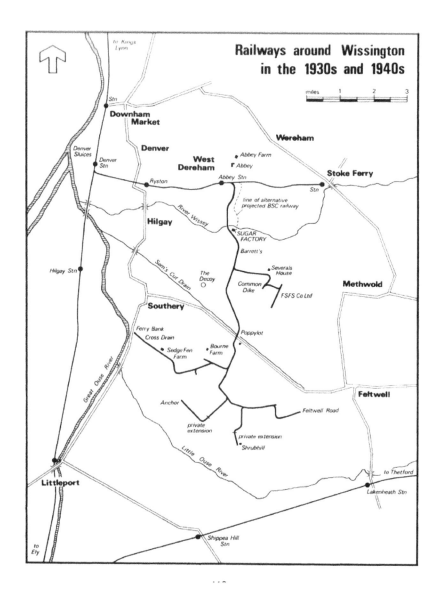

Engines using the Wissington Light Railway
The 'Wissington' crossing the Cut Off Channel, 1964 (above)
The 'Wissington' seemingly lost in the fen, 1957 (below left)
The 'Wissington' with 'Newcastle' and W.L.R. No. 17, 1964 (below right)

The 'Crab and Winkle' goods train (on the left) on its way to
Stoke Ferry, 1957

The Third Part

In which is described
the creation of the important town of
Stoke Ferry with fine houses,
hostelries, church,
schools and chapels

Chapter Eight

An Age of Affluence and Grand Designs

Between the late seventeenth and early twentieth centuries, Stoke Ferry achieved considerable wealth and prominence. The development of transport systems described in Part Two encouraged significant trade and facilitated this growth. Successful farmers and a small group of innovative entrepreneurs – see Part Four – capitalised. The result was an era of competitive building with almost all of Stoke Ferry's grand houses dating from the period between 1660 and 1800.

After the Civil War

At around the time of the Restoration of the Monarchy in 1660, the shape and structure of the village began to take on a form recognisable today. Some buildings and features are still in existence or well documented. There will also have been other farms, peasants' cottages, alehouses and work-premises of craftsmen such as wheelwrights, tanners, weavers and carpenters.

Since Stoke Ferry had no source of good building stone, cottages built in earlier times would have been made of wood, or local cobbles and flints bound together with inferior mortar made from sand, lime and horsehair. These buildings had a short life span and many of the original buildings were replaced over the years by more robust structures.

At the end of the seventeenth century, almost all of the land on both sides of the River Wissey was bog and fen, a region of reed and willow, wild and desolate except for the wildfowl. Marshes stretched from Whittington to the river at Stoke Ferry, crossed only by an ancient causeway. There was a bridge of sorts over the river, and the ferry was used when this was impassable. On dry land there were many acres of woodland and copse and about a third of the land was common land. Roads were dirt and stones, rutted and narrow.

The Church and The Hill were at the centre of the village. The church had occupied this site since the thirteenth century. By 1700 there were already two or three taverns around The Hill. Some parts of the Crown Hotel (now All Saints' Lodge) date from the fourteenth century, and by 1700 it was a substantial building. The King's Arms (later The Crown Hotel) was built in 1690. It is probable that by then a third inn stood on the south side of The Hill (re-built later as The Duke's Head). Adjacent to the churchyard, was the blacksmith's forge and house (this site is now occupied by two cottages).

Houses Dating from Around 1700

Along the High Street and bordering the east side of the churchyard is a group of buildings that date in part from the late seventeenth century. On ancient deeds Lodge Cottage, the Old Chemist's Shop and Moulsham House appear as one property, owned by Henry Tingay, a cordwainer[1] in 1729. In that year he repaid a mortgage of £40 to Francis Ward, his neighbour the blacksmith.

These premises housed craftsmen and trades-people throughout most of their history. Moulsham House was at one time two units, used by shoemakers, tailors and wool mercers at different periods. In 1803 it came into the possession of Abraham West, draper and grocer. From that time, and under various ownership it continued to be an important grocery and drapery store for at least the next 150 years, and was later used as the branch of a bank.

The house next to the churchyard was occupied by Henry Piggott, druggist, and this became the home and shop of the local chemist or pharmacist until at least the 1960s where medicines and other medical supplies were sold alongside other merchandise. An inscription over the door reads *Dealer in Tobacco and Snuff, Vinegar and Spices.*

Lodge Cottage, behind the chemists and abutting on the churchyard, was a bakery in the early eighteenth century. Its 'large baker's oven' is mentioned in a sale notice of 1777. Later it became the servants' wing of The Lodge, which was built in the early nineteenth century. These four premises are all Grade II listed buildings.

Elsewhere in the village, buildings already in existence by 1700 or a little later include *Canterbury House*, built in the reign of Elizabeth I in Wretton Road and thought to have been a hunting lodge for the Archbishop. On Lynn Road *The Cobbles*, a seventeenth-century merchant's house, and *Bayfield's* next door, with its bay window, also date from the seventeenth century. These are also Grade II listed buildings.

---

1   Shoe-maker.

Ancient Farms

Farmhouses bordered the village street, as was the custom of the time. They were usually long narrow buildings with substantial outbuildings set in a *homestall* or croft of about an acre, often with an orchard as well. Farm produce and stock were bought and sold either at the weekly market or at the annual horse and cattle fair. Farm hands and indoor servants were engaged at the Hiring Fair[2]. They worked for a few pounds a year and their keep, sharing meals with the farmer's family in the long, low rooms in a simple and spartan existence.

The sites of four of these farms can still be identified. One was at the junction of Oxborough Road and the High Street. Nothing original remains, but Osborne House, the Granary, and Brewery House were rebuilt on the site in the 1700s.

A second farm (known as Salmon's Farm) was situated on the triangle bounded by Lynn Road and Furlong Road. The original buildings were probably substantially re-built in the late eighteenth or early nineteenth century, the thatch and flint being replaced by tiles, stone and brick. This farm was still operative in 1890 when it was sold by auction. On 20th June, by order of the trustees of Miss Hegbin, the farmhouse and thirteen scattered parcels of land, held and occupied at the time by Benjamin Salmon, were auctioned at the Town Hall, Downham Market by Charles Hawkins (grandfather of the late Paul Hawkins, M.P. for South-west Norfolk from 1964 - 87).

The auctioneer's announcement states that the farmhouse contained:

> *A cellar, three lower rooms, store-room, five bedrooms, attic, two walled-in gardens, gig-house, riding-horse stable, out-buildings. There was also a malt-house with a 30-coomb[3] steep, a kiln, two lower and two upper floors and a malt chamber.*

The farm buildings comprised:

> *a meal-house, four loose boxes, cart-horse stable, harness and chaff houses, barn, granary, enclosed yard with open shed and cart-lodge. All stone and brick-built and tiled. Also a paddock of fine old pasture land enclosed with a high wall containing together 5 acres, 1 rood 30 perches[4].*

---

2   See Chapter 4.

3   A Coomb is a unit of volume, defined as 4 bushels, c 140 litres. In Norfolk it was used for both liquids and dry goods such as corn.

4   A rood is a quarter of an acre, a perch was a unit of length equal to 5½ yards.

A third farmhouse stood on the opposite side of Furlong Road, also surrounded by a high wall. The long narrow dwelling with its ancient outbuildings is still occupied today. It now comprises three houses, Kavenham House, The Apiary and Furlong House. Restoration of The Apiary in the 1980s revealed evidence of three hundred years' of history in the woodwork and general structure. A 1676 half-crown, found between a ceiling and the floorboards of a bedroom, could have been dropped there by the occupants in the reign of Charles II. The Kavenham House end, facing the village street, has a bow window, and used to have a fine staircase. This was probably added later as private quarters for the farmer's family, with a parlour and bedrooms superior to those of the servants. Outside at the opposite end is a 'back-house' where laundry, baking and dairy work took place.

When first built in the 1600s, this farm would have had a croft and orchard behind it. The removal of great quantities of lime and cobbles to form the present 'pit' occurred during the eighteenth and nineteenth centuries. This end of Stoke Ferry was under the jurisdiction of the Manor of Cavenham[5] and this farm was probably owned by that estate, hence its name. It is not to be confused with Cavenham Manor House, which is in Wereham.

The fourth seventeenth-century farm, Stoke Ferry Manor House, on Wretton Road, is well preserved and again restoration was undertaken in the 1980s. It is likely that the current building was constructed in the 1600s on the site of the original manor house from the Norman period. Lords of the Manor who lived there in more recent times include James Bradfield in the late eighteenth century, followed by his son-in-law Charles Sanders and grandson James Bradfield Sanders Bradfield[6]. Later, in the nineteenth century Anthony Horrex Micklefield[7] lived in The Manor House.

In the 1930s the property was divided into three dwellings: Manor House, Manor Farm and Manor Cottage. The latter was originally stables and a cart-lodge, with a cobbled yard. Restoration work at the west end of the complex revealed an outside staircase to the servants' bedrooms, where there were bells still connected to bell-pulls downstairs. In the wall between the main building and a later wing a King's Lynn farthing of 1669 was found.

---

5 Although the Manor of Cavenham is always spelt with a 'C' the Stoke Ferry house has always had a 'K'. Whether this was deliberate in order to avoid confusion, or simply resulted from some seventeenth century phonetic spelling is unclear.

6 See Chapter 12.

7 See Chapter 13.

The farmhouses were thatched with reeds and straw, like most buildings of the period. Both Manor Farm and Kavenham Farm show evidence in their gables of the roof being raised and the pitch altered to accommodate tiles at a later period.

The land which went with these farms consisted of scattered fields, as evidenced by the sale plan for Salmon's Farm. Many of the fields were ditched but not fenced, approached by droves, and interspersed with large tracts of common land and smallholdings, often of less than twenty acres. On the commons all parishioners had the right to graze cattle, pigs, sheep and geese, which were kept in large numbers. They could cut wood, turf and peat. On many of the unfenced fields villagers could graze their animals on the stubble after farmers had harvested their crops. These rights were important in maintaining the living standards of smallholders and labourers. Most people kept a milk-cow, poultry and pigs. Even craftsmen usually had a small piece of land: Henry Tingay, for example, the shoemaker, had three acres of pasture down Great Man's Way, according to the 1729 deed previously cited.

Corn was grown on the farms and ground at the local windmill, a wooden post-mill that was replaced by the present brick tower mill in the mid nineteenth century.

Social Change in the Eighteenth Century

During the 1700s Stoke Ferry reached the zenith of its wealth and local importance. The reasons for this increased prosperity are apparent from earlier chapters. It became a busy inland port, handling incoming goods for the merchants dealing in coal, grain, wool, wine, building materials and much else besides. The merchants flourished and so did the farmers, who now had better access to markets for their produce. The improvement of roads in the second half of the century made trade more profitable. Blacksmiths, wheelwrights, and other craftsmen also prospered.

Much of this extra wealth was invested in property, acquiring more land, rebuilding existing houses or building new ones. There was also a change in the social structure: merchants and craftsmen adopted middle-class pretensions and built themselves 'gentlemen's houses' in the Georgian style, with high square rooms and servants' quarters. The fronts of these houses usually faced the street, with a considerable area of grounds and gardens behind. There was also a departure from using local building materials since the merchants could now afford to have bricks which were made in Peterborough brought by barge to the wharf. The modern brick-built houses became status symbols, the newly rich vying with one another for the grandest residence. This often required borrowing money on mortgage to finance the ventures, and quite frequently it was the local solicitor who lent the money, considerably enhancing the fortune of the Micklefield family[8].

The New Farms

The greatly improved prospects for farmers allowed them to expand their properties and experiment with more modern methods of husbandry. This often entailed squeezing out their smaller neighbours and fencing some of their land, a process that occurred gradually over many years. The Enclosure Acts (see later in this Chapter) towards the end of the century enabled each farmer to consolidate his land into one convenient area, instead of in widely scattered strips. Like the merchants before them, some farmers now adopted a superior social style. Farmhouses were modernised, or new ones built on their recently acquired estates (Ivy Farm, Grange Farm and Lime Kiln Farm are all examples from the eighteenth century).

The shape of the new buildings made them unsuitable for housing the farm hands as had been the custom. Many workers had to resort to sleeping over stables and barns, but the better employers, in farming and in commerce, built cottages for their workers. These eighteenth-century cottages, which no doubt replaced earlier wooden buildings, are one of the pleasing features of Stoke Ferry today, particularly those in Oxborough Road.

The first half of the eighteenth century saw considerable building work in the village. Between 1700 - 12 the old Crown Inn was enlarged. In 1746 a wheelwright called Taylor built the present Osborne House. It was on the site of a former farmhouse and had its own brewery and granary (still standing but now separate houses). It had wrought iron gates in Oxborough Road so that the occupants could leave and enter without being stopped at the Toll House. This house was owned and occupied by the Winfield family and was let when Samuel Winfield moved to the Hall. In 1892 William Buckenham bought it from Winfield's Trustees and it remained with that family for the next century.

In the grounds of Osborne House and Park House are high 'crinkle-crankle' walls, whose serpentine shapes form a series of alcoves to provide shelter for tender plants or fruits such as peaches or nectarines. The art of building these walls, with their reversed semi-circles just one brick thick, was perfected in France. Examples in this country were usually the work of French prisoners-of-war in Napoleonic times.

---

8   See Chapter 13.

In Oxborough Road the nearest cottages to Osborne House were also dated 1746. It is likely that they were originally built for members of Osborne House staff. Trowell House (once the Trowell and Hammer Inn) was built in 1775 and the cottages on the opposite side of Oxborough Road are of similar age. White's Farm was probably built on newly acquired land at the time of the enclosures in the late 1700s.

Three other large houses in the High Street were all built in the mid-1700s. They are now called Homeleigh, Park House and Deanscroft. The builders vied with one another in the use of bricks, the size and height of rooms and the stylish doors and windows. Homeleigh was always connected with the merchant Etheridge family and the grain storage buildings and counting house were probably built and used by them.

Park House indeed had its own park with a fine avenue of walnut trees extending to Barker's Drove, so that carriages could bypass the toll bar. The Micklefield family may have built it; certainly it was in that family for many years.

On the opposite side of the road behind the chemist's shop and Moulsham House, retired naval surgeon, William Harvey, built another fine house known as *The Lodge*.

Other properties thought to date from this period are:

- The Grey House, built in the precincts of Kavenham Farm as a superior residence by the owner as his prosperity increased
- A number of the houses on either side of the forge in Lynn Road
- Clifton House, in Furlong Road, which was a private school from the 1840s to 1870s and later the premises of wheelwrights

Later chapters describe a number of the influential families of the village who were instrumental in this housing boom.

The Enclosures

There was, however, a much darker side to social change in this period, as the rich farmers, merchants and landowners became richer, and the poor in the community most definitely became much poorer.

This was, in considerable part the result of Enclosure. The old pattern of common land and grazing rights had made life tolerable for the 'one-field' farmer. Graziers, labourers and landless peasants could augment their inadequate diet and incomes by keeping geese, a few sheep, a milk-cow, or a few pigs, goats or poultry. Throughout England this was changing. Between 1760 and 1820 six million acres of open arable land and common land were redistributed and fenced. No wonder the Enclosure Acts, introduced separately for each parish towards the end of the 1700s and early 1800s aroused class hatred which endured for generations. The object of the operation is clear from the following quotation from the Act[9]:

Whereas there are within the Parishes …divers Open Fields, Half Year and Shack Lands, Lammas Meadows, Commons and Waste Grounds….

And whereas … George Robert Eyres, Esquire, Abraham Sewell, Esquire, Edward Roger Pratt Esquire, Charles Sanders, Esquire, Roger Micklefield Esquire, Henry Morley Esquire and divers other persons respectively are Owners and Proprietors of all the Messuages, Cottages, Lands, Grounds and Hereditaments within the said parishes…

And whereas it would be advantageous to the several Persons entitled to, and interested in the Premises, if the Rights of Sheepwalk, Common Shackage, and other rights were extinguished; and if the Open Fields, Half-Year or Shacklands, Lammas Meadows, Commons and Waste Grounds, were divided and inclosed, and specific Parts or Shares thereof allotted to the Respective Persons entitled to or interested in the same, according to their respective Estates, Rights and Interests therein; But such Extinguishment, Division and Allotment, cannot be effected without the Aid and Authority of Parliament:

May it therefore please Your MAJESTY,

That it may be Enacted….

So, with all the power of the law, the entitlement to use common land was taken from ordinary people and given to named landlords who divided it up between them. By law the land had to be enclosed with quick-thorn hedges. Smallholders' land was seized and in return they were offered poor patches of remote land. They could not afford to fence it or pay legal fees and so were forced out. The loss of common rights was, in theory, recompensed by the

---

9   *An Act for Inclosing lands in the Parishes of Stoke otherwise Stoke Ferry, Wretton and Wereham and the hamlet of Winnold in the County of Norfolk* received Royal Assent on 14th June 1815, four days before the Battle of Waterloo.

allocation of new commons at the edge of the parish, often marshy useless land the farmers did not want. The local fuel allotment at East Fen and Stoke Ferry Common were the result of this policy. Even these poor areas were of little use, as they had to be fenced and no cattle, sheep or lambs kept on them for seven years to allow the hedges to grow.

It was stipulated that:

> *No geese shall be turned, kept or pastured on any Common, Fen ground or Waste land within the parish. In case geese are kept after the said time it shall be lawful for the fen-reeves to take, kill or destroy the same.*

In addition, the ancient right of turf-cutting and 'firing' was restricted to occupiers of cottages with over twenty years' tenancy.

Across the country, this iniquitous process was enacted. The poor could do nothing to resist, though they could protest. This poem or song[10] aptly sums up their anger:

> *The law locks up the man or woman*
> *Who steals the goose from off the common*
> *But leaves the greater villain loose*
> *Who steals the common from off the goose*
>
> *The law demands that we atone*
> *When we take things we do not own*
> *But leaves the lords and ladies fine*
> *Who take things that are yours and mine*
>
> *The poor and wretched don't escape*
> *If they conspire the law to break*
> *This must be so but they endure*
> *Those who conspire to make the law*
>
> *The law locks up the man or woman*
> *Who steals the goose from off the common*
> *And geese will still a common lack*
> *Till they go and steal it back*

---

10 Late Eighteenth Century, origin unknown, quoted in unionsong.com.

Almost overnight, large numbers of families were destitute. Some were also homeless as their cottages were demolished on the newly enclosed farms. Many became vagrants, but with every rural area suffering the same plight this only increased the problem. It was decided that each parish should be responsible for its own poor. The effect on the rates was disastrous. One result was the building of 'Paupers' Cottages' where some of the most desperate cases could be housed in cramped quarters. It is likely that cottages at the junction of Boughton Road and Lynn Road, now demolished, were used for this purpose between 1790 and 1830. It was not until 1836 that the Workhouse was built at Downham Market to serve a 'Union' of parishes, each village contributing to its upkeep from the rates according to the number of its poor.

So began class bitterness in rural areas which was to last for generations. Even into the early twentieth century, working people were expressing grievance at the loss of their common land.

Stoke Ferry Mill

East Anglia has been a major grain producing area for over two hundred years, whilst Stoke Ferry was an important centre for grain processing and trade. Its slightly higher elevation overlooking the fens provided an ideal site for a windmill.

The first Ordnance Survey Map, published in 1824, shows a windmill on the present site (most probably a post-mill[11]) and also another on the other side of the road. The post-mill was probably built in the late 1700s or early 1800s. In the 1830s and '40s, directories show that both William Pollard and John Lock were millers, presumably one at each mill. It is not clear when John Lock's mill stopped working, or what happened to the building.

Around 1862, William Pollard built the current brick tower mill on the site, replacing the post-mill which had become unsafe. Initially, the mill had five stories until a further two were added in 1902 taking the height of the tower to 58 feet. At the same time a new set of sails and an onion-shaped cap, or ogee[12] were added, probably to replace others damaged in a severe gale in 1895.

William Pollard died in 1873 and his son, also William, kept it on for a number of years. By 1888, Kelly's Directory showed 'John Nix, Miller (wind)'. He mainly produced wheat flour for breadmaking and also milled barley.

The last man to manage a functioning mill was Ted Sharp assisted by his miller, Didley Carter. Up until its closure, their work mainly consisted of milling barley for local farmers for use as animal feed. Occasional bags of wheat for stone-ground flour were also processed. The mill finally closed for business in 1924, unable to compete with machine mills such as had been recently introduced by Favor Parker[13].

The mill itself fell into disuse, but the Mill House at its base was still inhabited by Wyborough Johnson, his wife and three school-age sons, Neville, Charlie[14] and Denny. One stormy night in 1936, two of the sails blew off, crashing through the roof of the house onto Neville's bed. By great good fortune, he was away for the night with some friends in the village, and everyone in the house was unhurt, though doubtless rather shaken. The remaining sails and the rest of the cap had to be removed because they were unsafe.

In more recent times, the mill has been used as a restaurant, a private home and a holiday rental, currently listed on Airbnb.

---

11 In a post-mill, the whole body of the mill that houses the machinery is mounted on a single vertical post, around which it can be turned manually to bring the sails into the wind.

12 This revolved in the wind automatically with the aid of a fan-tail. A survey of Norfolk windmills in 1949 stated that the ogee cap of this mill was the largest in the county (17 ft in diameter and 10 ft high).

13 See Chapter 18.

14 In the 1950s and 1960s, Charlie Johnson ran the village shop on the corner of Oxborough Road; he drove around Stoke Ferry and neighbouring villages with a large van, enabling householders to buy their groceries at the door, as well as delivering weekly groceries that had been pre-ordered (by phone or paper shopping list). This was a business model well before its time!

Chapter Nine

Hotels and Hostelries

Stoke Ferry's importance as a centre of social and commercial life can be measured by the number and diversity of inns and hotels that once flourished there. Even as late as 1953, when the author moved to Stoke Ferry, there were five licensed public houses in the village, as well as two in Boughton and one each in Wretton and Whittington no more than a mile away. Of these, only one – The Bell (or at times 'Bluebell' or 'Blue Bell') near the junction of Boughton Road - remains open, and the future of that, too, seems uncertain.

In Stoke Ferry's heyday as a market town in the eighteenth and nineteenth centuries, there were three busy hotels around The Hill - The Crown, The King's Arms and The Duke's Head. These served both locals and visitors to the market, as well as catering for long-distance stage-coach travellers through the town.

The Crown

The Crown was the oldest, largest and most important hotel in town. It was in the building on the east side of the High Street, now known as All Saints Lodge.

Recent residents may remember the pub next to The Hall as 'The Crown' but before 1902 this was The King's Arms. It was renamed when the original was closed in that year and the business transferred.

The original Crown Hotel is one of the oldest listed buildings in the district[1], and some experts think part of it may date from about 1380, making it one of the oldest buildings in West Norfolk. Among the features of early craftsmanship is a fine adze-cut beam in the present dining-room. The Queen Anne wing (the lower building to the left of All Saints Lodge) was added early

---

1   In fact there are three listings: one for the main house *All Saints Lodge* and one for the later Queen Anne wing *Crown House* and one for a third property at the back described as *House immediately east of All Saints Lodge*.

in the eighteenth century when, as trade expanded, the inn became one of the main coaching centres for travellers from north-west Norfolk to the south. All stage coaches needed to stop every fourteen or so miles to change horses and to allow the passengers to alight for rest and refreshment. (It is said that twelve-year-old Horatio Nelson called here on the way to join his first ship.)

There was ample stabling for the many horses required. The large staff of cooks, serving maids, tapsters, ostlers and stable boys was housed in an adjacent building[2]. Beer was brewed on the premises in the large outbuilding at the back which can be seen from the road. Bedrooms were approached from outside galleries. Market dinners were served in a large room on the second floor (now two bedrooms), and billiards matches, land sales and other functions also took place there. What is now a garage was once a skittle alley.

The earliest recorded licensee was Richard Curtis from 1790 - 94. He advised the public on 17th January 1791, that having taken the Crown Inn at Christmas, he had fitted it up in every respect, suitable for public accommodation.

Throughout the nineteenth century, numerous licensees were listed with none of them staying very long, suggesting challenging trading conditions.

There are several records of sales of the property, such as this one from 1864:

10th September 1864 - The Crown Hotel Stoke Ferry
Edward Banham
is favoured with directions from Mr. E. Castleton to sell by Auction, on Thursday and Friday, the 15th and 16th days of September 1864, the entire contents of this old-established inn, Posting Establishment.

Out door and Live and Dead Farming Effects.

First day – The principal furniture, plate, linen &c &c

Second day – Post horses, Flys, Harness, Agricultural Implements and Out-door effects

The decline of the market and the coming of the railway had a disastrous effect on trade at the hotel. The occupiers of The Crown in the 1901 census were William and Charlotte Fox.[3] It is not clear why they left in the following

---

2   This building was on the site where the village sign now stands but was demolished in the 1960s to ease traffic flow.

3   Not 'Mrs. Cox' as shown in the first edition.

year, but they were not experienced publicans - in 1891, William was listed as a carpenter and joiner in the St. Clement district of Norwich, and by 1911 he had reverted to this profession, at Sculthorpe in North Norfolk presumably because the business had failed.

The property was purchased by Frederick Charles Winfield whose history as a merchant and wharfinger is described in Chapter 16. He made alterations to transform it into a private residence, including removal of the great oak doors. He converted the archway to the coach-yard into an entrance hall, thus closing the way to underground rooms and cellars. He also demolished the outside galleries which gave access to the bedrooms.

When business at the wharf declined, Mr. Winfield sold his assets and had left the district before the 1911 Census. A subsequent owner split up the property. Part of the land was bought by Mr. E. Allen, and the former servants' quarters were bought by Mr. Herbert Morley, whose father, a craftsman in flint-work, had carried out the previous renovation of the façade.

The King's Arms (later The Crown)

Situated on the western side of The Hill, directly on the junction with Wretton Road, the building is now used as offices for Stoke Ferry Mill.

Dating from 1670, the beams and joists in the ceilings and cellar are tribute to the craftsmen of 350 years ago. During a renovation in the 1970s, vestiges of a mural painting were discovered on the wall behind a cupboard on the upper floor. It is medieval in style but could not have been painted before the seventeenth century. Behind the buildings was a paved yard and the ancient stabling.

The earliest record for The King's Arms shows that the landlord in 1794 was William Bravestow. During the nineteenth century, the building was owned at various times by James Bradfield Sanders Bradfield who owned the Hall, and by the Etheridge family, who owned the Cobbles. Landlords were usually in residence for only a few years at a time - in the 1830s William Tedder, from 1845 - 56 Henry Roberts who was followed by his widow for a further few years. In the 1860s William Smith and John Pond, and the 1870s James Bowers, James Carter, Mrs. Susan Boyce and Mrs. M. Leader in quick succession. In 1877, Kelly's Directory shows Mrs. M. Leader as landlady and in 1893 Thomas William Rumbolds.

When The Crown across the road closed in 1902, The King's Arms adopted its name, aspiring to the prestige and goodwill of its once-important neighbour. In the early part of the twentieth century, it was known as

Crown Commercial Hotel, selling Bagge's Ales and advertising 'Billiards' and 'Posting'. As early as the First World War, it carried the badge of the CTC (the Cyclists Touring Club), which had been founded in 1878 to promote cycling and recommend accommodation for cyclists. By the 1920s, the word 'Posting' had been replaced by 'Garage' as motor cars replaced horse drawn carriages.

As passing trade declined it continued as The Crown, a popular local pub until its closure in 1963.

The Duke (or The Duke's Head)

The Duke or Duke's Head enclosed the southern side of The Hill, but it is not clear which Duke – if any specific one – it celebrates.

The Duke is shown on old engravings and dates from the late seventeenth or early eighteenth century. It was the second largest of the inns on the Hill after the original Crown and is listed in 1845 as a Hotel and Posting House, so must have had ample stabling. Considerable renovation over the years gave it a more modern appearance, but some original features survived, including a magnificent cellar.

Early landlords are recorded as John Flowers and William Flower (are these in fact father and son, despite the slightly different spelling?) who had the license from 1794 -1824. In that year it was auctioned:

Commercial Hotel & Posting House

Freehold premises offered for sale by auction Friday 27th August 1824. Consisting of three parlours, bar, excellent kitchen, seven sleeping-rooms, two capital cellars, a detached brew-house lately built, and conveniently fitted up for brewing seven coombs of malt, stabling for 9 horses, granary, piggery, and other suitable outhouses, likewise a detached cottage and a garden near the above. Brewery Utensils, nearly new, to be taken at valuation by the purchaser.

It was a substantial property, bought in the 1850s by the Winfields, first Henry William and later his son Samuel Henry. On his death in 1891 it was sold again, as instructed in his will (see Stoke Ferry Brewery, below). At that time, the landlord was William Elderkin from 1875 – 96, followed by his widow, Susannah up until 1904. Another long-serving publican couple were the Bowns. In 1929 Ernest Bown, a retired Metropolitan Police detective, took the license and after his death in 1945 his widow Gladys Alexandra Bown continued up until the closure of the pub in 1975.

The Duke was known as a place where the game Penny in the Hole (sometimes known as Pitch Penny) was played with a local rule variant using brass discs instead of (old) pennies. By the 1960s and 70s, it was falling behind social developments such as eating out but continued as a beer-drinking house for its dwindling local clientele. There were no bars, as such – only rooms with wooden chairs and tables. Ordering a pint required Mrs. Bown to go out to the back room and draw the beer from a barrel (there were no pumps or pressurised casks). It is not surprising that, when she finally tired of this exercise, the brewery (Watney Mann) decided to close the Duke forever.

After closure as a pub in 1975, it served for some years as the canteen and social club of Favor Parker's Stoke Ferry Mill employees. This ceased in 1995 when the business was sold to Grampian Foods, and it was put up for sale. Increasingly derelict, the building is still on the market over twenty years later and now constitutes a dangerous eyesore in the heart of the village.

The Bull

Away from the village centre in a fine river-side position by the bridge over the river Wissey stood The Bull (possibly originally named The Black Bull).

In earlier centuries this was the site of the ferry and later the bridge across the river Wissey. There must, therefore, have been an inn on that spot for many centuries, providing refreshment and accommodation to both watermen and road travellers.

The earliest listing of a landlord is in 1794 when John Drew was the licensee, and in 1811, the following sale particulars give some idea of its scale:

The Bury & Norwich Post of Wednesday
Wednesday 18th December 1811

Announcement that the premises known as The Bull Inn were to be let from 6th January 1812, including cottage, or tap-room adjoining; stables, yard, garden, and two inclosures of rich pasture land, containing about 7 acres

*Additional 24 acres of pasture land could also available to the tenant
Exclusive of good road business, the premises command and enjoy the full trade*

of the weekly corn market, held at Stoke Ferry; also of the merchant's yard opposite, and navigation on the river Wissey to Lynn and other places;

Well worth the attention of some steady person, and particularly of a butcher, for whom it would be a most desirable situation

It is not clear why it might particularly suit a butcher, except to provide meat at a competitive price for the catering, or indeed whether it was acquired by one.

Throughout the nineteenth-century, all directories list The Bull as a Posting House, where coaches could change horses. It was the right distance from both Brandon and King's Lynn to be a regular stage in a journey to or from the south.

From 1839 - 65, the licensees were the Browns – John from 1839, William from 1845 – 56 followed by his daughter Catherine up to 1865.

In the 1880s and 90s they were followed by Alfred Williamson and subsequently his widow, Sarah. This was a very popular inn in that era, with boats for hire for pleasure trips on the river, as well as horses and conveyances for hire for those wanting an outing on dry land.

In the early twentieth century, from 1908 - 30 George followed by Walter William Leggett were licensees. In 1930 there was a disastrous fire and the Bull was completely destroyed. The present building was erected on the same site, and was taken over by a new landlord Fred Ford, who stayed until 1949.

Although The Bull outlived all of the Inns in the centre of the village, this too was permanently closed by its final owners, also Watney Mann, in 1990. It is now a private residence known, unsurprisingly, as The Old Bull.

The Bell

At various times, this pub has been known as The Bell, The Blue Bell or The Bluebell. It is the last surviving licensed premises in Stoke Ferry, and in recent years has frequently been closed for periods before opening again and its future seems precarious.

The Bell was a much more modest place than the four hotels already described. It stands at the junction of Boughton Road and Lynn Road and has always been traditional 'local' tavern. It did not cater for the gentry in their carriages, as the Crown did, but would have been used by drovers and the working people of the village.

Early records of licensees are incomplete: the earliest shows that John Drake was landlord in 1794, though it is not clear how long he remained. From 1830 - 39 William Miller followed by Martha Miller (his widow?) were licensees and from1845 - 51 the landlord was William Wilson, who supplemented his living by also being a baker. From 1854 - 56 Henry Williams is shown as licensee.

From 1858 for a hundred years, the license was held by three generations of the Lock family. From that year until his death in 1887 at the age of 81, the landlord was John Lock. His son, Edward, who had earlier been a Mail Coach Driver, then took over but already by 1888 the license had passed to his wife Mary Ann; Edward died in early 1890.

At the 1891 Census guests included Edmund G. Fuller and his wife Emma, Mary Anne's younger sister. Fuller listed his occupation as 'Marine Artist'. A recent description[4] of him states:

> On his death in 1940, Fuller was described as "painter, architect, comic artist and metal worker" and he distinguished himself in all these disciplines but it was as a marine artist that he achieved the highest renown. The son of a military father, who became a General, Fuller was born in Brompton, London and educated at Sandhurst. He married Emma Wing, a Suffolk girl, in 1882....

His works, prints and comic postcards are still widely available today.

In 1925 the licence for the Bell was transferred to Mary Ann's two spinster daughters, Bertha and Florence, and she stayed on in the pub until her death in 1938 at the age of 91. The sisters continued there until 1958, two very old, prim, Victorian ladies presiding with dignity in their little old-fashioned inn, still furnished as it had been a hundred years before. The death of Bertha and the ill-health of her sister brought to an end this remarkable reign of landladies. A correspondent[5] wrote:

> I knew well the delightful Lock sisters who kept the Bell in the 30s. I retain fond memories of them, Bertha the typical local simple country woman with her hair in a bun and a spotless apron, and the more sophisticated Florence who returned from London with bobbed hair and a refined accent.

---

4   Messum's Gallery website, based on research by David Tovey.
5   Letter to Doris Coates from Nancy Nuttall of Sutton Coldfield, 26ᵗʰ September 1980.

After the closure of The Bull in 1990 The Bell was the only remaining pub in Stoke Ferry. In August 2011 it appeared to close permanently and, fearing that the site would be redeveloped for housing, the Parish Council proposed reopening it as a community-owned and run establishment. This came to nothing, but the pub was active again in 2012, since when it has obviously had some ups and downs. As recently as 2016, the current landlords issued a plea through the Village Pump magazine to "use it or lose it". It would be a sad day if Stoke Ferry lost its last remaining licensed premises.

The Cock

Ale houses in Oxborough Road would have been popular with drovers, as well as with the craftsmen who carried on their cottage industries in that part of the village. One of these was The Cock (now a private house) which was licenced until the 1950s.

In the nineteenth century, James Nunn and his son, also James, were landlords for over fifty years (1845 – 1986), the latter also listed as a brewer and a carpenter. They were followed in the first part of the twentieth century by the lengthy tenancy of George Lusher (from 1906 until his death in 1941, when his wife took over for a further four years). He had worked at the maltings at Whittington before becoming a landlord. The last landlord was George Fodder before the pub was closed by the brewery (Bullards) in 1960.

There is no evidence that cock fighting took place here, but this was often the case in inns of that name. (Certainly The Cock at Methwold was notorious for this sport, and it is said that Charles II enjoyed a session there when he visited the inn during a trip to Norfolk to inspect the fen drainage which he had encouraged.)

Stoke Ferry Brewery

It is very likely that many local pubs, particularly in rural locations, brewed their own beer on the premises; the trend for larger breweries serving a group of houses started in the first half of the nineteenth century.

White's Directory of 1835 shows John Hawes as a brewer and maltster and in 1846 John Osbert Blackburn the same. There is no remaining evidence of the sites of their breweries.

By 1850, Henry William Winfield is shown as a brewer (as well as maltster, corn, cake, and coal merchant, and wharfinger) having a brewery in Stoke Ferry, most probably in the buildings on the river bank that he owned. When he died in 1868, the ownership of the brewery and all his other businesses passed to his son Samuel Henry Winfield. However, the brewing side of the business had been leased to Hogge & Seppings (Setch Brewery[6]) from 1864 onwards. In total, the Winfields acquired eighteen pubs within a ten-mile radius of Stoke Ferry to sell their beer, as was happening in many other places around the country. This all came to an end when Samuel died in 1891, and almost all of his businesses were sold at auction. Just how sizeable the brewing and pub business had become can be seen from the list of establishments for sale at that time:

VALUABLE FREEHOLD & COPYHOLD PROPERTY.

Comprising a desirable FAMILY RESIDENCE, with conservatory, vinery, forcing house, excellent garden and commodious premises;

BREWERY, with malt and store houses, stabling and Brewery premises;

18 PUBLIC HOUSES, 3 Cottages, 2 Blacksmith's Shops, 2 Feeding Rights on Walton Wash and Accommodation Lands.

The Public Houses were listed and sold separately (although in some cases a buyer bought more than one of them). They were -

- Stoke Ferry   The Duke's Head Inn
- Northwold   George and Dragon Inn
- Northwold   The Bricklayers Arms
- Methwold   The Windmill
- Methwold   The Cock
- Methwold   The Crown
- Feltwell   The Bell
- Feltwell   The Crown
- Feltwell   The Elm Tree
- Hockwold-cum-Wilton   The Ferry Boat Inn
- Brandon   The Swan Inn
- Lakenheath   The Chequers

---

6 Hogge and Seppings was a brewery company originally established as Hogge and Herbert at Setch / Setchey just south of King's Lynn as early as 1802. It stayed in business throughout the nineteenth century, eventually being acquired by Bullard and Sons in 1928.

- Lakenheath   The Plough Inn
- Wereham   Chequers Inn
- West Dereham   White Horse Inn
- Hilgay   Queen's Head Inn
- Southery   Nag's Head Inn

James Seppings bought The Dukes Head at Stoke Ferry, The Chequers at Wereham The White Horse at West Dereham and The Nag's Head at Southery for a total of £1,570[7]. W.A.J. Amherst bought The White Hart at Foulden for £360.[8] Not all sale records are available.

Lost Public Houses

Other small and humble establishments would have been the meeting places for drovers and local men, alehouses often selling beer brewed by the proprietor.

The Trowel and Hammer (at one time known as the Shovel and Hammer) stood almost opposite The Cock in Oxborough Road. It was owned by the Micklefields and also leased to Hogge and Seppings, later Bullards. It closed in 1932.

In 1794, an establishment called The Wounded Heart is mentioned in sale particulars, though it not clear where exactly it was located:

> *All that capital new-built and well situated Messuage or Tenement, with yard belonging, at the annual rent of £22 6s, now occupied by Mr. John Hewson, and others, and was formerly a public-house, known by the sign of the 'Wounded Heart.'*

White's Directory of 1835 also lists James Clarke and Thomas Hewson (son, perhaps, of John Hewson mentioned above?) as having 'Beer Houses' but again, it is not clear where these were.

***

---

7   Equivalent of c £192,000 in 2018.

8   Equivalent of c £44,000 in 2018.

It can be seen that a significant role has been played by hotels, posthouses, inns, public houses and simple alehouses in cottage parlours over many centuries. They were central to making Stoke Ferry a vibrant market town, trading and business centre, bustling with activity. Today, with the exception of the sporadic opening of the Bluebell, there are no licensed premises nor anywhere to stay or eat out in Stoke Ferry. Like many rural communities, it has progressively lost these amenities and another focus for 'the heart of the community' has gone, most probably permanently.

Chapter Ten

All Saints Church

The Church and its officers played a significant role in the life of many towns and villages, particularly in relatively isolated locations such as Stoke Ferry. The church was certainly one of the main foundations of the village and is likely to have played a role equally as important as more secular factors in shaping the life and activities of the community.

This ended in 2001, when All Saints Church was closed and sold to a private buyer. Since then, Anglican worship, christenings, marriages and funerals for Stoke Ferry residents have been held at the church in neighbouring Wretton[1]. For a considerable period of time the vicar of Stoke Ferry had also been vicar of Wretton and Whittington and lived in The Vicarage in Stoke Ferry. This too has now been sold (as *Godsold House*) and the parishes are currently part of a group of five – with Methwold, West Dereham and Wereham being added to 'Wretton with Stoke Ferry' and Whittington.

Early Church Buildings

The first simple church in Stoke Ferry was most probably built in the early 1200s under the jurisdiction of the Prior of Shouldham. As seen previously, The Earl of Clare, Lord of the Manor of Stoke Ferry, donated his interest and the Lordship of the Manor to Shouldham Priory in the early part of the 13th century. The original Charter for Stoke Ferry was granted by Henry III in 1248 and it is inconceivable that there was no church there at that time. Indeed, it is quite likely that some form of Christian worship had been held

---

1   One of the earliest 'Stoke Ferry' funerals, held at Wretton in February 2002, was for the author's father, George Coates, formerly Headmaster of Stoke Ferry school. The cortege set off from his home in Furlong Road, proceeded past the old school to Wretton for the service, and then all the way back to the cemetery, just beyond the hedge at the bottom of his garden for burial.

for centuries previously, from as early as the adoption of Christianity by East Anglia in the eighth century.

Before the English Reformation – Henry VIII's break with Rome – the church was Catholic and the monks from Shouldham Priory sang the mass in Latin. The Church had dominating power as the Abbott owned much of the area and local men were either his tenants or labourers. Some crops and stock belonged to the Church entirely, the rest were taxed at one-tenth (tithe) on all produce. However, only the monks had any role caring for the poor and sick and were amongst the very few who could read and write.

The church at Stoke Ferry was always dedicated to All Saints, as shown by two ancient wills in county records:

- In 1399 John Fyshere gave a legacy to St Mary's image in the belfry of All Saints Church, Stoke Ferry.
- In 1417 William Curteys, curate, in his will desired to be buried in the Churchyard of All Saints Stoke Ferry. He also made a legacy for the upkeep of the church.

In 1534, when Henry VIII dissolved the monasteries and expelled the Prior and his monks from Shouldham Priory, the control of Stoke Ferry Church and its lands was given to Edward Bedingfeld. This is somewhat surprising, as the Bedingfelds continued to be Roman Catholics with their own chapel and priest in residence at Oxburgh Hall (though presumably this was not known)[2]. At that time churches were compelled to become Protestant and recognise the King rather than the Pope as head of the Church, meaning that this would have been an awkward situation and control must have soon passed into other hands.

Blomefield[3] in 1797 stated that the right of patronage and the ability to appoint the curate was in the hands of one Edward Nightingale Esq. but little evidence is available about this long period of the church's history. Blomefield described the former church thus:

The church is dedicated to All Saints, and was a single pile of flint, chalk-stone, &c. about fifty-one feet long, and twenty-four broad, covered with

---

2   A notable feature of Oxburgh Hall is the Priest Hole, a secret and very confined chamber in the wall of one of the towers, where the priest could be hidden during any unwelcome visits or inspections by Henry's officers.

3   Blomefield ibid.

tile, with a four-square tower, embattled, and four pinnacles of stone and a shaft with a weather-cock; this tower falling unexpectedly in 1758, beat down (a) great part of the church. In this tower were two bells. At the west end of the steeple was a decayed little building, probably the station formerly of some hermit. There was formerly a chancel, but that has been dilapidated some many years past.

From the records at this time, we also know that there was a Rectory House with 30 acres of glebe land.

Disaster and Rebuilding

As Blomefield describes, in 1758 disaster struck the church. The tower collapsed, and in its fall destroyed so much of the fabric that the whole church had to be re-built. It took seven years to raise enough money to do this, and in 1765 the two bells were sold to raise the repair fund to £212[4]. Although the leading families of that time were prospering and building fine houses, they were evidently not over-generous to the church. Perhaps one exception was the Harvey family[5], since there are four large memorial stones for family members inside the church – a rare honour.

There is, however, little sign of the competitive church-building seen in other parts of East Anglia where the wealthy created magnificent edifices to show off both their wealth and their piety (see for example Lavenham, Long Melford and Southwold in Suffolk, all built on 'wool').

In 1766, the present church building was completed. It was smaller and simpler than the one it replaced, built of free-stone and flint, with chancel, vestry, nave, west porch and a bell turret with only one bell which bears the date 1766. Many old church records must have been lost or destroyed at the time of the collapse of the old church as the remaining church registers date only from 1736. Particularly during this period, the church had a lot of influence in the community. Despite their apparent lack of benefactions to All Saints, most of the gentry and farmers attended church regularly and expected their workers to do so too.

The church 'Vestry Committee', comprising the vicar, churchwardens and leading residents, governed the administration of the village. They were given powers by an Act of 1601 to manage the poor, law and order, local roads and

---

4   Equivalent of c. £37,000 in 2018.

5   See Chapter 15 for the story of the Harvey family in the 18th and 19th centuries.

the education of children in Sunday schools. They lost these responsibilities as new bodies were set up - the Poor Law in 1834, County Councils in 1888, and Parish Councils in 1894. Now the Vestry Meeting is an annual event when parishioners handle Church matters only.

Nineteenth and Twentieth Centuries

In the eighteenth and nineteenth centuries, Anglican ministers were often men of means, with private incomes in addition to the ample rewards of the living and the tithe payments most landowners had to contribute. Some vicars[6] spent their own money to improve the church. In 1847 - 48 the Rev. George Henry McGill paid £1,200[7] to have the church thoroughly restored and partially rebuilt. A gallery was built and an organ installed. (This organ was moved to the chancel in 1900 and was still in use until the closure of the church. It is now in Wretton Church.)

In 1901 when Charles E. H. Wilford was vicar, heating apparatus was installed and new cathedral glass put in seven windows. Now the only stained glass is in the west and east windows.

Writing in 2009, after the closure and part refurbishment of the church Simon Knott[8] says:

> *The nave is full of light, the windows large and the tracery in a flamboyante style. Flamboyante, literally 'blazing flame', was what the French had when we had Perpendicular, and it was popular with Gothick architects of the early 19th century. The pale coloured glass in an Art Nouveau style in the upper lights must be later. Interestingly, Pevsner[9] says that these patterns were also to be found on the font... The other striking feature of the nave is the set of painted shields decorated with heraldic devices.*

The only treasure which had survived from the original church was a small silver Chalice and Paten, unmarked but obviously very old. The communion plate in use until 2002 (Flagon, Chalice and Paten) were presented to the church by Mr. W.H. Winfield in May 1858 and are now on loan to Barton Bendish church.

---

6   A list of vicars who have served the parish of Stoke Ferry is shown at the end of this chapter.

7   C £135,000 in 2018.

8   The Norfolk Churches Site, www.norfolkchurches.co.uk.

9   Pevsner, Nikolaus, *The Buildings of England - North-West and South-East Norfolk,* Penguin, 1962.

In 1914, the parish of Stoke Ferry (and the whole of the Fincham Deanery) was transferred from the diocese of Norwich, to which it had belonged throughout the whole of its previous history, to the Diocese of Ely. This appears to have been part of a regular and on-going programme to balance the dioceses geographically. It is not clear what impact, if any, this had on parishioners.

In July 1959, the church was listed as a Grade II Building[10] (unlike many churches which receive the higher Grade I or II* listings). Locally, West Dereham church is Grade I, while those at Wereham, Wretton and Boughton are all Grade II*. Stoke Ferry's lower grading was significant when the church was decommissioned in 2002.

Decline and Closure

Up until the early 1960s, Stoke Ferry Church was thriving. The vicar, the Reverend Fred Willson was a genial and kindly man. He lived with his wife and daughter at The Vicarage, which was always open and welcoming. He particularly worked at getting young people into church activities, utilising the Parish Hall[11] as a youth club for badminton, social events and just a drop-in for anyone from the village. Tea and soft drinks were provided. Fred himself was usually there, joining in. He used this to encourage people to go to church, get baptised if they had not already been and study for confirmation. Church records of that period show regular groups of a dozen or so young people being confirmed – and all of them will have spent a number of evenings at The Vicarage, learning the catechism and gaining a better understanding of Christianity. It was a great loss to the church and the village when he moved to Bawburgh, another parish in Norfolk at the end of 1963.

The Reverend Willson died aged 80 in 1982. The obituary in his parish magazine[12] said:

> *Fr. Willson – as he was affectionately known…was a real man of God. During the frightening war years, he introduced the people of Rotherhithe to an inner peace. Later he joined the army and was chaplain to the 94th Field Regiment*

---

10 Listed Building Categories are as follows: Grade I for buildings of the highest significance; Grade II* for buildings of particular national importance and special interest; Grade II for buildings of special architectural or historic interest.

11 The Parish Hall is down the lane next to the defunct Duke's Head and before its closure was most recently used as the social club for Favor Parker. It is for sale (as it has been for well over a decade), along with the Dukes Head, with planning permission for four houses.

12 The extract is unreferenced, but this was most probably Bawburgh parish magazine, following his death in December 1982.

of the Royal Artillery and then returned to Rotherhithe.... And for the last 22 years has served the church in Norfolk.... He was a priest with time to listen, time to pray and a man capable of inspiring and leading people to God.

His replacement Frank Chadwick was very different. He came to Stoke Ferry in 1964 and was the incumbent for the next twenty years, living alone in The Vicarage (his family did not transfer with him from the Midlands). It is thought that he had had a tough time during the war, though it was never clear what that meant; his style and demeanour were the very opposite of welcoming. Not surprisingly, church attendance declined and the many young people who had joined during Fred Willson's time moved on, either to the chapel or in most cases to not attending church at all. Unfortunately, the universal memories of the Reverend Chadwick's time were of him travelling everywhere on his ancient bicycle (he did not have a car) and his almost daily habit of making home visits just when food was being served.

After his death, the church continued for another twenty years but struggled to recover and, more importantly, to raise sufficient funds for its ongoing maintenance. The Diocese of Ely[13] gave me this summary of the situation and events leading up to closure:

> *The fate of the church at Stoke Ferry was fairly typical, but in one way unusual.*
>
> *The typical part was that the congregation felt over-burdened by the repair needs of their building. Quite a lot of work seems to have been undertaken with the church and the village during the 1990s, including a "parish conference" trying to find ways in which the church could do more for the village, and become more valued by the village. However, by the end of the decade, the repair bills were mounting up, with, it seems, little support from the village to meet them. It is reported in 1998 that "villagers were canvassed by the PCC[14]...to see what measure of support might be forthcoming for restoration work. There was very little positive response, and certainly not enough to divert the PCC from requesting closure."*

---

13 Personal email to the author from Geoffrey Hunter, Church Buildings Consultant, Diocese of Ely, 11 December 2017.

14 Parochial Church Council.

So the PCC wrote to the Bishop, resolving to close the church. This was duly done, by Order in Council, on 16 July 2002. The building was appropriated to the uses of: "social, cultural and community purposes and for occasional religious worship in accordance with the rites and ceremonies of the Church of England."

The untypical part is what happened next. Most country churches are highly listed buildings (grades II* or I) and therefore eligible for vesting by the Churches Conservation Trust. At that time, vesting in the CCT would have been almost the expected outcome. There are other closed churches cared for by CCT in Feltwell, Hockwold and Barton Bendish. But because of its complete 19th century rebuilding, the church at Stoke Ferry is only Grade II listed, which is unusual for a country church, and therefore the CCT safety net was not available to it. The fate of the building at Stoke Ferry was, therefore, more in line with what one sees for Victorian churches in towns and cities: sale and re-purposing. The building would have been valued commercially .... and put on the open market.

I am certain that we would have approached the situation differently today, and I would hope a combined church/community use for the building might have sustained it; but the bottom line remains the same: the money to repair and maintain church buildings has to come from somewhere.

Stoke Ferry Church was put on the market through agents Joliffe of Peterborough asking for offers around £40,000. It was purchased by Christopher (Kit) Hesketh-Harvey, a long-time Stoke Ferry resident[15]. He believes that the existence of several Harvey gravestones in the church may have played some part in his successful bid for the property.

Since acquiring the church, Mr. Hesketh-Harvey has invested heavily in renovation and maintenance of the fabric, keeping the churchyard in good condition and making it available for art exhibitions, musical shows and occasional village events. As such, he is a considerable benefactor to the village.

Since the closure, the parish is now officially known as Wretton with Stoke Ferry. In the long period between vicars, the church and its spirit have been kept alive by a dedicated team of lay preachers, lead by Carol Nicholas-Letch.

---

15 See Chapter 17.

All Saints Church Stoke Ferry
Incumbents since 1726

1726	Robert Rushbrooke, Sen.
1768	Thomas Ibbot
1774	Thomas Whiston
1803	Richard Golding
1810	Henry Howard
1843	Henry Sims
1846	George Henry McGill, M.A.
1856	Edward Thomas Scott
1858 - 99	John McGill
1900 - 05	Charles Edward Hignett Wilford, B.A.
1905 - 09	H. J. Adams
1910 - 20	Edward T. Woollard
1920 - 21	Paul H. Chamney
1922 - 28	O G Bolton, B.A., Canon
1928 - 31	George H. Dwyer Wright, B.A.
1931 - 41	William Place, M.A.
1941 - 51	J. C. Paterson-Morgan
1952 - 58	Herbert Law, M.A.
1958 - 63	Frederick James Willson, B.Sc.
1964 - 86	Frank Chadwick, M.A.
1986 - 97	Alan Bennett
1997 - 2002	Nigel Tufnell (Rector of Northwold[16])
2017 -	Ken Waters[17]

---

16 As well as Northwold, Nigel Tufnell covered the parishes of Methwold, Whittington, Stoke Ferry and Wretton until 2002

17 Now part of a group of five churches: Methwold, Wereham, West Dereham, Wretton with Stoke Ferry, and Whittington

All Saints Parish Church, Stoke Ferry
Grade II Listing

Originally 15th Century, tower fell 1578, nave rebuilt 18th Century, nave and chancel entirely rebuilt by W.J. Donthorn 1848.

Ashlar, clunch and flint[18] with slate roofs. Stepped angle buttresses to west wall. Central portico porch. Single bellcote at apex of western gable.

3 2-light south nave windows between stepped buttresses: cusped lights below flamboyant tracery head. Moulded jambs and hood on head stops. North nave with 4 similar windows and parapet.

Gabled nave roof. Large gabled vestry obscures much of south chancel and is entered through arched doorway in west wall. 3 irregularly spaced lancets punctuate south gable wall.

One 2-light chancel south window as nave. Angle buttresses to chancel. 4-light east window by W.F. Cullyer of Norwich with Geometric lay-out and flamboyant tracery details. Moulded jambs and hood.2 2-light north chancel, windows as before.

Interior. All of 19th Century re-construction. Octagonal font with tracery in style of fenestration. Open timber roofs, adorned with shields.

---

18 All types of stone used in Norfolk

Chapter Eleven

Education, Chapels and the Community

The development of education in Stoke Ferry over the last three hundred years has been closely tied to the Church of England. The role of non-conformist churches and the entirely secular community facilities are also included here, since in 1987, albeit briefly, these all came together in the new School, Sports and Community Centre[1].

Education

In 1819, many decades before a series of Education Acts made elementary schooling compulsory (1880) and free (1891) for children up to the age of 10, The James Bradfield School was opened. The successor of that school, All Saints Academy, celebrates the bicentenary of its foundation in the 2018 - 19 academic year.

Early Schools

This was not the first school for Stoke Ferry and Wretton, however. As far back as 1713, the Subscription Books[2] included the following entries for church-linked educational establishments in both villages:

Date of Registration	Parish	Master
11th June 1713	Wretton	Joseph Clarke
9th May 1717	Stoke Ferry	Stephen Aliothe Warner
24th Sept 1753	Stoke Ferry	Robert Young

---

1   See Chapter 19.

2   These were diocesan records, listing educational establishments (as well as clergy, doctors and midwives). The 'subscription' was in effect a listing by the individual, which included making an oath of faith. From E.H. Carter, *The Norwich Subscription Books – A study of the Subscription Books of the Diocese of Norwich 1637-1800,* Thomas Nelson & Sons Ltd, London 1937.

15th Aug 1760	Stoke Ferry	William Attmore
3rd June 1777	Stoke Ferry	John Rush
1779	Stoke Ferry	John Baynes

These schools were both called 'English Schools', offering reading, writing and arithmetic, as well as religious studies. It appears that the school at Stoke Ferry was in operation for at least sixty years, but there is no mention in the records of its size or where it was located. It would undoubtedly have been fee-paying, most probably for boys only and obviously closely linked to the church. In such a wealthy place, there may also have been a school for young ladies at this time, but no records survive.

James Bradfield's Will[3]
James Bradfield was Lord of the Manor of Stoke Ferry and Wereham and a major landowner in the two villages, as well as in Wretton. He had acquired his wealth from serving as agent to the Earl of Mountrath and other Irish nobility and through investing in land and property locally, also benefitting from the enclosures. His home was the Manor House on Wretton Road until 1806, the year before his death, when he acquired The Hall from the estate of Dr. Henry Helsham, who died in that year.

Bradfield had lived in Stoke Ferry from some time before 1767, when he married Sarah Worns and he would have been familiar with the school listed above. In a series of codicils to his will, written only a few days before his death in Ireland in 1807, he made a significant bequest to establish a Free School for poor children from the two parishes of Stoke Ferry and Wretton.

In the third codicil, dated 13th October 1807, he begins with a general explanation of why he is doing this:

> *God almighty having been very bountiful to me and having enabled me through prosperous industry to acquire a valuable estate in my native place of Stoke Ferry I feel it a duty incumbent on me to leave some public token of my affection for the good people of that village and of the neighbouring village of Wretton.*

He goes on to instruct his wife and son-in-law:

---

3 For further information about James Bradfield and his legacy, see Chapter 12.

I therefore order and direct that my dear wife Gertrude Bradfield[4] and my son-in-law John Land…. shall hand and be seized and possessed of that plot of ground at Stoke Ferry … near Charles Sanders house and containing about one acre and a quarter marked out by me for the purpose of building a schoolhouse.

In this and the fifth codicil, he makes a number of detailed stipulations about establishing the school:

at the end of seven years after (my death) there shall be created and built on (that) lot of ground a plain substantial schoolhouse in which there shall be convenient apartments for the residence of a schoolmaster…

… in creating such building and enclosing that ground at the rear (of it) there should be expended a sum of two hundred and fifty pounds English money[5] …

I … direct that twenty-five pounds a year English money[6] should forever be paid to the schoolmaster of (the) school … and he shall have his residence in the … schoolhouse and the garden to the rear is to belong (to it) rent free.

…I desire that there shall be …taught in the … school Reading, Writing and Arithmetic and the principles and duties of the established Church of England.

Twenty-five poor children to be selected from amongst those whose parents are least able to pay for the education of their children, (and these) children are to be educated and instituted (enrolled) free of all charge or expense to them or their parents.

I desire that my wife and my son-in-law John Land … shall have the selection and appointment (of) ten of the … poor children … and the appointment of the remaining fifteen shall be (made by) Ministers and the Churchwardens … of the parishes of Stoke Ferry and Wretton.

…further I desire that (these) shall be in the proportion of sixteen children from the parish of Stoke Ferry and nine children from the parish of Wretton

---

4   Gertrude was James Bradfield's second wife who he married in Ireland in 1797, his first wife, Sarah, having died in 1793.

5   Equivalent to c £21,500 in 2018.

6   Equivalent to £2,150 in 2018.

and that in selecting (these) poor children a preference shall be given to the poor children working on my own estates in the parishes.

The following day, 14th October 1807, he remembers something else to add:

I hereby direct that the schoolmaster of the school that I directed to be built at Stoke Ferry shall be ... appointed by my wife and my son-in-law John Land ... and shall be removable by (either of them) provided that if the office of schoolmaster shall at any time be vacant for six calendar months that such a vacancy may be filled up by appointment by the Minister and Churchwardens of Stoke Ferry.

James Bradfield died in Dublin ten days later on 24th October 1807. His wife Gertrude, together with his sons-in-law John Land and Charles Sanders were present and heard at first hand his detailed stipulations for establishing the school, no doubt clarifying his intentions, as required.

As with many major projects, the time frame for completion of the school slipped from seven years, as stated in his will, to nearly twelve years. It is not clear why this was, but Mrs. Bradfield moved away from Stoke Ferry and back to Ireland about two years after James's death and so, presumably, the whole burden of the construction and establishment of the school fell on John Land. He was the husband of James Bradfield's younger daughter Susannah, who had inherited land in her father's will and undoubtedly he had many other responsibilities in addition to the school. Sadly, Susannah died in 1819, the same year as the eventual opening of the school.

It is interesting to note that although Bradfield mentions only *children*, by the time the school was built the trustees had interpreted this as *boys* as can be seen from the inscription over the schoolhouse door. It should also be noted that he states that preference should be given to poor children *working on his estate* (rather than the children of parents working on the estate).

A Board of Trustees was set up, comprising the Vicar of Stoke Ferry and Churchwardens of the two parishes. The schoolmaster had to be a member of the Church of England and obey any conditions imposed by the Board. Initially, he was also expected to take Sunday School, train the choir and play the church organ[7].

---

7   In later years, this body became the School Managers and continued to be chaired by the Vicar of Stoke Ferry. In 1953, when my father, George Coates, was appointed as Head, this was the decision-making body (not the Norfolk Education Committee). George had been a life-long Baptist but transferred his allegiance to the Church of England to comply with this requirement. He later became secretary of the Parochial Church Council for many years and sang in the choir but was spared the duty of playing the organ.

Other children could be accepted in the school, paying their *School Pence* so long as this was no detriment to the chosen free pupils. By 1833, records show that there were 32 boys and 18 girls in total, half of them James Bradfield's free pupils[8].

Thus, local children had educational opportunities much earlier than most villages, not only in Norfolk but throughout the country. Later in the century, as the Church of England became more concerned about education, three classrooms were constructed behind the original school in 1848 and in 1866. This building, with later extensions, continued in use until July 1987, while the original School House became the headmaster's home.

Elementary Education Acts 1870 - 1902

The Education Act of 1870 placed local education under the control of School Boards. Stoke Ferry's Board of five members, which was established in 1875, incorporated the Bradfield School into the State system, though still under the patronage of the Church, with the Vicar as chairman of the Board. Under this Act, education was neither free nor compulsory, but Acts in 1880 made attendance to age ten[9] compulsory and in 1891 elementary schooling became free in all schools up to that age.

The capacity of Stoke Ferry School was set at 100 boys and 80 girls and infants, which must have been very crowded in the three available classrooms. In 1888[10] the average attendance was 98 boys and 75 girls and infants. There were three teachers, Charles William Brown, Master; Miss Alice Welham, Mistress; and Miss Amelia Pearson, Infants' Mistress.

Correspondence from Alton Jones[11], who was a pupil of the school under headmaster Charles Brown and then served as a pupil teacher until 1895, speaks of overcrowding in the school and the way older children were discouraged from staying on:

Rather than build an additional class-room.... the school management devised the scheme of graduated increases as you advanced in class. The highest grade was Class 7, and every child in there had to pay 5 pence a week, in a community where an agricultural labourer could not earn more than eleven shillings a week.

---

8   House of Commons records for May 1833, published in March 1835.

9   The age for compulsory education was progressively raised to 11 in 1893, 12 in 1899, 14 in 1918, 15 in 1944 and 16 in 1972.

10 Kelly's *Directory of Norfolk,* 1888.

11 See Chapter 17 for Alton Jones's story.

No wonder parents of large families let their children leave school as early as possible.

The 1902 Education Act replaced the School Boards with Local Education Authorities (LEA), ending local management of schools, in an attempt to harmonise and upgrade schools. The LEA's took over the payment of teachers, also ensuring that they were properly qualified. The Bradfield Trust continued as a charity which owned the School House and all the land used by the school[12].

Other Local Schools

Among the wealthier members of the community, private schooling was in demand and many small establishments have existed from time to time. John Bird Hill (1816-91) had a 'Gentleman's Day and Boarding Academy' at Clifton House in The Furlong for many years from about 1840 until the 1870s. He was the husband of Sarah Etheridge, a great-granddaughter of James Bradfield.

In 1888 Miss Mary Steele[13] had a 'School for Young Ladies' at the Lodge and Miss Flora Barber ran another private school in Boughton Road in a cottage near the mill. Both these schools continued until the early part of the twentieth century.

---

12 George Coates, the last headmaster to rent the School House (for one pound per week – equivalent to £12.60 in 2018) used to receive a 'peppercorn rent' of 7s 6d (37½p) annually from the Norfolk Education Committee for the use of the playing area, which was the garden of the house, as stipulated by James Bradfield's will.

13 One of Dr. Henry Steele's sisters – see Chapter 17.

SCHOOL CONCERT
A Crowded House At Stoke Ferry

Careful Training

Stoke Ferry school concert was patronised by a full house. Successful as previous school concerts have been that held on Friday, at the Village Hall, eclipsed them all. The seating accommodation proved inadequate and many had to be satisfied with standing room. Not only in point of attendance and financial result was a record established, but the consensus of opinion was that in the excellence of the programme this concert surpassed any previously held. It would be invidious to single out any for special mention in connection with Friday's concert where all reached such a high standard.

Messrs. E.G.Eggett and W.A. Buckenham (school managers) rendered valuable assistanceas stewards, and the Rev. W.Place (chairman of the managers) presided. The indispensible Mrs. Hinde was, as usual, at the piano and Miss Rolfe (headmistress South Wootton) and Mrs. Spooner assisted as dressers. The stage presented a most pleasing spectacle, the design and scheme being the work of Miss C.I.Rolfe. The first part of the programme consisted of a play, "The Princess and the Little Grey Dream." The wonderful costumes and dresses worn by the twenty-five characters were made by Miss C. Rolfe, who was entirely responsible for this part of the programme. The children taking part were Ernest Best, the dream-maker; Margery Payne, wise woman; Freda Payne, grey dream; Dick Heygate, blacksmith; Pamela White, Steven, his son; Jack Manning, Simple Simon; William Ward, Tom Farmer; Jack Wilby, Dick Doughty; Eric Phillips, Peter Knowall; Sylvia Kiddell, Mrs Sarsenet; Peggy Bonnett, Jenny; Gwendolen Kiddell, Mrs. Goodenough; Clarice Bent, Mrs Pipchin; George Carter, The King; Violet Reeve, The Queen; Doreen Kiddell, Princess Chrystal; Margaret Spooner, nurse; Geoffrey Allen, herald; Joan Hildreth, Lord high-master of music; Leslie Taylor, Stanley Barnett and Hayden Phillips, musicians; Joan Arter, citizen; Vera Allen and Tony Bonnett, boys.

Part two included some miscellaneous items which reflected much credit on the training of Miss Long, infants' teacher. These very juvenile actors acquitted themselves well and afforded a great deal of amusement, all their numbers receiving hearty applause. Miss Chapman's girls in "Grandmothers old" were very entertaining. Other items were, action song "The Aeroplane," infants recitation, "Queen Mob," Clarice Bent; dance, six infants; song "Grandmothers old," junior girls; song "Soldier, soldier, will you marry me?", infant girls and Angus Longmuir; dances, "Hit and Miss" and "Heartease," Doreen Kiddell, Peggy Bonnett, Freda Payne and Vera Allen.

At this stage, the chairman thanked the head-teacher and staff for the work they had done in producing the concert..

Part 3 consisted of a musical sketch "Matrimonee." This was a real side-splitter, six husbands dissatisfied with their respective wives' housekeeping arrangements and management determined to show them how to do it properly and the wives are told they need only to come in at meal-times. Taken at their word, the husbands find that with the babies to mind, the housework to do, and the dinner to cook – things they know nothing about whatever – they have bitten off a good deal more than they can chew. The complications that arise lead to situations that are better visualized than described. The characters were sustained by the following senior boys and girls, Jack Carter, Eric White, Cecil Taylor, Ernest Manning, Jim Carter, and Gordon Bent as the six grumbling husbands; Winnie Larner, Doris White, Clarice Phillips, Evelyn Longmuir, Frances Watson and May Cowles as their doleful wives, Phyllis White as Mary Anne, a nursemaid and Jack Wilson, a police man.

This is an undated newspaper report of a School Concert from the 1930s. A 1983 letter to Doris Coates from one of the participants, Cecil Taylor, suggests that it was 1932. He says, *I took part in one of those plays and my brother in the other…these school plays were one of the highlights of our year.*

Stoke Ferry School in the 1950s

When I started at Stoke Ferry School at the age of seven in 1953[14], the school catered for pupils up to the age of 14, at which time they transferred to Methwold village school for their final year. Others left at the age of eleven to go to the local Grammar School, if they 'passed' the 11+ exams. There were four classes, each with its own full-time teacher – Mrs. Ashby for the infants, Mr. Norman Errington for ages 7-8, Mrs. Daisy Williamson for 9-10 and Mr. George Coates for 11-14. In all there were about 120 children. The classrooms were spacious with high ceilings up to the rafters and could be very hot or cold depending on the season. The installation of coke-burning stoves helped with the heating but emitted noxious fumes; the teachers themselves had to keep these fires going. The toilets were outside and often froze up in winter. School milk was delivered and taken daily at morning break in one third of a pint bottles. There was a large playground and extensive school gardens – George Coates was an enthusiastic horticulturalist.

I vividly remember being taught 'joined-up' writing by Mr. Errington using a dip-pen and ink, guaranteed to create blots and splotches across the work. After a year, I moved to Mrs. Williamson's class; this remarkable teacher, with a class of nearly thirty pupils covering two year-groups and the full range of academic capability, engaged each person individually, encouraging and enabling us to do our very best. We had regular spelling, 'reading age' and mental arithmetic tests. We read books out loud as a class – not text books but great stories such as *Treasure Island*. And we did 'projects' requiring research, analysis and presentation on a range of topics – historical, geographical, scientific and the practical world around us. School was fun!

My commute to school required opening the back door of School House and stepping outside. There was no excuse for lateness or absence and it would, in any case, have been difficult to skive! There were no school lunches at that time, so lunch was taken at home. At 3.45 when school was done for the day, the playground, buildings and garden became my personal back yard.

My father believed (and I agreed!) that it would not be good for either of us for me to be in his class (getting the right balance of strictness and favouritism would have been difficult). So very shortly after my tenth birthday, I successfully took the 11+ and in September 1956 started at Downham Grammar School, a year young for my class.

---

14 George Coates was appointed Headmaster in April 1953 and we moved from Long Eaton in industrial south Derbyshire to Stoke Ferry to take up residence in School House, my home for the next 20 years.

After My Time

In 1957, the year after I left Stoke Ferry School local education changed with the opening of Methwold Secondary Modern School (now Iceni Academy)[15]. Stoke Ferry School lost its older pupils and reduced to three classes, with Norman Errington leaving to become head of another local school.

In the early 1960s, school lunches arrived at Stoke Ferry (delivered daily by van and served from a new kitchen extension). There were two 'dinner ladies' and a midday supervisor. In 1968 the school appointed Eleanor Grimsey née Weedon, a former pupil, to this role. In October 2018 the School celebrated Eleanor's 50 years' continuous service, most recently as assistant to her daughter, now the school cook.

George Coates retired in 1973, to be followed as Head by Chris Young. The new school (long-promised but always at some distant future date) was still more than a decade away[16].

Nonconformist Churches

In the nineteenth century there were two chapels in Stoke Ferry, a Wesleyan and a Primitive Methodist. The Wesleyan Chapel was in Wretton Road, built in 1834 at a cost of £500[17] and a gallery was added in 1854. The Primitive Methodist[18] chapel whose location cannot now be identified, fell into disuse after 1864, but another chapel, 'Ebenezer', was built in Furlong Road by the Free Wesleyans[19], appearing in Directories from 1877 onwards.

After a national decision to unite the main divisions of the Methodist Church, these chapels were closed, and nonconformist worship was combined in a new Methodist Church in the High Street.

The inspiration for this spacious building came in the first place from a Methodist philanthropist, Richard Harwin (1825 - 1912) who settled in Boughton after a successful trading career in Durban, South Africa. In memory of his wife who died in 1890, he built The Manse at Stoke Ferry as a home for a resident minister and handed it over to the Methodist Circuit in 1897.

The house occupied part of a field which he had purchased for the purpose of building a church and schoolroom. It was some years before this could be done, but in 1902 the Trustees of the old Wesleyan chapel and schoolroom in

---

15 My mother, Doris Coates joined Methwold Secondary Modern School as Senior Mistress (later Deputy Head) and remained there until her retirement in 1975

16 See Chapter 19.

17 Equivalent to c£57,000 in 2018.

18 A breakaway group from the main Wesleyan church, founded in 1810.

19 Yet another breakaway group, founded in 1849.

Wretton Road were given permission to sell their premises. They were sold to Mrs. Martha Bader[20] for £500. A bazaar in the grounds of Homeleigh (then the home of the Tuck family) raised further funds and building work started for the new chapel and schoolroom at a cost of £550[21]. The first services in the new building were held in January 1903.

There were two vestries on the south side and a large schoolroom to the west, with a kitchen and separate classroom. A two-manual organ was installed in 1908, which needed to be reconditioned in 1961 and the same year, oil-fired central heating was installed.

Throughout this period, the Methodist Church continued to play an important role in village life. Important occasions, such as Remembrance Services and St. George's Day parades were shared with All Saints Church, services alternating annually between Church and Chapel[22]. Eventually, however, the decision was taken to close the Chapel and take up residence in a small Sanctuary in the new School and Community Centre, which was opened in September 1987. The old Chapel buildings were converted into two houses and sold.

Community Centres

Village Halls still play a significant part in community life, but they were of even more importance in the early part of the twentieth century, when lack of public transport made people dependent on local facilities for social gatherings and entertainment. In Stoke Ferry such halls were first opened as private business ventures and for a time between the early 1960s and the 1980s there were two – The Parish Hall and The Village Hall.

The Parish Hall is the older of the two and was described by the Rev. Hugh T. Bryant in his book, *Norfolk Churches*[23]. He calls it the Village Hall and says:

It was opened in 1902. It is private property, but it is leased by the Vicar for the profit of the parish. Originally it was a private house, but it was converted by its owner (Mr. George Salmon) at the instigation of the Vicar, to its present form. It makes a fine lofty hall, with a match-board interior to the roof, and plaster and cement walls. The length is 90ft and the breadth 19ft. It will accommodate 350 people.

20 Wife of a Harley Street eye specialist – see Chapter 17.

21 £550 is equivalent to c£64,000 in 2018 and the sale value of £500 equivalent to c£58,000.

22 Until the arrival of Reverend Chadwick as Vicar in 1964, who refused to collaborate with the Methodists.

23 Reverend Hugh T. Bryant *Norfolk Churches* Norwich Mercury Office 1905.

This refers to the building opposite Church Cottages and the old cemetery, later used as the Favor Parker Social Club but now derelict. Bryant also mentions a Reading Room, of which there is no present trace:

An Institute and Reading Room was erected by the Vicar and Church-Wardens (who are the trustees) in 1900... It is open during the winter months for young men of the parish, and it has a library attached to it. A small reading room was (first) opened in 1874.

The current Village Hall, still in use, is in a building that was once part of Salmon's Farm which occupied the triangle of land between Lynn Road and Furlong Road. After World War I, the building and the one adjoining were used as a coach garage, first by Eastern Counties Bus Company and then by the Ward Brothers whose business was local transport. In 1926 it was sold by Thomas Ward, William Ward and Albert Cecil Ward to H. Gordon Parker and five other young businessmen, including Charles Buckenham, Charles Hewitt and Herbert Morley and converted into a hall to be run as a commercial enterprise.

This group of young businessmen were impatient with the 'old guard' (the vicar, Dr. Steele and Mr. Hinde) who had the monopoly of the use of the Parish Hall and could block activities of the younger generation. By 1968, Gordon Parker was the sole shareholder; he offered the Village Hall to the community for a token payment and it was conveyed to the Village Hall Committee in 1968 to be run as a charity.

The Trust Deed specifies that it should be used for:

meetings, lectures and classes and for other forms of recreation and leisure-time occupation with the object of improving the conditions of life for the inhabitants

By 1989 the operating committee determined that the hall had no reasonable prospects of fulfilling these aims, particularly in view of the recent construction of the new school which incorporated a Community Centre. It had, in any case, become expensive to maintain and its position, with no parking, was very inconvenient. And so, it was resolved that it should be closed and sold. However, this is not what happened.

***

The new School, Chapel and Community Centre first opened in 1987. Chapter 19 takes up the story.

The Hall, built by Henry Linhook Helsham in 1790, later owned by J.B.S. Bradfield and Samuel Winfield

The Manor House on Wretton Road, home to James Bradfield and later, Charles and Sarah Sanders and their children

Rear view of All Saints Place, formerly the original Crown Hotel, later the childhood home of Sir Percy Winfield

The Church, Stoke Ferry.

Views from The Hill – the old
Saxon word for 'market'

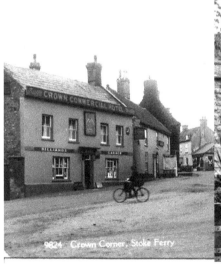

9824 Crown Corner, Stoke Ferry

*The Windmill before and after the 1936
storm and as it is today (bottom right)*

Hostelries through the years. Clockwise from top:
The original Crown Hotel (c. 1905)
The new Crown during WWI
The Cock (1930s)
The Bell Inn (1950s)
The Duke's Head (1950s)

High Street showing Homeleigh and Park House on the right

The Chemist's Shop in the early 1900s (above) and renewed plaque over the door today (below)

The corner of Oxborough Road. In the 1800s this was Hogge and Seppings Wine Store, Maltings and Brewery. Following a fire in 1909 a shop was built which is still open today (below)

147

All Saints Church –
closed in 2001

Stoke Ferry.

Stoke Ferry School c.1905

*School House and old Stoke Ferry School
converted to houses*

All Saints Academy

149

Plaque over the door of James Bradfield's School established in 1819

Headmaster George Coates in 1973, showing the classroom decorated for Christmas

Official opening of Stoke Ferry new school in 1988, originally also named after James Bradfield

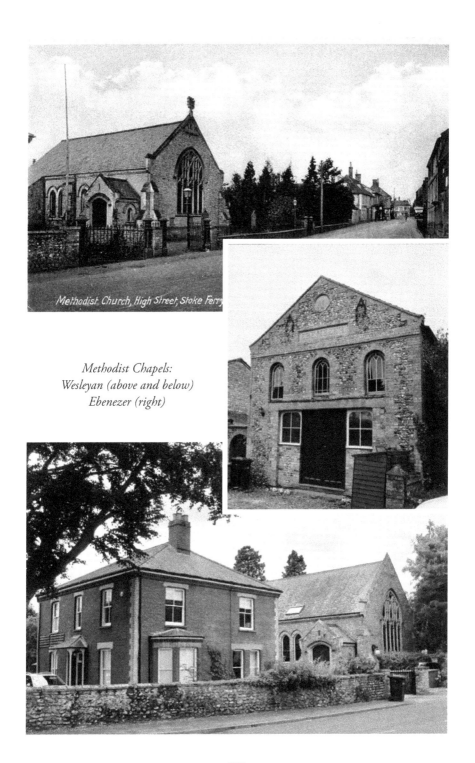

Methodist Church, High Street, Stoke Ferry

Methodist Chapels:
Wesleyan (above and below)
Ebenezer (right)

Oxborough Road Cottages

*Furlong Road
Cottages*

*The former Parish Hall showing
typical Norfolk flint construction*

High Street, Stoke Ferry.

High Street showing numerous shops on left and right

Wretton Road (left)

*Lynn Road
(below and left)*

The Fourth Part

In which is exposed
the lives, loves, exploits and deeds
of the great and sometimes good
families and citizens of
Stoke Ferry

Chapter Twelve

James Bradfield – Benefactor

The name of James Bradfield was, until recently, perhaps the best-known locally of any former Stoke Ferry resident, since both the old and the new schools were named after him. A plaque over my childhood home at School House stated:

Free School
For twenty-five Boys
From the Parishes of
STOKE FERRY and WRETTON
Founded by the late *Js BRADFIELD Esq.*
Anno Domini 1819

Until as recently as 2014, when it changed its name to All Saints Academy, the 'new' school was known as The James Bradfield Church of England Community Primary School. So, who was this remarkable man?

Origins

James Bradfield was born in the village of Beetley, near East Dereham and baptized on 12th June 1736. His was a very large family. His father Thomas (c. 1700 - 66) married three times, while living in Beetley and the neighbouring village of East Bilney:

- In 1724 to Alice Hawes who died in 1734, with whom he had five children
- In 1735 to Sarah Harrison who died in 1748, with whom he had eight children including James
- In 1749 to Alice Jarvis who outlived him, with whom he had four children

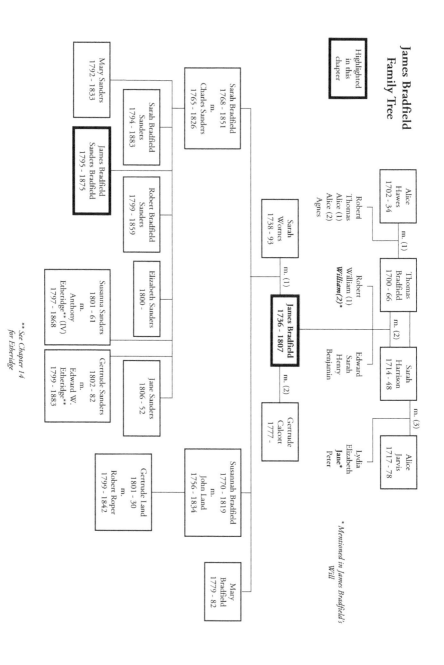

James Bradfield
Family Tree

Highlighted
in this
chapter

Alice
Hawes
1702 - 34

m. (1)

Robert
Thomas
Alice (1)
Alice (2)
Agnes

Thomas
Bradfield
1700 - 66

Robert
William (1)
William (2)*

m. (2)

Edward
Sarah
Henry
Benjamin

Sarah Harrison
1714 - 48

Lydia
Elizabeth
Jane*
Peter

m. (3)

Alice
Jarvis
1717 - 78

*Mentioned in James Bradfield's
Will

Mary Sanders
1792 - 1833

Sarah Bradfield
1768 - 1851
m.
Charles Sanders
1765 - 1826

Sarah Bradfield
Sanders
1794 - 1883

James Bradfield
Sanders Bradfield
1795 - 1875

Robert Bradfield
Sanders
1799 - 1859

Sarah
Worries
1738 - 93

m. (1)

James Bradfield
1736 - 1807

m. (2)

Gertrude
Calcott
1777 -

Elizabeth Sanders
1800 -

Susanna Sanders
1801 - 61
m.
Anthony
Etheridge** (IV)
1797 - 1868

Gertrude Sanders
1802 - 82
m.
Edward W.
Etheridge**
1799 - 1883

Jane Sanders
1806 - 52

Gertrude Land
1801 - 30
m.
Robert Roper
1799 - 1842

Susannah Bradfield
1770 - 1819
m.
John Land
1756 - 1834

Mary
Bradfield
1779 - 82

** See Chapter 14
for Etheridge

At least two of these children died before they were one year old. There is no record of Thomas's status or employment or whether he was a gentleman of means. He was buried at East Bilney at the old church, later demolished.

James was the second son of Thomas and his second wife Sarah[1] but his early life is something of a mystery. What is clear from his later achievements is that he must have been formally educated to a high level and had considerable talent and ambition to advance himself and his career. However, I have not found any school records for him in Norfolk or at the University of Cambridge (where his grandson was later educated).

James Bradfield and Stoke Ferry

The first record of James Bradfield in Stoke Ferry was in 1767, when the Banns were published for his marriage to Sarah Worns:

> *Banns of Marriage between James Bradfield singleman and Sarah Worns singlewoman were published on the 1st 8th and 15th March 1767.*

> *James Bradfield of the parish of Wearham (sic) and Sarah Worns of the Parish of Stoke*

> *By me, Thos Weatherhead, Curate*

They were married on 15th March and it appears that they lived in Stoke Ferry after that. In time, they had three daughters Sarah (1768 - 1851), Susannah (1770 - 1819) and Mary (1779 - 82) who died at the age of three. James's wife, Sarah, died in 1793 and is buried in Stoke Ferry churchyard. Her raised tomb (which also contains the bodies of daughter Sarah and her husband Charles Sanders and her grandson James Bradfield Sanders Bradfield – of whom more later) is just inside the church gate, one of the few graves still standing in the churchyard.

After Sarah's death, James remarried in Ireland to a lady named Gertrude Calcott. Little can be traced of her background, but they married in October 1897, as recorded by Walker's Hibernian Magazine.

Over his lifetime James became very wealthy, acquiring land in Stoke Ferry and the neighbouring villages. At some point he became Lord of the Manor;

---

1 Supporting evidence that this is indeed the 'Stoke Ferry James Bradfield' is that in his will he mentions a brother William, next younger to him, and a sister Jane, who is a much younger half-sister, daughter of Thomas and his third wife, Alice Jarvis.

there are records of him taking on apprentices, being exempted from Land Tax and later of being on the electoral register at a time when only a very few wealthy landowners were (only fourteen in Stoke Ferry). It is thought that he and his family lived in the Manor House on Wretton Road.

Irish Land Agent

However, he was not merely a local landowner and farmer. In addition, he was an important Land Agent in Ireland, employed by various titled landowners to manage their vast estates there. For this he was presumably paid handsomely, in addition to any income generated from his own land, enabling him to continue building his wealth and estates in Norfolk.

A collection of letters, written by James Bradfield to one of his employers, The Earl of Mountrath[2], has been preserved[3]. These give a fascinating insight into the levels of society in which he operated, the scale of his responsibilities and the character and personality of the man himself. Written during 1800 - 02, the letters were addressed either to the Earl himself, or more usually to a 'Mrs. Preston', who, by deduction, is likely to have been the Earl's housekeeper and was fully conversant with the business.

The first few extracts refer to ongoing business matters:

5th July 1800 to The Earl of Mountrath: summary of income for the Irish and English estates

Money from Ireland	£4,750	18s	9d
Walsall	£1,150	0s	0d
Total[4]	£5,901	18s	9d

26th September 1800 to Mrs. Preston:

> *I have a great deal of trouble with the Commissioners of the income tax. They refuse to accept my Lord's offer of payment delivered to them and this day had a letter from Mr. Wright of Swaffham, the Commissioners Clerk, to desire me to state to them how and from what part of My Lord's income the*

2 Charles Henry Coote, Seventh Earl of Mountrath (1725 - 1802). His primary home was at Strawberry Hill near Collumpton in Devon; in Norfolk, he built and owned Weeting Hall, which was completed in 1770. The Earl had a phobia about smallpox which was still prevalent and would not stay at any inns in case he contracted it, and so he built five houses to use when travelling between his two main properties. By the period of these letters, the Earl was very elderly and almost reclusive, leaving all the management of his Irish estates to James Bradfield.

3 Held in The Norfolk Record Office in Norwich.

4 Equivalent to £645,000 in 2018.

calculation of the tax is levied.

30th November 1800 to the Earl of Mountrath (from Weeting):
(obviously fighting a losing battle against the Tax Commissioners)

I will pay the tax due. Write to Child (the Earl's Solicitor) to order him to pay me £996

My Lord's assessment for the English Estates is   £2,681 10s
For the Irish Estates   £7,278 10s

Total [5]   £9,960 –
Tax   £996 –

27th April 1801 to Mrs. Preston:

I returned here from Connaught last night safe and well with my treasure and the Connaught rents all pretty well paid…

But to my astonishment on my arrival here I find on the 13 instant the mail coach was robbed and all my pacquets (sic) to the printer and my first letter to you and every director of the business all stolen and gone but thank god no money or bills lost…

5th May 1801 to Mrs. Preston:

I shall be in Dublin on 15 inst and will then send My Lord all the money I have in hand and in the bank which will make up the sum I prepared…

23rd May 1801 to Mrs. Preston:

I also send you to Childs £4,000[6] English pounds at the enormous rate of 14 per 6! (market price was 15)[7]

---

5   Equivalent to £1,058,000 in 2018.

6   Equivalent to £318,000 in 2018.

7   The Irish Pound was not the same value as the English Pound at that time, but the exchange rates available (not officially set by the central bank) seem to have fluctuated wildly.

21ˢᵗ August 1801 to Mrs. Preston:

Made progress letting 2 acres plus 36 pockets of land for intended railway[8]

VIZ a railway is a cast iron road laid down to transport great weights at small expense of horses from the coalfields to the wharfs or from one wharf to another as one horse on a railway will draw the load of six on the common roads – so far for explanation

26ᵗʰ September 1801 to Mrs. Preston (from Mountrath, Ireland):

- Have ejected Sandys – he begged me to withdraw, offered £400 for arrears. Asked him for £500 now and the remainder in 12 months, but he couldn't do that. *I'm afraid he will always be a bad tenant*
- Death of a tenant – the farm is out of lease. 300+ acres at about £300+ pa rent

20ᵗʰ October 1801 to Mrs. Preston:

Sent Child and Co for my Lord Mountrath's use £5,500 English pounds[9] - in Irish at 11 for 10 £6,105 Irish Pounds

I hope my Lord will approve of my management of his business

The following extracts illustrate an informed and active interest in Irish politics –

11ᵗʰ December 1801 to The Earl of Mountrath:

The unfortunate and sudden Devolution of Sir John Parnell will in all probability create an immediate election in the Queen's County

JB writes that he heard about the death of Sir John on the road. A Mr. Pole has offered himself as a candidate but do any of Sir John's family wish to stand?

- What should I do?

---

8   This is nearly 20 years before George Stephenson's steam railway started the great railway boom.

9   Equivalent to £438,000 in 2018.

- Will there be a contest?

I hope there will not as there are now so many papist votes, a contest would create great confusion in the country

5th January 1802 from Mountrath to Mrs. Preston:

I have delayed writing to you for some time hoping my Lord would have given me some direction about the voting in Queen's County.

- Henry Parnell (Sir John's eldest) is late canvassing. My Lord did not promise (endorse) him.

Official accounts of the election state:
Parnell, who was evidently disappointed in his hope of gaining James Bradfield, one of the trustees of the Mountrath interest, declined a contest…[10]

10th January 1802 to Lord Mountrath:

There has since the Catholics were admitted into the Electoral Franchise in this Kingdom been a custom of increasing lease lengths to help voter registration. I think it is a bad practice as it breeds great corruption and many poor wretches go to the hustings at forty shillings freehold when they really have none at all…

The following extracts suggest that, as well as being a sound businessman, James Bradfield also empathised with the employees and others dependent on the Earl.

16th October 1800 to Mrs. Preston:

Poor Mrs. J is to be buried this night. She has had a very hard struggle indeed – all the inoculated people are perfectly well, thank god, and Mrs. Watson and children go home tomorrow and the little Sanders on Sunday. Indeed, I am much alarmed at the progress of the fever as almost all the people who attended on Hunter's family who brought it into the town have

---

10 R.G. Thorne, *The History of the House of Commons 1790-1820,* Published for The History of Parliament Trust by Secker and Warburg, London, 1986.

caught it and some of them has had it very severe indeed.

30ᵗʰ November 1800 To Earl of Mountrath (from Weeting):

I have waited ever since Friday last hoping I should have it in my power to inform you of the inoculation of Brandon but they still hold off and it is now four families in Town Street[11].

For god's sake give me leave to raise the labourers' wages. There is the greatest necessity for it or I would not ask it. I have prevented them going to the Justice in hopes you would raise them as everyone else gives 2s per day.

6ᵗʰ January 1801 to Mrs. Preston:

As soon as I came home I paid Bet Leach her mother's annuity to her death (viz) New Year 1800 and of all the poor mortals I ever saw a more distressed creature than she appears to be and if his Lordship would please to continue the £5 yearly I think a greater act of charity could not be done. You cannot conceive what apparent wretchedness there is attached to her.

30ᵗʰ March 1801 to Mrs. Preston:

Since I came here my Lord was pleased to send an order to pay Mr. Griffith £200 for the relief of the poor in and about this town which was indeed much wanted. The people here are in a very wretched state...

6ᵗʰ April 1801 to Mrs. Preston:

God forbid I should do anything to prevent my Lord doing any act of charity but after he has subscribed so liberally I think them imposing on him in soliciting him to contribute to their subscription when they have done nothing for their own poor....[12]

---

11 This refers to an outbreak of smallpox.

12 Objecting to a further appeal to Earl Mountrath for funds for the poor, when they themselves have contributed nothing.

8ᵗʰ October 1801 to Mrs. Preston (from Weeting):

I now have the pleasure to tell you I think all the inoculated people at Weeting are well and most of them perfectly clear, except a few who had a sprinkling of it…[13]

And finally, a few more personal comments and irritations:

5ᵗʰ May 1801 to Mrs. Preston:

I am very much distressed and disappointed that my letters to my Lord and you are not answered as they so much require it. I wish my Lord would answer on the Jamestown Borough business as it will be too late in June.

23ʳᵈ May 1801 to Earl of Mountrath:

I wish to god your Lordship would write to him (Sir Wm Glendower) about the matter of the remittance which cost you exactly £200 more than my original bargain.

30ᵗʰ May 1801 to Earl of Mountrath:

P.S. I am sorry to say I have got a bad cold and am but poorly but no part of my old disorder, thank god.

20ᵗʰ October 1801 to Mrs. Preston:

I hope to be home to my Christmas Dinner and thank god my business is in great forwardness.

5ᵗʰ January 1802 from Mountrath to Mrs. Preston:

Mrs. Bradfield beg her dutiful respects to my Lord and your self – thank heaven there is now peace and plenty in this country. I have had a bad cold for a long time back with great pain in the head which is general here for some time and many have died here of the disorder…

---

13 Further news on the smallpox outbreak.

And, in the style of the time, he would always end every letter as follows:

I beg my duty to my Lord and best respects to Mr. Pratt and family and to all friends in the west

And am your ever
Dutiful obed't and humble serv't
Jas Bradfield

The Earl of Mountrath died in 1802, leaving no direct heir to the Earldom (he never married). The title lapsed, but much of his estate was left to two distant kinsmen. It is not clear whether James continued working for the new owners but given his intimate knowledge of the estate and its business, it would seem likely that they would, at least for a while, have needed his knowledge and expertise.

Death and Will

James Bradfield died in 1807 in Dublin, Queen's County in Ireland and was buried there. As already mentioned, he had married an Irish woman ten years earlier and seems to have spent much of his time in Ireland.

His obituary[14] states:

At Dublin in the 73rd year of his age, much regretted, James Bradfield Esq, of Stoke Ferry, Norfolk. Mr. B. although not born to affluence, was of that active and industrious disposition, that by great exertions in business, in this country as well as Ireland (where he was the faithful steward upwards of 25 years to the late Earl of Mountrath and many other noblemen), he acquired a very fine landed estate and considerable fortune with great credit and distinguished reputation. As a mark of affection for his native place, he has by will endowed a school at Stoke Ferry for the education of 25 poor children.

It is clear that by the time of his death, James Bradfield had a very large and valuable estate. In his main will, written in July 1807, this was left to his wife Gertrude, his two daughters Sarah Sanders and Susannah Land and his grandchildren in particular to his eldest grandson, James Bradfield Sanders.

---

14 Possibly from the London Times, following the publication of his will in December 1807.

A series of codicils were drawn up in the last few days of his life in October 1807, including detailed provisions for the school[15].

The principal bequests were:

- For Gertrude (wife) – living rent free in his Mansion House[16] for her lifetime together with the furniture and several named parcels of land around Stoke Ferry plus stocks and shares which would generate an income; also all the furniture in his house in Ireland
- For Sarah (daughter) – an income of £200[17] (which would pass to her husband Charles Sanders if she died first)
- For Mary, Sarah, Susanna, Elizabeth, Gertrude and Jane Sanders (grandchildren, daughters of Sarah and Charles Sanders) £1000[18] at age of 25 or when marrying younger with parental consent
- For Robert and Thomas Sanders (grandchildren, sons of Sarah and Charles Sanders) £1000 at age 25, or after age 21 if they have *an advantageous opportunity of getting into business* or get married with parental consent
- For Gertrude Land (granddaughter, daughter of Susannah and John Land), £1000 and the same stipulations as for Sarah's daughters.
- For Jane Jacob (sister) her two sons £100[19] each
- For James Bradfield Sanders (eldest grandson, son of Sarah and Charles Sanders), all remaining houses, land and other interests, whether freehold or copyhold, in Stoke Ferry, Wereham and Wretton, provided that he adopts the surname of Bradfield
- Other land and property in West Dereham and Boughton to be held for further bequests and codicils.

The codicils followed in October 1807 in quick succession. He obviously believed (correctly) that he had only a few days to live, stating at one point:

…the codicils to my will are hastily drawn in Ireland at a time when I am extremely ill and cannot resort to legal advice respecting the proper forms of carrying my intentions into execution…

---

15 See Chapter 11.

16 This refers to The Hall at Stoke Ferry, acquired after the death of Henry Helsham in 1806.

17 Equivalent of £17,200 in 2018.

18 Equivalent of £85,800 in 2018.

19 Equivalent of £8,580 in 2018.

First Codicil – 11ᵗʰ October 1807

- For Gertrude an annuity of £200 in addition to the rents
- For James Bradfield Sanders – additionally all lands in Northwold and West Dereham and provision for his whole legacy to transfer to his younger brother Robert if he does not survive to 25 then on to succeeding male heirs
- For Susannah, all land recently purchased in Boughton
- For all the grandchildren, an additional allowance for maintenance, clothing and education during their minorities
- Other small bequests

Second Codicil – 11ᵗʰ October 1807

- Small bequest to Gertrude's niece

Third Codicil – 13ᵗʰ October 1807

- Concerning founding the school

Fourth Codicil – 14ᵗʰ October 1807

- Further stipulations about the school
- Provision for an allowance for James Bradfield Sanders' maintenance, clothing and education

Fifth Codicil – 15ᵗʰ October 1807

- For Sarah Sanders – all freehold and copyhold estates in Wimbotsham, Stow Bardolph and Downham, consitituting the estate of James's late brother William Bradfield

Sixth Codicil – 16ᵗʰ October 1807

- To complete the purchase of several parcels of land in Stoke Ferry from Edward Youngman and these to also form part of the bequest to James Bradfield Sanders

- Other detailed provisions on the legacy to Susannah Land
- Resolving other current financial transactions.

James's wife, Gertrude, and his two sons-in-law Charles Sanders and John Land were present in Dublin for the dictation of this last codicil.

After completing these extensive amendments and additions to his will, James Bradfield died in Dublin on 24th October 1807; the will was proved in London on 15th December the same year.

Succeeding Generations

It is impossible to estimate the value of James Bradfield's estate, since much of it was in land, buildings and rents in Stoke Ferry and several nearby villages, as well, it seems, as some property in Ireland. The 'minor' monetary legacies to his grandchildren and others alone amounted to several hundred thousand pounds in today's money, so it is obvious that the whole estate would have been worth multi-millions of pounds.

As can be seen from the summary above, the vast majority of the estate was left to his eldest grandchild, James Bradfield Sanders, who was twelve when his grandfather died. He would acquire his full inheritance once he had reached the age of 25 and changed his surname to Bradfield. This he duly did, with the help of his father, in 1814:

The London Gazette
Whitehall, November 14th 1814

His Royal Highness the Prince Regent hath been pleased, in the name and on behalf of His Majesty, to give and to grant to Charles Sanders of Stoke Ferry in the County of Norfolk, Gentleman, on behalf of James Bradfield Sanders, his eldest son (a minor), His Majesty's royal licence and permission that his said son may, in compliance with an injunction contained in the last will and testament of James Bradfield, late of Stoke Ferry aforesaid, Esquire, deceased (father-in-law of the said Charles Sanders), take and use the surname of Bradfield, in addition to and after that of Sanders, and that he may also bear the arms of Bradfield; provided the same be first duly exemplified according to the laws of arms, and recorded in the Heralds' Office, otherwise His Majesty's said licence and permission to be void and of none effect:

And also to command, that the said royal concession and declaration be registered in His Majesty's College of Arms.

He was subsequently known as James Bradfield Sanders Bradfield, or JBSB for short. In Michaelmas Term 1815, he was admitted to Jesus College Cambridge to read Law, graduating with a BA degree in 1819. He later gained a Doctorate of Law and was made a JP. On a Stoke Ferry map of 1817 showing land ownership, the village is covered with his initials, but his legal work, rather than the estate seems to have been his primary interest. He never married and lived alone with servants at The Hall in Stoke Ferry until his death in 1875, since by 1809 Mrs. Gertrude Bradfield had moved back to Ireland and remarried[20].

It appears that much of the estate was mortgaged during Charles Sanders' guardianship and JBSB's ownership. One mortgage, but by no means the only one, was a loan of £10,000[21] from the Reverend Jermyn Pratt, curate of Wretton and obviously a man of some wealth. Until his death JBSB continued to pay interest on this loan, but never repaid the capital.

After his death, his heirs, nephews Edward Etheridge and the Reverend Sanders Etheridge had to sell the estate to repay all the debts and mortgages associated with it. It was bought by the village solicitor (an ambitious acquirer of property) Anthony Horrex Roger Micklefield[22], who had taken over the mortgage from Reverend Pratt. The price – for 433 acres of land in Stoke Ferry, 56 acres in Wretton as well as houses, farms and cottages – was £26,941[23].

When JBSB's will was proved on 5th July 1875, the net effects were recorded as being less than £10,000[24]. It seems that he had managed to spend a great deal of his inheritance, though this was still a considerable sum. The Bradfield name, recreated for JBSB, died out again except for its association with Stoke Ferry School and the countless children, including me, who attended it over the next 140 years.

---

20 To the Reverend Francis Green Despard.

21 Equivalent of £992,000 in 2018.

22 See Chapter 13 for more on the Micklefield dynasty of solicitors.

23 Equivalent of £2.9m in 2018.

24 Equivalent of c £1.1m in 2008.

Chapter Thirteen

Micklefields – Solicitors

In the eighteenth and nineteenth centuries sons, grandsons and great-grandsons often followed a traditional family profession, in the case of the Micklefields the law. They were often also given the same Christian name, so the name of *Roger Micklefield* appears on legal documents in and around Stoke Ferry and Wretton for nearly 170 years from 1750 to 1920.

The country solicitor during that period had a much broader function than his modern counterpart. Known as a 'man of affairs', in addition to dealing with wills, property, conveyancing and litigation, the solicitor also acted as banker, money-lender and financial adviser. With a virtual local monopoly, he was likely to be involved in almost every legal transaction, knew everyone's secrets and had every opportunity to manipulate matters to his own benefit. No wonder 'The Lawyer' was a power in the community, with influence and wealth increasing over the generations.

Roger Micklefield (1722 - 1809)

The first Roger Micklefield we know about was born in about 1722 (according to the church record of his burial in 1809 which stated he was 87) and was living in Stoke Ferry from at least the 1760s when he appears on the Electoral Register. In his fifties, he fathered three children with a lady called Mary Fundery; Roger, Mary and Elizabeth Fundery were born in 1773, 1776 and 1779 respectively and baptised at Wretton Church with the entries in the church register reading, for example:

1774, 7 October - Baptised Roger, son of Mary Fundery, singlewoman

Roger (senior) and Mary Fundery eventually married in September 1785. It seems likely that Mary was Roger's housekeeper – certainly she was not an educated woman from his own class and signed the Banns of Marriage with a cross. After they married, Roger junior took on his father's surname (though the girls appear to have retained the Fundery name)[1].

Data on these earlier generations is sketchy, though deeds, wills and other documents of that period bear Micklefield signatures and they also acquired land on their own accounts.

Roger Micklefield (1773 -1849)

Roger (junior) also married relatively late in life (to Elizabeth Horrex from Foulden) and although the date and place of marriage are not known, his three children Anthony Horrex Roger (b. 1815), Elizabeth Horrex (b. 1818) and Georgeana (b. 1822) were all born when he was in his forties.

It is known that in 1817 he had half shares in the Maltings[2] and Staithe at Whittington and that in 1833 he was the owner of the chemist's shop next to the churchyard. His tenant was a Mr Piggott, druggist. In White's 1845 Directory he and J. B. S. Bradfield are listed as the two principal landowners in both Stoke Ferry and Wretton. Roger Micklefield died in July 1849 and is buried in Stoke Ferry churchyard; his tombstone is still visible.

Anthony Horrex Roger Micklefield (1815 - 92)

By the time of Roger (junior's) death, his son, Anthony Horrex Roger Micklefield (AHRM) was in practice too. He had become an articled clerk for five years in his father's practice in June 1832. They worked together until 1849, when AHRM took over fully on his father's death.

Between 1845 and 1890 few local property transactions happened without his involvement. Documents show how successful he was in his ruling obsession - acquiring land. Most landowners in the district were his clients and of these many found it necessary from time to time to borrow money on the security of their property and so became indebted to him. Even when large sums were borrowed from other sources AHRM frequently managed to buy out the original lender and take over the mortgage[3]. He must have had a

---

1   Doris Coates speculated that there might be another generation between Roger (senior) and Roger (junior) but the evidence now shows that this was not the case.

2   This was, in the twentieth century, owned by Whitbreads, the brewers and recently converted to a housing development.

3   See Chapter 11 with regard to JBSB's debt to the Reverend Pratt.

very large income from interest payments alone, far exceeding the legal fees paid by his clients.

He continually invested in more property. Building on his father's holdings, he bought up adjoining lands, sometimes by foreclosing mortgages, sometimes buying at public auction after a death or a bankruptcy. In Wretton he acquired the farm and lands of the Townley family (about 70 acres) in 1851; over 500 acres of the Bradfield estate in 1876[4]; about 30 acres of the King Estate at an auction in 1885; and 70 acres of the Hegbin estate auctioned in 1890, were some of the more notable acquisitions. He continuously extended the boundaries of his estate until he owned most of the village of Stoke Ferry, all of the land on the Stoke Ferry side of the Wissey from the Bridge to Wretton, much of the farm land in Wretton and further land on the Boughton side of the village. The rental income for this land – he did not farm it himself – will also have been significant.

On the death of James Bradfield Sanders Bradfield in 1875, AHRM became Lord of the Manor of Stoke Ferry and of 'Wretton and Irunhall'[5]. The main Micklefield residence was a house in the High Street, known as Park House but for part of his life he lived at the Manor House in Wretton Road.

AHRM married Augusta Ferrar from Wramplingham in mid-Norfolk in 1840, when he was 25. They had seven children – Thomas Ferrar Roger (b. 1842 and died in infancy), Augustus Edward Roger (b. 1846), Georgiana Elizabeth (b. 1847), Albert Ernest Roger (b. 1848), Arthur Farrer Roger (b. 1852), Ida Augusta (b. 1853) and Kate Farrer (b. 1855). AHRM's wife, Augusta died in 1856 at the age of only 41. In the corner of the churchyard is an undated marble memorial cross, topped with a carved angel for her. AHRM lived until 1892 dying aged 77.

---

4   As stated in Chapter 11, he paid £26,941, equivalent of c £2.9m in 2018. The Manor and its Lordship were acquired as part of this purchase.

5   An ancient name for Wereham.

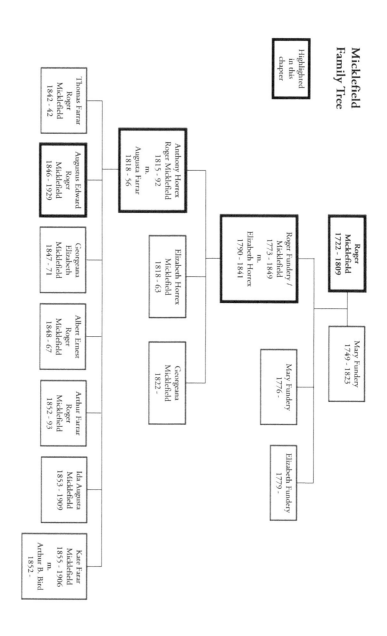

**Micklefield
Family Tree**

Highlighted
in this
chapter

Roger
Micklefield
1722 - 1809

Mary Fundery
1749 - 1823

Roger Fundery /
Micklefield
1773 - 1849
m.
Elizabeth Horrex
1790 - 1841

Mary Fundery
1776 -

Elizabeth Fundery
1779 -

Anthony Horrex
Roger Micklefield
1815 - 92
m.
Augussa Farrar
1818 - 56

Elizabeth Horrex
Micklefield
1818 - 63

Georgeana
Micklefield
1822 -

Thomas Farrar
Roger
Micklefield
1842 - 42

Augustus Edward
Roger
Micklefield
1846 - 1929

Georgeana
Elizabeth
Micklefield
1847 - 71

Albert Ernest
Roger
Micklefield
1848 - 67

Arthur Farrar
Roger
Micklefield
1852 - 93

Ida Augusta
Micklefield
1853 - 1909

Kate Farar
Micklefield
1855 - 1906
m.
Arthur B. Bird
1852 -

Augustus Edward Roger Micklefield (1846 - 1920)

On his death, the huge estate was inherited by his oldest son, Augustus Edward Roger Micklefield (AERM) the fourth generation of this family of lawyers, usually known as 'The Squire'. He attended King's School, Ely before going to St. John's College, Cambridge in Michaelmas Term 1865. He was awarded a BA in 1873 and MA in 1876.

After he graduated, AERM, like his father before him, was articled. The Deed states:

In the Queen's Bench

I Henry Braxton Branwhite Mason of Wereham in the County of Norfolk, Attorney at Law Make oath and say:

That Articles of Clerkship, bearing date the tenth day of June in the year of our Lord 1873 made between Anthony Roger Horrex Micklefield of Stoke Ferry in the County of Norfolk who has been duly admitted an Attorney of this Honourable Court and a Solicitor in the High Court of Chancery … and Augustus Edward Roger Micklefield of Stoke Ferry … son of the said Anthony Horrex Roger Micklefield …

Augustus Edward Roger Micklefield did with the consent of … Anthony Horrex Roger Micklefield … bind himself Clerk to the said Anthony Horrex Roger Micklefield for the term of three years …to serve him in the profession of an Attorney at Law and a Solicitor in Chancery from the day of the date of the …articles …

In the presence of me this deponent[6] and of one William Ashley of Stoke Ferry …, Draper.

Sworn at Swaffham in the County of Norfolk the tenth day of June 1873.

Following his Articles, AERM worked with his father until the latter's death in 1892, when he took over the family business in his own right.

He did not marry and lived at Park House in the High Street with a housekeeper, cook and maids and employed ostlers, a coachman, a gamekeeper

6   Someone who makes a deposition.

and gardeners to care for his large park and grounds. At times of celebration and festivals, he entertained the whole village and, with William Buckenham and Ernest Hinde, founded the annual Horticultural Show which was a feature of Stoke Ferry social life for over fifty years.

In addition to running his legal practice, for nearly thirty years AERM was the last of the 'gentlemen landowners.' He supervised the farming and kept a benevolent eye on tenants. He jealously guarded his woodlands and frequently invited friends to enjoy the excellent shooting and fishing on his estate.

The Sale of the Micklefield Estate

When he died in October 1920, AERM had outlived all his six siblings (one of whom had died in infancy). Of them, only Kate Ferrar Micklefield had married and none of them had children. Thus there were no near family members to inherit his large estate, which was valued at probate at £37,831[7]. In total, this comprised 1,457 acres of land in Stoke Ferry and Wretton and many farm buildings, as well The Manor House, Park House and Deanscroft.

Initially, the aim was to sell the *Stoke Ferry Estate* as one lot but this failed and was withdrawn, later to be sold piecemeal in separate lots. The Stoke Ferry estate alone comprised 648 acres, of which about 263 acres were arable, 290 acres pasture and 94 acres woodland, with two farmhouses – Manor Farm on Wretton Road and Limehouse Farm near Stoke Ferry Common (demolished in the 1960s). It was described in the sale particulars as an *Attractive and Desirable Freehold Sporting Property.*

Additionally, at Wretton the estate included Home Farm with the Steward's house opposite (now called Haringay Farm), Church Farm, Willow Farm, three smallholdings and eight cottages., as well as a considerable amount of land.

In Stoke Ferry High Street there were four shops (the old chemist's shop and three other double-fronted shops on the other side of the road). There were many more scattered parcels of land, including 173½ acres in the area between Furlong Road and Boughton. Finally, there were two 'family residences', the buildings now known as Dean's Croft and Park House.

The dispersal of this large estate signified the end of an era and it came at an unfortunate time for beneficiaries of the estate. By 1921 there were ominous signs of the post-war slump and a general reluctance to invest in land. Most of the bidding was low, even by 1921 standards.

---

7   Equivalent to approximately £1.86m in 2018.

Some of the deals made on the day of the auction in October 1921 were:

Lot	Buyer	Price 1921 £	Price 2018 [8] £
Farm, Wretton, 14 acres	S. Fretwell	550	23,400
Willow Farm, Wretton, 107 acres	A. Walker	2,050	87,100
4-bedroom house + 4 acres, Wretton	G. Drewery	400	17,000
Pasture Land, Wretton, 7 acres	G. Drewery	210	8,900
Arable land, Stoke Ferry, 14 acres	B. Gathercole	300	12,750
4-roomed Cottage, Stoke Ferry	H. Norman	90	3,825
Arable land, Stoke Ferry, 4 acres	H. Green	110	4,675
Pasture land, Stoke Ferry, 6 acres	G. Drewery	240	10,200
Pasture land, Wretton, 1 acre	W. Fendick	105	4,450
4-roomed cottage, Wretton	W. Fendick	80	3,400
5-roomed cottage + 5 acres, Wretton	F. Rickard	230	9,775
2 x 4-roomed cottages, Wretton	Mr. Blade	90	3,825
5-roomed cottage, Wretton	F. Stannard	170	7,225
2 x 4-roomed cottages, Wretton	Mr. Wilson	150	6,375
Arable and Pasture lands, Wretton, 20 acres	M. Garrod	360	15,300
Pasture land, Wretton, 13 acres	M. Garrod	230	9,775
Pasture land, Wretton, 13 acres	M. Garrod	255	10,850
Arable land, Wretton, 7 acres	D. Churchill	115	4,900
Pasture Land, Wretton, 8 acres	D. Churchill	130	5,525
Pasture Land, Wretton, 11 acres	A. Rickard	230	9,775

---

8 Equivalent price in 2018. It can be seen that the land, cottages and houses were all sold at very low prices by today's standards.

Fen pasture, Wretton, 13 acres	A. Rickard	160	6,800
Freehold Family Residence (Park House)	Mr. Hewitt	1,750	74,375
Arable land, Stoke Ferry, 13 acres	Mr. Salmon	420	17,850
Arable land, Stoke Ferry, 5 acres	H. Darkins	130	5,525
Arable and pasture land, Stoke Ferry, 44 acres	S. Fretwell	100	4,250
Residence (Dean's Croft)	Mr. Hewitt	450	19,125
Double-fronted shop and 5-roomed house	C. Hegbin	290	12,325
Double-fronted shop	D. Steele	340	14,450

Amongst Lots withdrawn at auction to be sold later were:

Farm at Wretton, 67 acres
Pasture land, Wretton, 15 acres
Arable and Pasture lands, Wretton, 34 acres
Arable, Pasture and wood lands, 138 acres
Pasture land, Stoke Ferry, 13 acres
Freehold arable land, Stoke Ferry, 173 acres
Pasture land, Stoke Ferry, 5 acres
Pasture land, Stoke Ferry, 7 acres
Pasture land, Wretton, 8 acres
Fen pasture land, Stoke Ferry, 13 acres
Double-fronted shop, Stoke Ferry

So the estate and fortune so painstakingly built up by four generations of the highly influential Micklefield family came to an end. The family name disappeared from Stoke Ferry and never since has one person owned and controlled so much property in the area.

Chapter Fourteen

Etheridges – Merchants

Another family with significant commercial interests in Stoke Ferry for nearly 130 years from 1791 – 1921 were the Etheridges. Unlike the Bradfield and Micklefield families[1] which literally died out, at the end of this period the Etheridges left Stoke Ferry and continued to thrive, firstly around the UK and then far and wide across the old Dominions – in Australia, Canada, New Zealand and South Africa[2].

The Etheridges were an old Norfolk family whose ancestry can be traced back to 1573 and earlier, when a Robert Etrich married Marion Francis at Necton. For the next several generations, the family lived at various times in Necton, Sporle, Hindringham, Swaffham and Narborough, in Norfolk and the name gradually migrated from Etridge to Ettridge and finally to Etheridge.

Coming to Stoke Ferry - Anthonys I and II

The Stoke Ferry connection can be traced back to Anthony Etheridge (1712 - 75), Gentleman and Farmer, of Hindringham. As with other families, Christian names tended to be repeated down the generations and for the Etheridges there is a repetition of Anthony[3]. His eldest son, Anthony II (1739 - 1806 - an almost exact contemporary of James Bradfield), was a 'Gentleman and Farmer' at Stanhoe, Norfolk for forty years.

In 1791 he bought an agricultural merchant's business in Stoke Ferry from Thomas Seppings[4] for his eldest son, Anthony III (1769 - 1843), to set

---

1   See Chapters 12 and 13.

2   Because of this, there is much more data and family research and a very extensive family tree. This chapter focuses mainly on the Stoke Ferry branch and period.

3   For ease of reference, I will number the Anthonys I, II, III, IV and V, this being Anthony I.

4   This was probably an ancestor of the Seppings who later owned the brewery in Stoke Ferry – see Chapter 9.

him up in a business of his own at the age of 21. In addition to dealing in grain, wool and wine, he also described himself as a 'grocer and draper'. This business thrived for much of the nineteenth century and the Etheridges were one of the wealthiest families in the village during that time.

Setting up Business – Anthony III

In 1794, Anthony III married Alice Drosier (1770 - 1808) and had three sons and four daughters: Mary (1795 - 1884), Anthony IV (1797 - 1868), Edward Wright (1799 - 1883), Alice (1800 - 75), John Drosier (1802 - 54), Ann (1806 - 69) and Charlotte (1808 - 66). A year after the death of his wife Alice in 1808, Anthony III married his cousin Sophia, but they had no further children.

Two of the sons married daughters of Charles Sanders (Lord of the Manor at the time) and granddaughters of James Bradfield. Anthony IV married Susanna in 1820 and Edward Wright married Gertrude in 1827. Each girl would have claimed her grandfather's bequest of £1,000 at the time of her marriage. Thus, a very strong link between two of Stoke Ferry's wealthiest families was created.

Anthony III acquired 'The Cobbles' with its granary and storehouses for his residence and also had other property interests in the village. In 1833 he bought a large shop in the High Street (now Moulsham House) selling it to his son Edward Wright for £800[5] in 1836. It appears that Edward sublet the property to tenants, at one time Wm. Jaggard, Tailor & Mercer. He continued to own the shop, with chaise house, storehouses, stables and other outbuildings and one acre of land until 1878 when it was sold to Wm. Ashley for £1,000[6], a fairly modest profit over 42 years.

Anthony III was not a particularly successful businessman but despite this the business did well enough during his time.

---

5   Equivalent to c. £97,000 in 2018.
6   Equivalent to c £110,000 in 2018.

Etheridge Family Tree

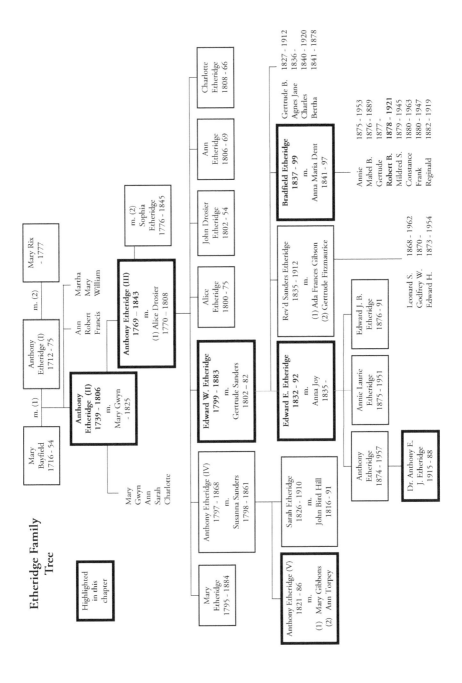

Thriving in the Next Generation

His eldest son, Anthony IV, preferred to follow the earlier family tradition of farming, initially owning land at Ickburgh, ten miles away, but he retained his main residence at Stoke Ferry. He presumably had another house with his farm, since both of his children - Anthony V (1821 - 86) and Sarah (1826 -1910) were born there. By the time of the 1851 Census, Anthony IV and his wife Susanna had moved to Chigwell in Essex, where he farmed 157 acres and employed six men. By 1861 they had moved again to Binfield in Berkshire where he had 280 acres and employed four men and four boys. Anthony and Sarah died and were buried in Binfield.

Anthony III's two younger sons, Edward Wright and John Drosier continued the Stoke Ferry businesses and built them up considerably over the following years. The 1845 Directory[7] describes Edward Wright Etheridge as 'Spirit, seed and hop merchant, chandler and maltster' John Drosier Etheridge as 'Wine merchant'. Their sister, Charlotte also married into a local business when she married Richard Piggott, the local chemist.

John Drosier married Sarah Hegbin of Fincham in 1828. After John Drosier's relatively early death (he was 52) the wine business was incorporated into Edward Wright's business, since John's only child (later the Reverend John Hegbin Etheridge) was a baby of two years at his father's death.

Edward Wright and Gertrude Sanders had seven children: Gertrude Bradfield (1827 - 1912), Edward E. (1832 - 92), Sanders (1835 - 1912), Agnes Jane (born 1836), Bradfield (1837 - 99), Charles (1840 - 1920) and Bertha (1841 - 78). Two of the sons, Edward and Bradfield, played significant roles in running the business and when their father died at the age of 84 in 1843, they took over its ownership and management. The 1888 Directory lists:

E & B Etheridge, maltsters, corn, seed, hop, wool, wine, spirit, ale and porter merchants (and at King's Lynn)

The business was known as E & B Etheridge until it was eventually sold in 1922.

In practice, it seems to have been Edward who ran the business. He lived at 'The Cobbles' and owned the premises there, while Bradfield lived with his large family at 'Homeleigh' and seems to have had little to do with the day-to-day running of the firm.

---

7   Kelly's Directory of Norfolk, 1845.

Business in Decline 1892 - 1922

Edward made his will in early 1892, leaving his property in trust to his executors - Sanders Etheridge, John Joseph Nunn and Charles Hawkins of Downham Market.

Sanders was the brother between Edward and Bradfield (Rector of Haslemere in Surrey). He was also appointed guardian to Edward's daughter, Annie Laurie.

By a codicil to his will, he later added the name of his brother Bradfield - it seems he had little confidence in his brother's ability to manage the business after his death. He stated in the will that he wished the property to be sold but the executors could postpone the sale as long as they thought fit. Edward died a few months later in May 1892, age 60.

This started a long period of decline for the business. After Edward's death it was run by a manager, Mr Yorke, who lived in 'The Cobbles' for a while. Bradfield kept a general supervisory view of affairs until his own death in 1899 but he did not have his brother's acumen. After his death, his eldest son Robert Bradfield Etheridge took over management when he was only 21 years old.

John Joseph Nunn also died in 1899 and the Rev. Sanders Etheridge died in 1912. Charles Hawkins, by then the sole trustee, declined to continue in that role and put the business in the hands of the Public Trustee. Although Robert Bradfield Etheridge continued to manage the trade in wine, wool, seeds and grain, the business, already declining, was further hit by the outbreak of war.

In 1915, the Public Trustee put the property up for auction and it was bought by Robert Bradfield Etheridge for £500[8]. To meet this relatively small sum, he borrowed £350 on mortgage from Mrs Edith Annie Plowright at 3¾% interest, which he continued to pay, but did not repay any of the capital.

In 1921, Robert Bradfield Etheridge died of tuberculosis at the age of 43, by which time the business was virtually bankrupt. None of his brothers or sisters was interested in running it; indeed, most of them had left the area or the country. Frank was a Lt. Colonel in the Indian Army, Reginald (Rex) migrated to Canada, Mildred had gone to New Zealand and Constance to South Africa. Annie had travelled as far as Hull.

In April 1922, Trustees and personal associates of the late Robert Bradfield Etheridge sold the premises to Mr Favor Parker, farmer and auctioneer, for the sum of £525 plus the outstanding mortgage of £350, making a total of £875[9] in all, for:

---

8   Equivalent to £55,000 in 2018, a very small sum for a once thriving business.

9   By then equivalent to c £41,000.

Dwelling House, yards, walled garden, stables, warehouses, wine and spirit vaults and other buildings

His son, H. Gordon Parker, moved into 'The Cobbles' and immediately took over the management of the business, which was to trade under the name Favor Parker for the rest of the twentieth century.

This marked the end of a very successful local business lasting four generations.

Other Noteworthy Etheridges

The Etheridge family is now spread far and wide around the world and doubtless contains many individuals of note. Here are the stories of just three of them, which cover a broad spectrum of achievement and notoriety.

Reverend Sanders Etheridge (1835 – 1912)

Sanders was the second son of Edward Wright Etheridge and Gertrude Sanders and great-grandson of James Bradfield. Born in Stoke Ferry, he went to a private boarding school called Wick Hall in Hackney, London and later to King's College London. In 1855, aged 19, he was admitted to Caius College, Cambridge where he gained his BA in 1859 and MA in 1862, presumably reading Divinity, in light of his later career.

His clerical career was as follows-

1859	Ordained as Deacon in the Peterborough diocese and a priest in 1860
1859 - 62	Curate of Kettering, Northants
1862 - 66	Curate of St Paul's Clapham, London
1866 - 67	Curate of Farnham, Surrey
1867 - 68	Curate of Hinton Ampner, Hampshire
1868 - 97	Rector of Haslemere, Surrey
1897 - 99	Vicar of Moulsford, Berkshire

On at least two occasions, the Reverend Sanders Bradfield acted as Executor of significant Stoke Ferry wills. When his uncle James Bradfield Sanders Bradfield (JBSB) died in 1875 with no direct heir, Sanders and his brother Edward were beneficiaries as well as executors. Because of the debts, the estate was sold to Anthony Horrex Roger Micklefield, but the brothers are still likely to have received a reasonably significant sum. As mentioned earlier in the chapter, in 1892 he was also executor of his brother Edward's estate and appointed guardian of Edward's daughter Annie Laurie.

Sander's life ended in unfortunate circumstances, killed by a train on the railway at Haslemere. A newspaper report of the incident in The Times stated:

> *The Rev. Sanders Etheridge, formerly rector of Haslemere, was seen to walk onto the railway line at Haslemere on Saturday, when he was knocked down and killed by an express. For some months he had been under medical care for a mental breakdown, and a professional nurse had also been engaged.*

The inquest held a few days later gave a verdict of suicide while of unsound mind, a sad end to a long life of service.

Anthony Etheridge V

Anthony Etheridge V (1821 - 86) was born in Ickburgh to Anthony Etheridge IV and Susanna Sanders, and so was a first cousin of the Reverend Sanders Etheridge, above and also a great grandson of James Bradfield.

By the age of 27 in 1849, Anthony V had emigrated to South Australia and married Mary Gibbons, with whom he had five children, one dying in infancy. Within three months of Mary's death he married Ann Torpey and had a further four children.

Anthony V had joined the police force in Adelaide and his conduct attracted media attention. Under the headline

1872 SA Metropolitan Police Enquiry

In 1872 a police enquiry was set up to investigate the conduct of police officers in the SA[10] Metropolitan Police Force....

Various allegations were being investigated, including:

> *Other police officers were accused of coercing publicans to open their bars at all hours to serve police officers drinks. Some police officers were also accused of entering Simms Brewery at night and helping themselves to beer.*

---

10 South Australia.

Inspector Bee and Sergeant Anthony Etheridge were directly accused of setting up publicans in order in order to personally profit. One witness states that Sergeant Anthony Etheridge would bring persons in on charges of being drunk when perfectly sober, then offer to let them off with a deal to try and gain access to pubs after hours, entrapping the publicans and putting the fine money into a collective slush fund. Anthony Etheridge is also accused of being a habitual drunk by other officers, claims Anthony denied - stating that the officers' statements were vindictive and unreliable. He none the less was forced to resign from the force.

A further article in The Argus on 5 February 1873 states, with some irony:

The unsatisfactory state of the police force is still being intermittently kept before the public.

Sergeant Etheridge, who was recently authorised to resign, on the ground of habitual drunkenness, has been doing his best to vindicate the leniency of the Government towards him, and to prove his utter unfitness for the post he occupied during 20 years or thereabouts, by creating violent disturbances in the most crowded thoroughfares of the city. With a moderation perfectly incomprehensible the police declined to interfere and allowed the stalwart ex sergeant and his amiable wife to continue on the rampage for hours together. The neighbours, scandalised by the scenes they were compelled to witness, appealed first to the inspector and then to the commissioner for redress, but without avail. Etheridge still makes night hideous with his violent behaviour, the public still protest against his conduct, and the police still refuse to interpose.

The article refers to Anthony V's second wife Ann. They continued to live in the Adelaide area until his death in 1886.

Anthony Edward John Etheridge (1915 - 88) MRCS, LRCP[11]

Anthony E. J. Etheridge was the grandson of Edward Etheridge (1832 - 92) who ran E & B Etheridge for many years. His father, another Anthony Etheridge, was the brother of Annie Laurie, mentioned earlier, for whom the Reverend Sanders Etheridge became guardian.

---

11 Member of the Royal College of Surgeons, Licentiate of the Royal College of Physicians.

Anthony E. J. (later colloquially known as 'Dr John') was born at Docking in Norfolk in 1915 and was firstly educated at Hurstpierpoint College near Brighton. When he had completed his studies there, he was still too young to start a medical degree, so spent the next two years at Malvern College in Worcestershire, before entering Guy's Hospital Medical School. After qualifying in 1939, he started his career in General Practice in Cambridgeshire before joining a private practice in Hampstead in 1948, which he later took over and where he continued for the rest of his career.

In addition, he specialised in ear, nose and throat surgery and held clinical assistantships at The London, The Royal Free and Manor House Hospitals and at the Royal National Throat, Nose and Ear Hospital.

As well as being a distinguished physician, Dr John was also a highly successful athlete. He was cross-country champion at school, won the Ledbury Run at Malvern and continued his running career with South London Harriers whilst at Guy's. He specialised in cross-country and, on the track, the 3 Miles[12]. Coming second in the AAA Championships in 1939, he was selected to run for Britain in an International with France, scheduled for 3rd September 1939[13]. He had thought that he would be selected for the 1940 Olympics in Tokyo but these too were inevitably cancelled.

His obituary[14] states:

> *John Etheridge never married and devoted all his energies to his work. Time was of no importance to him when he was treating his patients, and he had been known to spend a whole morning or afternoon on one consultation when he thought it necessary. His interests included cabinet making, antiques and reading. He was an occasional writer and in the 1950s read some of his short stories on the radio under the name of John Price[15].*

He died in August 1988, a distinguished and highly respected doctor.

---

12 Roughly equivalent to the 5,000 metres.

13 The day the Second World War broke out – unsurprisingly, the match was cancelled.

14 British Medical Journal, Volume 298, 4 February 1989.

15 Price was his mother's maiden name.

Chapter Fifteen

Harveys and Helshams – Medicine & Wealth

The name Harvey has long associations with Stoke Ferry; in the eighteenth and early nineteenth century Harveys (together with their sons-in-law Helsham and Forby) had a considerable impact on the health, wealth and architecture of the village. Their significance can be seen from the number of Harvey gravestones inside All Saints Church (four), while none of the other notable families are buried or commemorated inside the church. In the twenty-first century, another Harvey saved the church after its closure[1].

The surname Harvey is believed to originate from the Breton *Haerviu*, meaning battle-worthy and is likely to have come to Britain with the Norman invasion of 1066. There are significant branches of the family in East Anglia, including Stoke Ferry, and in the west country, particularly in Devon and Cornwall.

Two Robert Harveys

In the first half of the eighteenth century there were, somewhat confusingly, two Robert Harveys of some importance in Stoke Ferry.

The Surgeon

The first of these, Robert Harvey, a surgeon[2], was born at Beachamwell in 1727 and died at the young age of 28 in 1754. There is a memorial on the outside of Beachamwell church to him and other members of his family - Robert

---

1   See Chapters 10 and 17.

2   'Surgeon' denotes a medical practitioner who has a lower level of qualification than a Doctor of Medicine, but who nevertheless acted as the local doctor.

Harvey Senior of Hilborough, Gent. (died 1740), John Harvey of Caldecot, Gent. (eldest son, died 1742, Ellen, John's wife (died 1742) and lastly:

> *And Robert youngest son of the*
> *aforesaid John and Ellen Harvey*
> *Late of Stoke Ferry in Norfolk, Surgeon*
> *Who died February 28th 1754*
> *Aged 28 Years*

Assuming that this Robert Harvey had undertaken some medical qualifications[3], he is very unlikely to have started practice in Stoke Ferry until at least the age of 21 in 1747 so was active there for no more than seven years before his untimely death.

The Grocer

The second Robert Harvey was a grocer – and a very wealthy one at that[4]. This Robert Harvey died on 29th July 1756, aged 56 (suggesting he was born in late 1699 or early 1700). His wife, Mary, is described on their tombstone inside the vestry of Stoke Ferry church as daughter of William Wheasenham, Gent. Late of Runcton Holme, died in September 1777.

This Robert was also born in Beachamwell and later moved with his family to Crimplesham (including his older brother William who graduated from the University of Cambridge and went on to become Rector of Fincham, West Winch and Crimplesham for over forty years). It is likely that Robert and his family lived at Crimplesham before moving to Stoke Ferry sometime in the late 1720s or very early 30s. He may have acquired a business in Stoke Ferry (or moved an existing one). By 1744, the business was large enough to support an apprentice, and one was registered in that year.

At some point he acquired and occupied substantial premises on the High Street later known as Osborne House[5]. The eventual scale of Robert's business can be seen from his will, written in July 1754, two years before he died. In addition to specific bequests to his wife and children (listed below), his will also refers to:

---

3 I have not been able to find a record of his academic qualifications.

4 They were not closely related, if at all. In the earlier edition of this book, *Stoke Ferry – The Story of a Norfolk Village*, Doris Coates, perhaps understandably, conflated these individuals.

5 This property was later owned by the Winfields and W.A. Buckenham and included large granaries and other outbuildings.

Harvey, Helsham & Forby
Family Tree

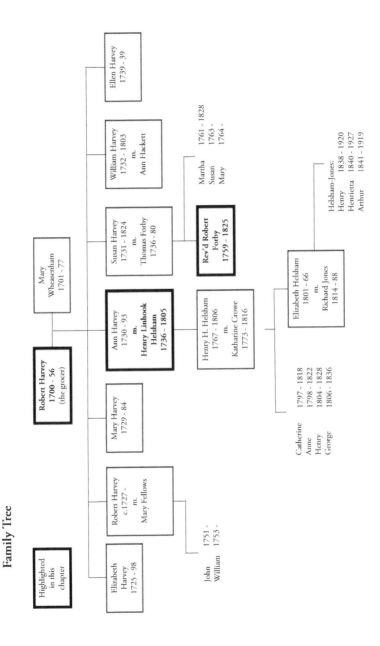

all and every my Messuages[6], Lands, Tenements and Hereditaments…… as well freehold as copyhold together with their … Appurtenances

and also all … my Goods, Chattels, Store in Trade, Corn, Cattle, household Goods, furniture, Silver and Plate….. Bills, Bonds, Notes of Land Mortgages, ready Money Debts, and all other my personal Estate of what kind or Nature soever

These were to be sold after his death.

This description (together with the amount of the bequests to his children – see below) suggests that Robert's estate was quite substantial with a total equivalent to a few million pounds in today's values.

Other than his will, there is little evidence of the scope and scale of the grocery business, but this suggests rather more than just a village store. Perhaps, like the Etheridges and Winfields[7] described in other chapters, the business included a wide range of both domestic and agricultural supplies and was, in effect, a wholesale business covering a wide geographic area. It appears that he also had some financial interests including shares and mortgages.

Robert (who died in 1756) and his wife Mary (died in 1777) are buried in the vestry of the All Saints Church and their memorial is on the vestry wall. This is an honour not bestowed on many parishioners and suggests that the Harveys were both very important in the village and, most likely, had made some significant financial contributions to the church.

---

6   A dwelling house with outbuildings and land.
7   See Chapters 14 and 16.

> Here lieth the body of
> **ROBERT HARVEY**
> **Late of this Parish Gent**
> **Who died July 29, 1756**
> **Aged 56**
>
> **Also the body of**
> **Mary relict of**
> **Robert Harvey**
> **And daughter of William Wheasenham, Gent**
> **Late of Runcton Holme**
> **Who died Sepr 27 1777**
>
> **Whose remains**
> **With those of her husband**
> **Are Inclosed**
> **In the tomb below**

Children and Grandchildren of Robert Harvey - Grocer

Assuming Robert and Mary Harvey moved to Stoke Ferry in 1731, they already had four young children: Elizabeth (c1725 - 98), Robert (b c.1727), Mary (1729 - 84), and Ann (1731 - 93). Records show that Susan (1831 - 24) and William (1732 - 1803) were born and baptised in Stoke Ferry on 8th September 1731 and 16th July 1732 respectively. A seventh child, Ellen, was born and died in Stoke Ferry in 1739.

After Robert's death, the financial bequests to each of his children were:

- Elizabeth - £1,000[8]
- Mary - £1,000
- Robert - £300[9] (the will states ...*which with what I have already given him and what he will enjoy at the death of his mother is all I intend him by this my will*)
- Ann - £1,000
- Susan - £1,000
- William - £500[10]

---

8   Equivalent to £215,000 in 2018.

9   Equivalent to £64,200 in 2018.

10 Equivalent to £107,000 in 2018.

The size of the legacies, particularly to the daughters, will have allowed them to live lives of some luxury. Elizabeth and Mary did not marry and most probably continued to live with their mother, Mary, until her death in 1777. It is not clear what happened after that and it seems probable that Elizabeth stayed in Stoke Ferry until she died in 1798. Mary died in London in 1784, whether on a visit or because she had moved there to live. Her burial record on 17th November 1784 states that she was *brt from London* and a fee of 18s 4d was paid[11]. Both their names are inscribed on a memorial stone in the chancel of Stoke Ferry church.

The other sisters, Ann and Susan, both married – Susan to Robert Forby in 1757 and Ann to Henry Linhook Hesham in 1761 – see below.

It would appear that Robert senior's relationship with his son Robert had been somewhat strained. In addition to the slightly barbed comment, quoted above, the will goes on to say that if Robert junior did not co-operate with the executors in the sale of property and other matters, he would forfeit his legacy altogether and it would be divided amongst the other children. Robert junior had already moved to King's Lynn by this time and appears not to have had much to do with the family or family business in Stoke Ferry afterwards. He is listed as a merchant, but by 1772, he was listed as bankrupt. He is not commemorated in the church, unlike four of his siblings.

The remaining siblings are described in more detail in the following sections, but to summarise –

- Ann Harvey married, in 1761, Henry Linhook Helsham, a doctor who had already been in practice in Stoke Ferry for a number of years and was the successor (though, given his age, probably not immediately) of Robert Harvey, the doctor.
- Susan Harvey married, in 1757, Thomas Forby, who took over the grocery business on the death of Robert Snr.
- William Harvey, the second son, was a Naval Surgeon for many years, before retiring to Stoke Ferry, buying property and marrying late in life.

Ann Harvey and Henry Linhook Helsham

Five years after her father's death, in December 1761, Ann Harvey married Henry Linhook Helsham, a 'surgeon' who had been living and practicing in

---

11 Equivalent to £134 in 2018.

Stoke Ferry since 1759[12]. The wedding was in Wretton church and Elizabeth Harvey and Thomas Forby (both members of Ann's family) were witnesses.

They had one son born in 1767, also named Henry, who was to follow his father into the medical profession. There are records of Henry L. Helsham taking on apprentices in 1779 (Edmund Shand) and 1787, and later, along with his son in 1794 (Charles Toulmin) and 1803. He also appears on the electoral lists for Stoke Ferry during this period, confirming that he was a property owner, although it is not clear which was his residence at these dates.

As with the medical Robert Harvey, mentioned above, Henry L. Helsham was a 'surgeon' not a doctor, although late in life (in 1798) he was awarded an M.D. degree by the University of St. Andrews, on the recommendation of two eminent Norwich doctors.

In addition to his profession, Henry accumulated considerable wealth from inheritances and through property ownership and dealing, sufficient to build The Hall in Stoke Ferry, which was completed in 1790[13]. In addition to his wife's legacy from her father, they both may have received further inheritances on the deaths of his mother in 1774 and Ann's mother in 1777. In 1778 he raised further finance (£500) from the sale of land in Shipdham, near East Dereham. In all, the cost of construction seems to have been about £1,400,[14] and apparently completed without a mortgage.

The Hall was, and is, a substantial building, described[15] when it was being put up for sale after the death if Henry Helsham Jnr, as:

> *An elegant modern-built Dwelling House, with all requisite and detached offices, suitable for the residence and accommodation of a gentleman's family, situated in the pleasant village of Stoke Ferry together with pleasure and kitchen gardens, well planted with choice fruit trees, farm-yard, requisite buildings and paddock adjoining containing about 3 acres and 2 roods, together with ten acres of pasture near the house and 24 acres of arable land in the adjacent open fields.*

---

12 Little is known of Henry Linhook Helsham's previous history surprisingly, given his very unusual middle name (most probably his mother's maiden name). There are a few records of Linhook(e)s near King's Lynn in the early eighteenth century, so it is possible that they were connections.

13 In the earlier edition of this book, Doris Coates suggested that The Hall was built by James Bradfield, but this is incorrect. Bradfield acquired the property after the deaths of Henry Linhook Hesham in 1805 and his son Henry Helsham in 1806.

14 C £205,000 at 2018 prices.

15 Bury and Norwich Post, Wednesday 25th June 1806.

Just why the village doctor wanted to build such a 'statement property' is not clear. Shortly after moving in to The Hall, Ann died (in February 1793). Henry Helsham junior married in 1795 and brought his new wife to live in The Hall, where they proceeded to have five children.

Henry Linhook Helsham died in April 1805 and is buried, along with his wife, in Stoke Ferry church. Their memorial also includes Ann's spinster sisters Mary (who had died in 1784) and Elizabeth, who died later, in 1798.

Mary the daughter of
Robert and Mary Harvey
Died in the year 1784
Also
Elizabeth Harvey her Sister
who died 5th June 1798

Near this place lay the Remains of
Ann, daughter of Robert and Mary Harvey
and Wife of
Henry Linhhook Helsham
Who departed this Life
January 29th 1793 in the 63rd Year
Of her Age

Henry Helsham M.D.
Died April 25th 1805
Aged 69 Years

Henry Helsham (1767 - 1806) – son of Ann Harvey and Henry Linhook Helsham

Following his father's death, in 1805 Henry Helsham continued the medical practice, but only for about a year until his own early death, aged 39.

Henry had married Katharine Crowe from Burnham Westgate in 1795. They had five children – Catherine (1797 - 1818), Anne (1798 - 1822), Elizabeth (1801 - 66), Henry (1804 - 28) and George (1806 - 36). Other than Elizabeth, the others all died relatively young (21, 24, 24 and 30).

Katharine and the children moved away from Stoke Ferry after her husband's death, initially to Fincham and later to Norwich.

Henry Helsham (the son) was yet another Stoke Ferry resident who attended the University of Cambridge (Corpus Christi College) but left with ill-health before graduating[16] although it is not recorded what subject he was studying. He died (and was buried) in Bath the following year where he had been staying with his uncle, the Reverend Henry Crowe. He had presumably gone there to seek a cure.

Elizabeth married another doctor, Richard Jones, thirteen years her junior, in 1837 and lived in Woodbridge, Essex. They had three children Henry (later Colonel Henry Helsham-Jones), Henrietta and Arthur. In her later years Elizabeth wrote a journal reminiscing about her distant memories of early childhood in Stoke Ferry and her Harvey, Helsham and Forby forbears, on which some of this chapter is based.

Susan Harvey and Robert Forby

Susan Harvey was the youngest daughter of Robert and Mary, born in 1732. Robert's will specified that she should not receive her legacy of £1,000 until she had reached the age of 24, with no proviso that this should be earlier if she married before that age. Fortuitously, she became 24 in the same year that her father Robert died. The following year, she married Thomas Forby, son of the Reverend Joseph Forby, Rector of Fincham, who was born in 1736, and was 21 at the time of marriage.

It seems likely that Thomas had been working in some capacity in Robert Harvey's business and took over running it after he died. While it is not clear how much of the business was kept in the family, records show that Thomas Forby, *Grocer of Stoke Ferry*, registered apprentices in 1762 (George Swarner), 1766 (Hugh Gibbins), 1769 (William Rodwell) and 1772 (Edward Gillam).

Susan and Robert had four children – Robert (1759-1825)[17], Martha (1761 - 1828), Susan (b. 1763) and Mary (1765-1845). In 1776, Robert was admitted to Gonville and Caius College, Cambridge and here, too, his father is described as *Grocer of Stoke Ferry*.

It is believed that Thomas got into financial difficulties, died in 1780 at the relatively young age of 44 and was buried at Stoke Ferry. Much later, his widow moved to Fincham, where her son Robert was Rector from 1801 onwards. She died and was buried in Fincham at the age of 92.

---

16 He was awarded an Aegrotat degree, awarded to someone who had completed their studies, but not taken final exams through ill health.

17 See section below in the Reverend Robert Forby.

Reverend Robert Forby (1759-1825) – son of Susan Harvey and Thomas Forby

The Reverend Robert Forby published a study of the dialects found in Norfolk and Suffolk entitled:

> *The Vocabulary of East Anglia; an attempt to record the Vulgar Tongue of the twin sister counties, Norfolk and Suffolk, as it existed in the last twenty years of the Eighteenth Century, and still exists: with Proof of its Antiquity from Etymology and Authority*[18]

Robert Forby was born at Stoke Ferry in 1759, son of Susan Harvey and Thomas Forby, Grocer. He was educated at King's Lynn and Caius College, Cambridge, where he became a fellow. On leaving Cambridge he moved to Barton Bendish and became tutor to the sons of Sir John Berney but when the Berneys lost a considerable amount of money, they dispensed with his services. He took in pupils at his home to earn money to support himself and his family. As the number of his pupils increased, he moved his private school to a larger house in Wereham (probably The Hall).

In 1799, his financial affairs became more secure when he was appointed Vicar to the well-paid living at Fincham, succeeding his uncle. He was very active in public affairs, holding the positions of Justice of the Peace, Deputy Lieutenant of Norfolk and Commissioner of the Land Tax. But he also had other, more academic, interests. He was a keen botanist and spent much time studying the flora of Shouldham Common.

His main claim to fame lies in his one published book. He was afraid that dialect words would disappear as local craftsmen and labourers acquired education at the Mechanics' Institutes then being established. Unfortunately, he died suddenly in 1825 before his book was quite finished. It was completed by his friend, the Rev. George Turner and published in 1830.

Most of the dialect words recorded in this book have indeed been forgotten. Some of the more colourful ones were 'bandy-wicket' - a game of cricket, 'plumpendicular' - upright, 'asosh' - slanting, while 'fapes' were unripe gooseberries. There are also chapters on customs and games such as 'bandyhoshoe', 'nine-holes' and 'camp-ball'.

William Harvey

William Harvey was a naval surgeon for many years before retiring to Stoke Ferry some time before 1777. It is not known where William served or

---

18 Published in London in two volumes, 1830.

whether he was ship-based or land-based. Assuming that he joined the Navy aged about 21 (following qualification as a surgeon) his service will have covered the years of the Seven Years War (against France) and the period in the run-up to the American War of Independence.

There is no evidence that he continued with any medical practice after returning to Stoke Ferry, nor mention of any involvement in his brother-in-law's (Henry Linhook Helsham) practice.

In 1767, he bought the property of a grocer and mercer, Thomas Smith, who had been declared bankrupt the year before.

Lot 1 in this substantial sale comprised:

> *two messuages adjoining in Stoke Ferry… in good repair, also a warehouse and stable, an exceeding good baker's oven, a dove house, yard, garden and orchard planted with the best fruit-trees, now in perfection; containing by estimation one acre; also a piece of meadow ground containing by estimation three acres, and let with the said houses and other premises to Mr. William Bull, baker…*

These had been in the ownership of the Tingay family for more than forty years but sold to Smith in October 1774 for £335[19]. He obviously struggled financially, taking out a mortgage of £200 at the end of that year and another loan of £100 the following year. Yet another loan of over £100 in 1776 year created a situation where the debts exceeded the property value and Thomas Smith was declared bankrupt, owing money to a number of people, including William Harvey and Henry Linhook Helsham.

The premises were put up for auction with William Harvey the highest bidder at £378. It seems that he moved into the main house and later built a new house further from the road, known as The Lodge.

In January 1880, William married Ann Hacket, a widow from Costessy in Norfolk at St. Benedict's Church in Norwich. William's niece, Mary Forby, was one of the witnesses. Ann was presumably a fairly wealthy woman in her own right, since William is careful to specify in his will that:

> *…all such household furniture, plate, linen, china, ornaments, trinkets, books and pictures as were her own property previous to our marriage…*

were to be returned to her.

---

19 Equivalent to about £50,000 in 2018.

William died in 1803 and his new house, along with the other properties in the group, was sold to Abraham West. He in turn advertised it to let in July 1803[20]:

> *An eligible and new-erected Messuage or Dwelling-house, stable, chaise-house, and all requisite outbuildings*

A few years later, this property was initially rented and then purchased by the first of three generations of Doctors Henry Steele who all lived there, serving Stoke Ferry's medical needs for the following 120 years[21]. The Lodge was known as *The Doctor's House* well into the twentieth century. Later owners of The Lodge found a print of an earlier, more renowned William Harvey (1578 - 1657) who discovered the circulation of the blood and the working of the heart. Although not direct descendants, since this William Harvey had no offspring, there was clearly some family pride in a famous Harvey ancestor.

---

20 Extract from The Norfolk Chronicle Saturday 23 July 1803.
21 See Chapter 17.

Chapter Sixteen

Winfields – Merchants, Wharfingers and a Knighthood

The Winfield family was another to benefit from Stoke Ferry's affluence, particularly in the nineteenth century. They owned the wharf with its granaries, storehouses and maltings near the bridge where all goods came in and out of the area[1]. As well as being merchants in their own right, they benefited from every cargo using the wharf during this very prosperous era of water-borne traffic and over three generations from the 1830s onwards, became very rich. However, the arrival of the railway at Stoke Ferry in 1882 began a rapid decline in trade on the river, and commercial downfall was inevitable.

John Winfield – Gardener (Late Eighteenth Century)

One of the earliest Winfield records was of John Winfield (1752 - 1811) who was described as a gardener, but able to take on an official apprentice - Christopher Horn - in August 1783. He married twice. By Elizabeth Richardson he had sons John (1778 - 1837) and Michael who died at a few weeks old in 1880, while his mother, Elizabeth had died in giving birth to him. A month after Elizabeth's death, John married Sarah Bunkall, by whom he had one son, William (1781 - 1851).

Early Business – William Winfield (Merchant and Maltster)

William started a coal and corn merchant's business in Stoke Ferry some time before 1839[2], because Pigot's Directory of that year shows:

---

1   See Chapter 5 for the role that trade on the River Wissey played in increasing Stoke Ferry's wealth.

2   Pigot's Directory of 1830 shows a 'Henry Winfield' as a Corn and Seed Merchant, but it is not clear whether it was Henry William, who would have been 23 at the time.

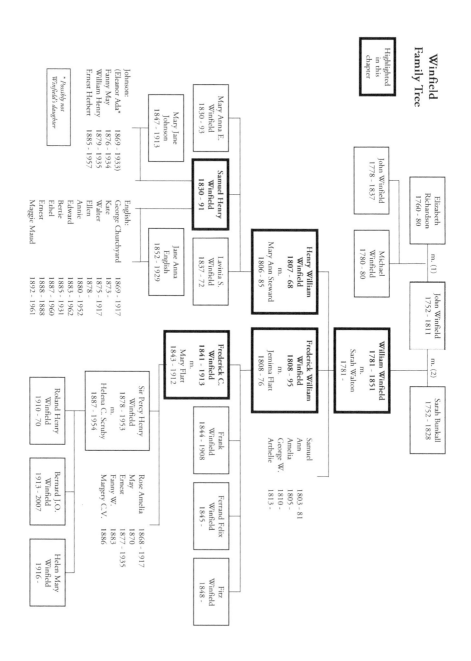

Winfield Family Tree

Highlighted in this chapter

* Possibly not Winfield's daughter

John Winfield 1778 - 1837

Elizabeth Richardson 1760 - 80

Michael Winfield 1780 - 80

m. (1)

John Winfield 1752 - 1811

m. (2)

Sarah Bunkall 1752 - 1828

William Winfield 1781 - 1851
m.
Sarah Walton 1781 -

Samuel 1803 - 81
Ann 1805 -
Amelia 1805 -
George W. 1810 -
Arthelie 1813 -

Frederick William Winfield 1808 - 95
m.
Jemima Flart 1808 - 76

Rose Amelia 1868 - 1917
May 1870
Ernest 1877 - 1935
Fanny W. 1883
Margery C.V. 1886

Frederick C. Winfield 1841 - 1913
m.
Mary Flart 1843 - 1912

Frank Winfield 1844 - 1908

Ferrand Felix Winfield 1845 -

Fitz Winfield 1848 -

Sir Percy Henry Winfield 1878 - 1953
m.
Helena C. Scruby 1887 - 1954

Roland Henry Winfield 1910 - 70

Bernard J.O. Winfield 1913 - 2007

Helen Mary Winfield 1916 -

Henry William Winfield 1807 - 68
m.
Mary Ann Steward 1806 - 85

Lavinia S. Winfield 1837 - 72

Jane Anna English 1852 - 1929

English:
George Churchyard 1869 - 1917
Kate 1873 -
Walter 1875 - 1917
Ellen 1878 -
Annie 1880 - 1952
Edward 1883 - 1962
Bertie 1885 - 1931
Ethel 1887 - 1960
Ernest 1888 - 1888
Maggie Maud 1892 - 1961

Samuel Henry Winfield 1830 - 91

Mary Anna E. Winfield 1830 - 93

Mary Jane Johnson 1847 - 1913

Johnson:
(Eleanor Ada* 1869 - 1933)
Fanny May 1876 - 1934
William Henry 1879 - 1935
Ernest Herbert 1885 - 1957

Winfield, William	Coal and corn merchant
Winfield, Henry William	Coal and corn merchant and Maltster
Winfield, Frederick William	Coal and corn merchant

Henry William (1807 - 68) and Frederick William (1808 - 95) were the two eldest of William's four sons (the others being George William, born in 1810 and Samuel). He also had three daughters - Ann (1803 - 81), Amelia, born 1805 and Arthelie, born 1813.

It is not clear whether this was a combined business and if so why only Henry William is listed as additionally having a maltings. The Directory explains the prevalence of maltings in Stoke Ferry and Whittington:

> *The malting business is carried on extensively – Messrs Whitbread and Co, the great brewers of London, have very large kilns here, upon the best principle, which employ a considerable number of hands. Lime of a very superior quality is obtained in the vicinity of the town, with which the fine and fertile country around is supplied.*

Henry William Winfield – Growth into Brewing

William (father) died in 1851, by which time his sons were running the business(es). In Craven and Co's Commercial Directory of Norfolk of 1856, they had changed their scope by dropping coal, but adding seeds and brewing:

| Winfield, Henry William | Maltster, brewer and corn merchant |
| Winfield, Frederick William | Corn and seed merchant |

Henry William married Mary Ann Steward (1806 - 85) of Boughton and they had one son, Samuel Henry (1833 - 91) and two daughters, Mary Anna Elizabeth (1830 - 93) and Lavinia Steward (1837 - 72). When Henry William died in 1868, he left the business to his son. Probate shows effects under £35,000[3], a very substantial sum.

Frederick William married Jemima Flatt (1808 - 76) of Methwold and they had four sons – Frederick Charles (1841 - 1913), Frank (1844 - 1908), Ferrand Felix (born 1845) and Fitz (born 1848), displaying a strong preference for names beginning with 'F'.

---

3 Equivalent of £3.7m in 2018.

In the late 1850s, the brothers seem to have gone in different directions. By the census of 1861 Frederick William is no longer listed as a merchant but as a farmer of 80 acres, employing 16 men and 4 boys.

Henry William is listed as a merchant, brewer and maltster, and his son Samuel Henry as merchant and brewer.

As described earlier[4], in the early 1860s the Winfields (Henry William and his son Samuel Henry) started a brewery, either in the buildings at the wharf that they owned or in a building near the corner of Oxborough Road. In 1864, this brewery was leased to Hogge and Seppings (Setch Brewery), but the Winfields built up a chain of tied houses through which to sell their beer. After his father's death, Samuel Henry continued to acquire licensed premises as well as running the coal and corn businesses and the malting until his own death in 1891.

Meanwhile by 1871, Frederick William's farm had expanded to 300 acres, employing (somewhat more efficiently) 10 men and 5 boys, and he continued farming for the rest of his life. His son, Frederick Charles, is also listed in 1871 as a farmer of 400 acres, employing 6 men and 5 boys.

Samuel Henry and Frederick Charles Winfield – Peak Prosperity

By 1881, however, Frederick Charles had given up farming and worked alongside his cousin Henry William, reverting to the description of Corn Coal and Cake Merchant. In 1891 he was listed as Corn Merchant, in 1901 Grain Coal and Seed Merchant, and in 1911 Corn and Coal Merchant. Given the contents of Samuel Henry's will (see below) it looks as though the ownership was in his hands, with Frederick Charles having a managerial, rather than an ownership role.

It was during this period that the family reached the peak of its prosperity. Samuel invested in land and houses. For a period, he lived in Osborne House and later (after the death of James Bradfield Sanders Bradfield – JBSB – in 1875) he bought The Hall from the Bradfield estate. He continued to live there until his death in 1891, employing a large staff of indoor and out-door servants. Frederick bought the original Crown Hotel when it closed in 1902 and lived there for a number of years before moving to Chesterton in Cambridgeshire for the last few years of his life.

After Samuel's death in 1891, he left a share of his estate and his business to his cousin, Frederick, mentioning specifically:

The Bridge premises at Stoke Ferry, namely The Counting House, Granaries,

4   See Chapter 9.

Malt-houses Stores, yards, Boat-houses, Stables and the Wharf on the North side of the River Wissey.'

He also ordered the sale by auction of his 'guns, boats, dogs, carriages, horses, harness, hay, straw, etc.

The rest of the business, including the brewery and the portfolio of public houses were sold at auction. Just how sizeable the brewing and pub business had become can be seen from the list of establishments for sale at that time[5]:

VALUABLE FREEHOLD & COPYHOLD PROPERTY[6]

Comprising a desirable FAMILY RESIDENCE, with conservatory, vinery, forcing house, excellent garden and commodious premises;

BREWERY, with malt and store houses, stabling and Brewery premises;

18 PUBLIC HOUSES, 3 Cottages, 2 Blacksmith's Shops, 2 Feeding Rights on Walton Wash and Accommodation Lands.

Frederick Charles Winfield inherited a diminishing business because of competition from the railways and sold out early in the 1900s. Most of the buildings stood, largely unused, at the wharf until the 1980s.

Private Lives and Children

As described, cousins Samuel and Frederick worked together successfully for many years. However, their personal lives were strikingly different and, for very different reasons, neither of them had heirs who were willing or able to prolong the business into the next generation.

Samuel never married. However, he fathered at least thirteen children with two separate women, one his housekeeper Mary Jane Johnson, the second Jane Anna English, who lived in Whittington.

In an Indenture made during his lifetime (exact date unknown), Samuel Winfield:

Was desirous of making some provision for ... Mrs (Mary Jane) Johnson and her three children in consideration of the valuable services rendered by (her)

---

5   For a full list of the Public Houses sold at auction, see Chapter 9.

6   Osborne House.

and for the natural love and affection (he) had for (her).

The children are named later in the document as Fanny May Johnson, William Henry Johnson and Ernest Herbert Johnson. Mary Jane had an older daughter, Eleanor Ada, presumably by another father.

In his will, dated 11th July 1889 Samuel left the contents of The Hall to Mary Jane Johnson and her children[7] (and to any other children born to her within nine months of his death). She was also granted an annuity. Additionally:

> *I give to … Mary Jane Johnson all the furniture plate linen pictures china glass books prints jewels and articles of household use or ornament, wines liqors and consumable stores as they now are in my residence … for her life provided she remains single as it is my express wish that the same should not be disturbed but remain precisely as they now are during her life and continuance to reside in The Hall…*

Samuel's will also made financial provision for Jane Anna English and her children, with the same stipulation about further offspring (with prescience in this case as a daughter, Maggie Maud, was born six months after his death). She was also granted an annuity, but much a smaller one.

Samuel and Jane's first child, George, was born when Jane was only 16, and christened George Churchyard English[8]. He died in France in 1917 and is commemorated on the Whittington War Memorial. The table below shows all thirteen children with their dates of birth (plus Eleanor Ada). Samuel appears to have been very loyal, in his way, to the two mothers of his children, but one can only imagine the opprobrium that this lifestyle would have engendered in Victorian England. Perhaps his wealth and the fact that he employed a large number of men in his various businesses somewhat muted the comments.

The Hall was to be kept in trust by the Executors to be sold after the death or marriage (whichever the earlier) of Mary Jane Johnson.

---

7   Mary Jane Johnson had four children, the first of whom, Eleanor Ada, was born in 1869. It is not clear who fathered this child. In the 1891 census, aged 20, she is shown as 'daughter' and 'cook', while Fanny May Johnson is shown as 'daughter' and 'housemaid'.

8   Was this an early example of naming a baby after the place where it was conceived?

Year	Mary Jane Johnson 1847 - 1913	Jane Anna English 1852 - 1929
1869	*Eleanor Ada*	George Churchyard
1870		
1872		
1873		Kate M
1874		
1875		Walter
1876	Fanny May	
1877		
1878		Ellen
1879	William Henry	
1880		Annie
1882		
1883		Edward
1884		
1885	Ernest Herbert	Bertie
1886		
1887		Ethel
1888		Ernest
1889		
1890		
1891	**Death of Samuel Henry Winfield**	
1892		Maggie Maud

Frederick's domestic arrangements were more conventional. He married Mary Flatt from Gooderstone in 1865 and they had seven children – Rose Amelia (1868 - 1917), May (born 1870), Ernest (1877 - 1935), Percy Henry (1878 - 1953), Fanny Winifred (born 1883) and Margery Charlotte Victoria (born 1886).

Rose Amelia emigrated to New Zealand in 1913, where she died four years later. May continued to live with her parents and moved with them to Chesterton in Cambridgeshire. Ernest was a musician, making his living as a church organist. Margery emigrated to Canada and Fanny Winifred married in 1905 and moved to Wales.

By far the most distinguished, and in his time famous, member of the family was Percy Henry Winfield, a lawyer of some note. His brief resume on the University of Cambridge website reads:

Sir Percy Winfield (1978 – 1953)

Personal
- Born 16th September 1878
- Son of Fred(erick) Winfield, Merchant of Stoke Ferry and Mary Flatt
- 17th August 1909 – Married Helena, fifth daughter of W.T. Scruby of Cambridge
- Died 7th July 1953

Academic
- Attended King's Lynn Grammar School
- 1896 - Admitted to Cambridge, Michaelmas Term
- 1898 - Law Tripos, Part I, 1st Class
- 1898 - Scholar
- 1899 - B.A. and LL.B. (Law Tripos Part II, 1st Class) – *Bachelor of Law*
- 1900 - Whewell Scholar
- 1906 - LL.M. – *Master of Law*
- 1918 - LL.D. – *Doctor of Law*
- 1921 - 53 – Machmahon Student (University of Cambridge)
- 1923 - Lecturer in English Legal History Harvard Law School
- 1926 - 28 - Lecturer in Law, Cambridge University
- 1928 - 43 - Rouse Ball Professor of English Law, Cambridge University
- 1930 - Tagore Law Professor, Calcutta University

Judicial Appointments
- 8 March 1900 - Admitted to the Inner Temple
- 24 June 1903 – Called to the Bar
- On the South-Eastern Circuit. Deputy County Court Judge

War Service
- 1914 - 18 – Served in the Great War as Captain in the Cambridgeshire Regiment
- 1914 – wounded; subsequently employed at The War Office

Other Appointments and Honours
- Federal Bar Association Hon LL.D. Harvard and Leeds
- 1925 – JP for Cambridge Borough
- 1943 – Member, Lord Chancellor's Law Revision Committee
- 1938 - 43 – Reader in Common Law to Council of Legal Education
- 1949 - Knighted

Publications
- *The Law of Torts*
- *Text-book on Torts*
- *History of Abuse of Legal Procedure*
- *Province of the Law of Torts*
- *Foundations and Future of International Law*

Salmon and Winfield
- *Law of Contracts*

Contribution to **Pollock**
- *On Contract*

Editor of *Law Quarterly Review* (1929)
Editor of *Cambridge Law Journal* (1927 - 47)

Sir Percy is, without doubt, one of Stoke Ferry's most distinguished sons. The Winfield businesses had thrived in the nineteenth century, creating wealth for the family. This, in part, enabled Percy to pursue his education at Cambridge and become one of the leading lawyers of his generation. He did not forget his birthplace – a later occupant of his family home, Maurice Place, remembered him visiting Stoke Ferry and coming to the house in the early 1950s.

Chapter Seventeen

Some Notable Local Characters

The enduring families covered in the previous chapters had considerable impact on the wealth and development of Stoke Ferry, particularly in the eighteenth and nineteenth centuries. There are, of course, many remarkable or interesting people who never achieve fame or wealth. Most local families will have tales to tell of their ancestors but it is only possible to mention a few whose names and stories have been reported in some way.

Many individuals from Stoke Ferry made their mark, either on the local community or on the wider world, and many 'outsiders', having achieved some fame or notoriety have made their homes there. This chapter includes brief descriptions of a few of their lives and claims to fame.

Three Henry Steeles (1781 - 1932) – Doctors

Following the death of Henry Helsham (Jnr) in 1806, the medical practice in Stoke Ferry was taken on by a surgeon from Witham in Essex called Henry Steele (1781 - 1845), the son of another Doctor, Peter Steele. Followed by his son and grandson, both named Henry, the Steele family provided medical services to Stoke Ferry for the next 125 years.

The Steeles were a Cumbrian family who could trace their ancestry back to the sixteenth century. In the latter half of the eighteenth century, Peter Steele, M.D. (1747 - 1815), moved south to Essex and set up practice at Witham. His eldest son, Henry, followed his father's profession and may have helped in his practice before moving to Stoke Ferry. Initially renting The Lodge, by 1817 he had acquired the property.

He and his wife Mary (formerly Mary Browne of Diss in Norfolk) had eleven children, five of whom died in infancy[1] and were buried in the churchyard just a few feet from the house.

When Henry Steele died in 1845, he was buried in Stoke Ferry churchyard very near the rear windows of The Lodge. His tomb is inscribed to the memory of:

Henry Steele, Surgeon,
died 25th October 1845, aged 63
Also Mary his wife, died 1851
Also 5 infant children of the above
who are buried near this place.

Following Henry's death, the practice was taken over by his eldest son, Henry Charles Browne Steele (1808 - 74) who was listed as *Surgeon* and *Registrar, Lunatic Asylum*[2]. Two attic windows of the Lodge are heavily barred and it is said that this was because the 'lunatics' were held there. If this is true, there must have been an uncomfortably close proximity between the patients and the doctor's family. At the age of 44, he married Elizabeth Jane Forest from Fordham in Norfolk, twenty-three years his junior. They had eleven children but four also died in infancy[3].

When Henry C. B. Steele died in 1874, his eldest son, Henry Frederick Steele, was only 21 and not yet qualified. For four years a locum looked after the practice until H. F. Steele took over and was Stoke Ferry's doctor for fifty years until his retirement in 1928. Dr. Steele would ride his horse for home visits, until he bought one of the first cars in the village in 1912. The horse he had at that time was called 'Syntax' and is seen in the picture of him. Though available at the time, Dr. Steele would never have a telephone in the house, insisting that if he were needed someone must call in person. He was still remembered by some of the village's older inhabitants in the 1970s, though not always fondly since he was an austere and rather frightening figure to children.

---

1   Elizabeth Hester (aged 4 months), James (3 months), Frederic (a few days), Mary Ann (3 years) and Letitia (4 months). By contrast, their sister Emma, who married local farmer Richard Salmon, lived to the age of 92.

2   The 1841 Census lists four patients living at the property, but later Census returns only show members of the Doctor's household and staff.

3   Edward (age 4), Alfred (2), Herbert Augustus (1) and one other, perhaps unnamed.

Henry did not marry until late in life, in part because he had spent a great deal of time educating his six surviving brothers and sisters[4]. He looked set to remain a bachelor for the rest of his days when, in 1908 at the age of 54, he married Clara Rebecca Vine of Oxborough, thirty-one years younger than himself. He joked that when he qualified as a doctor, his wife was not yet born. Their only child, a son (Henry Jack[5]), was born in 1910, but chose not to continue the family tradition of medicine. Dr. Steele retired to Gloucestershire in 1928, where he died four years later. Clara, his widow, lived until 1971.

The Lodge is reputedly haunted, especially the oldest part of the house. The last Dr. Steele and his wife experienced a number of strange happenings. One night, all the heavy venetian blinds came down from the windows and on another occasion everything on Mrs. Steele's dressing-table fell to the floor. Sometimes, an apparition was seen shortly before a death in the family and a lady was seen walking through the room with barred windows. Whether the disturbances or spirits result from some gruesome happening when the house was partially used as a lunatic asylum, or whether it is Mary Steele grieving for her five dead infants buried just outside the back window is a matter for speculation. The witnesses were convinced that these events actually happened and were not merely figments of imagination.

William Sparrow Springfield (1803 - 85) – Prize Fighter

Born in Stoke Ferry in 1803, William Springfield's name appears in White's Directory of 1845 as a lime merchant. Apparently, at various times he described himself as a glazier, a merchant and a 'Gent'. However, according to Springfield family papers he had a much more exciting career as a prize fighter[6].

Many stories have been told of the bare-knuckle prize-rings of the 19th century. This was a brutal sport, a far cry from boxing under Queensbury rules. Every kind of punching, gouging and kicking was permissible and there was no set length of rounds, or any regulations on the number of rounds. The fight simply went on to the finish, when one of the participants

---

4 With somewhat mixed results. His youngest sister, Bertha became the Principal of a girls boarding school by the age of 36; another sister Helen Frances was a governess. Brother Ernest owned a laundry in Manchester. Arthur was a clerk and later an assistant in an off-licence, while Edwin had a chequered naval career which included at least six spells in the cells and absconding for nine months, later working for his brother Ernest in the laundry.

5 In a letter to Doris Coates in 1981, H.J. Steele wrote that he was still the owner of The Chemist's Shop and unable to sell it because of the pre-bypass traffic.

6 Another fighter recorded in Stoke Ferry was Thomas Reginald Bowers, Boxer, of Methwold who married Queenie Phyllis Angela Hildreth at Stoke Ferry Church in October 1928.

had been beaten senseless. It was quite illegal, of course, but that did not deter backers (members of the 'Fancy' as they called themselves) setting up a ring in a remote place where they hoped to evade the forces of the law. Large sums of money were exchanged as bets.

It appears that in the early 1850s William Springfield killed a man in a prize fight and had to flee the country to escape the consequences. In letters in his family's possession he says that when he left Stoke Ferry he left his 'silver plate' in charge of his cousin, William Henry Winfield, owner of the wharf opposite The Bull Inn in Stoke Ferry. He complained that when he eventually returned to England he never got it back.

Evidently, some years later, believing that the police were no longer looking for him, he resumed life in his native village, where he died in 1885.

Thomas Jones (1853 - 1918) - Overcoming severe handicaps

Athletic ability was denied the next 'character', Thomas Jones of Wretton. At 28, he had sustained terrible injuries when knocked down by a train at a level crossing. His left leg and left arm had to be amputated, his cheekbone and right eye were severely injured and he lost two fingers of his right hand.

Born in 1853, before his accident he had been a teacher at Brentwood Grammar School in Essex. After months in hospital, he came with his wife and family to live at the railway gatehouse at Wretton. Here, he brought up a family of five boys and two girls who grew up to be successful in business or the professions.

The struggle against poverty must have been hard for one so severely handicapped but he refused to be discouraged. In those days, when school fees had to be paid, most village children left school early, at eleven or twelve years of age. But all the Jones children stayed on until the maximum schooling age, although the expense must have made huge inroads on their frugal resources.

Thomas Jones was held in high regard locally and when Wretton had its first Parish Council, he was unanimously elected Chairman. He was leader of the choir in Wretton Church and People's Warden. He was concerned about the dilapidation of the church and was the prime mover and money-raiser responsible for the extensive restoration of the roof, floor and seating in the early 1900s. Later, he raised money for the first paraffin lamps, so that evening services could be held in the church.

His money raising methods were prodigious[7]:

---

7 Letters from Alton M Jones (son of Thomas Jones) to F. T Bush, 1958.

He went whole-heartedly into the past history of the church, reading old records of income and expenditure, and tracing records of payments to the Lords of the Manor, and the rentals and tithes received. And then he planned a series of personally written appeals because of what the families had taken out of the Parish! In twenty years, he wrote many hundreds of letters, over 400 in one year. He studied The Times for lists of subscribers to National Calamity Funds, and families like the Cadburys, Frys and other philanthropic Quakers heard from him regularly.

He also collected money locally:

He borrowed a harmonium from one, a farm wagon from another to cart it round on; got a farmer to lend him a horse; found someone who could play the violin; organised a choir of folk from the church; got old Crabbe, the insurance man, who knew some music to get some accord into their renderings, and toured the neighbouring villages singing carols and folk songs. Crabbe, with his tuning-fork led the singers and Bertha White, the butcher's daughter, strummed the tune on the harmonium.

Wretton owes a debt of gratitude to this courageous man.

William English (1855 - 1927) - Gardener

English is a common surname in the district and crops up in many aspects of everyday life. William English with his wife and fourteen children can be seen in one of the illustrations. William was a gardener whose services were always in demand by the 'gentry'. At the Micklefields, one of his perquisites was the crop of walnuts on the fine avenue of trees which stretched across his park. William's children and later his grandchildren, were pressed into service to gather, clean and bag the nuts, which were sold at markets to make a welcome addition to the family income. The coming of the railway made it possible for this crop to be sent to Covent Garden.

Standing second from the right in the photograph is his eldest son, William English junior. He was born in 1876 and died in 1975 in his hundredth year, having spent his lifetime in the village.

William junior's first job (about 1890) was with Mr Edward Etheridge at The Cobbles. He worked at the 'wool-pack', dealing with fleeces, and also on the wine-cart, delivering orders as far afield as Castle Acre in all weathers. He later became gardener and groom for Roger Micklefield at Park House. He created beautiful flower gardens and from 1899 onwards frequently carried off the top prizes at the local Horticultural Show.

Accounts of his prowess as an athlete have become legend. Apparently, he was unsurpassed as a high-jumper and runner in West Norfolk. He won many athletics prizes at events held with no formal running-tracks or AAA rules. It is told that there was once a race from 'The Bell' at Stoke Ferry to 'The Bell' at Whittington[8] which he won by a great distance.

Alton M. Jones (1880 -1965) - Local Boy Makes Good

Alton Jones was one of Thomas Jones' sons, growing up in the railway gatehouse at Wretton. A bright boy at Stoke Ferry School, he became a pupil teacher there before, in 1895, embarking on a career which would take him far. He was aided initially by two of Stoke Ferry's notable residents, Frederick Barnes and Dr. Charles Bader (or more specifically his wife, Mrs. Martha Bader).

Frederick Barnes had held various responsible positions in Maple & Co's[9] upmarket furniture store in London, before coming to Stoke Ferry sometime in the late 1880s to run a grocery and drapery store in the High Street. He and his large family lived in Moulsham House. Deciding against teaching as a career, Alton went to ask for work at Barnes' shop. Mr Barnes objected to employing local boys behind his counter but offered to recommend him if he applied for a job at Maple's, his former employer.

Meanwhile, Dr. Charles Bader was an eminent Harley Street eye specialist, who spent his weekends in Stoke Ferry. In late Victorian times he built Border House,[10] and also owned The Limes, further along Wretton Road. He used this as a nursing home for his patients and gave free treatment to local poor people. His wife, Martha, was kind and very popular in the village. They also had a home at Fen House, Wretton.

Alton wrote[11]:

> *When I left Mr Barnes [that day], disappointed that he would not take me into his shop, and was walking home, I was overtaken by a governess cart, and the driver was Mrs Bader. Very courteously she told me that she was*

8   About 1 mile.

9   In Tottenham Court Road. Maple became one of the prime makers and suppliers of furniture to the aristocracy and royalty in the United Kingdom.

10 Later known as 'Catleughs' on Wretton Road opposite the School, now demolished.

11 Letter from Alton M Jones to F. T Bush, 1958.

driving to Wretton Fen and would take me home. Boy-like, I blurted out my troubles. I still don't know if she took up cudgels on my behalf, but she was certainly well informed.

When my letter of acceptance arrived she sent for me, ordered out the trap, drove to Barnes' shop and fitted me out from head to foot – overcoat, hat, shoes, clothing and under-clothing and a bag to put them in! Subsequently, she called at Maple's to inquire into my progress, and as she was a substantial shareholder, that didn't do me any harm.

Alton stayed with Maple's for twenty years in an era when it was patronised by the elite of society. He reminisced that he once saw four queens in the shop together.

Later in his career, after working for a firm of chartered accountants, he became Company Secretary of the Firestone Tyre and Rubber Company. He rewrote the company's Articles of Association, enabling them to manufacture in the UK. He was then instrumental in floating the Firestone Plantation Company to grow rubber, obtaining a million-acre concession in Liberia. He became Managing Director of this Company.

Sergeant James Walter Bent (1917 - 41) – Casualty of War

James Bent's father, Charles, was a policeman born in North Runcton in about 1885. During the course of his career Charles moved to various towns and villages in West Norfolk and Cambridgeshire, coming to Stoke Ferry in the 1920s with his wife, Zilpha and their seven children. They lived in a house on Lynn Road which doubled up as the police station and occasional Magistrate's Court. The family story tells that felons awaiting a hearing or waiting to be transported into custody were handcuffed to Zilpha's mangle to restrain them.

James, the second-eldest child was born in November 1917. In April 1940 he enlisted into the RAF and was based at RAF Marham nearby (Marham is still a major RAF base) with 115 Squadron of Wellington Bombers as a Wireless Operator / Gunner and had the rank of Sergeant. On the evening of 6th July 1941, his aircraft, together with 6 crew members took off from Marham as part of the raids on Munster.

On its return journey, the plane was shot down over the Dutch coast by a German night fighter. Although an SOS was sent, an air and sea search failed to find the crew. Their bodies were later washed up on a chain of islands, including one called Schiermonnikoog, but although some of the crew could be identified by their name-tags James's body could not and he was buried with this inscription on his gravestone:

An Airman of the 1939 - 1945 War
Royal Air Force
7 August 1941
Known unto God

Amazingly, in 2015, following extensive research by James's family[12] and with the active assistance of the RAF Historical Wing, RAF Marham Historical Wing and the Commonwealth War Graves Commission, it was confirmed that his body was lying in an unmarked grave in the Vredenhof Cemetery on the island of Schiermonnikog. It transpired that he had been buried with full military honours in 1941 by the German forces occupying the island, along with two other identified crew members.

On 16th June 2016, 75 years after James was killed, a rededication service was held in Vredenhof Cemetery, attended by family members[13], the British Defence Attaché of the Netherlands, Belgium and Luxembourg as well as local dignitaries and islanders. Also present were representatives of the Dutch and Commonwealth War Graves Commissions, the RAF and a representative of the Dutch Resistance Movement (at 93, one of only four still alive at that time).

The service was very moving; James's niece, Mary, was presented with the Bomber Command Clasp for her uncle.

Christopher (Kit) J Hesketh-Harvey (1957-) – Cabaret and Philanthropy

Kit Hesketh-Harvey, his wife Catherine and their new-born daughter Augusta (Gus) moved to Stoke Ferry in early 1988, acquiring and lovingly restoring Park House, the former Micklefield house on Stoke Ferry High Street. Their son Rollo was born in Norfolk in 1990.

In 2002, Kit acquired All Saints Church when it was deconsecrated, preventing its proposed use as commercial premises – a tyre depot, in fact.

---

12 His niece Mary and her husband Julian Cox.

13 Including James's great-great nephew Teddy Parker, who read a dedication, and whose report forms the basis for this section.

His generosity in doing so preserves a historic church (if only the building) in the village. It is now frequently used for art exhibitions, concerts and other local events. He is locally active as a member of the Parish Council and is a leading campaigner against the continued siting of Stoke Ferry Mill at the heart of the village[14].

Born in Nyasaland (now Malawi), Kit spent his early childhood as the son of a colonial administrator in the capital, Zomba, where he was born, and on the shores of Lake Nyasa. When asked for a newspaper article[15] about his dream house, he sought to recapture these idyllic early days. It would be, he said:

> *On the shores of Lake Malawi…where I spent my childhood. We had a house there which we used at weekends and on holidays. Lake Malawi is about 350 miles long and terribly deep. Alarmingly beautiful, its shores are fringed with rainforest, white sand and African fishing villages.*

More recently, Kit has described his early years as a magical childhood.

There are significant branches of the Harvey family in both East Anglia and the west country, particularly Devon and Cornwall. Kit can trace his Harvey roots in Devon for at least nine generations to William Harvy, born in 1645[16]. The Hesketh part of the name (solidly Anglo-Saxon in origin) stems from the marriage of Kit's grandfather Bernard Harvey (1899 - 1969) to Minnie Hesketh (1901 - 74) in 1926 in Kiangsu (Shanghai) where Bernard was a Wesleyan minister. Minnie's Hesketh line can be traced to several generations of landowners and millowners in Cheshire and Lancashire.

At age six, Kit was sent to boarding school in England at Canterbury Cathedral Choir School, where he became Head Chorister. This was the first step in an eclectic career based on music and entertainment. Later at Tonbridge School he was able to develop his interests in literature, drama and music, before going to Clare College Cambridge as an English and Music Scholar. There, in addition to his regular academic studies, he was a very active member of the Cambridge Footlights, at that point enjoying one of its several 'golden ages'. Contemporaries included Stephen Fry, Hugh

---

14 See Chapter 19.

15 Article by Rosanna Greenstreet, The Independent, Sunday 26th March 1995.

16 Coming from a Devonian branch of the family, Kit is not directly descended from the Stoke Ferry Harveys in Chapter 15. William is a very common Harvey name, the most illustrious being William Harvey (1578 - 1657) who discovered the circulation of the blood and who had no children.

Laurie, Griff Rhys-Jones, Emma Thompson, Robert Bathurst, Sandi Toksvig and Tony Slattery.

After graduation Kit worked as a Staff Producer in the BBC Music and Arts Department in London, augmenting his modest salary with frequent cabaret performances in Soho. A career breakthrough occurred when he was asked to co-write a film script with James Ivory of E.M. Forster's novel *Maurice*. Forster had also attended Tonbridge School and the novel was partly set in Cambridge. Ivory was to say of Kit's contribution[17]:

> *What Kit brought to the script was his social background. He went to Cambridge and a fancy prep school. His knowledge of the British upper middle class was incredibly useful – the dialect, the speech, the slang, and so many other things. As an American, I could not have possibly written the script without him.*

Maurice was released by Merchant-Ivory in 1987 with a cast including Hugh Grant, James Wilby, Rupert Graves, Denholm Elliot, Simon Callow, Billie Whitelaw and Ben Kingsley. It received outstanding reviews when released and again more recently, winning the Silver Lion at the Venice Film Festival. Playing the sister to Hugh Grant's role as Clive Durham, Maurice's friend at Cambridge, was Catherine Rabett[18], who had become Kit's wife in 1985.

Since then Kit has had a number of other TV and film screenwriting credits, including *The Vicar of Dibley*. His opera translations include *The Daughter of the Regiment, The Turk in Italy, La Belle Helene, The Bartered Bride, Die Fledermaus, The Magic Flute, The Marriage of Figaro, Veronique* and *The Merry Widow*. He has written librettos for West End Shows, including *The Beautiful and Damned, Edna: The Spectacle* and *The Caribbean Tempest*, which starred Kylie Minogue. He frequently presents TV and radio programmes on antiques, cabaret, shanson and domestic architecture, is a regular panellist on BBC Radio 4's *Just a Minute* and a columnist for Country Life Magazine.

However, ever since his student days, Kit's first love has been cabaret. From 1982 to 2011 he appeared in *Kit and The Widow*, a two-man musical satire with Richard Sisson. In recent years, he has created a similar format with James McConnel as *Kit and McConnel*. They are the resident cabaret at The Pheasantry in Chelsea and perform every year at numerous festivals, including

---

17 Article by Christopher McKittrick, *James Ivory on Screenwriting* creativescreenwriting.com, May 2017.
18 Born in 1960, she is described on Kit's website (kitandmcconnell.co.uk) as *actress, academic and Bond Girl*.

Edinburgh. Open to offers to appear around the world, they recently visited venues as diverse as Afghanistan and Barbados. Every year Kit spends a few weeks as a pantomime baddie at the Yvonne Arnaud Theatre in Guildford.

***

These are just a few names from the many thousands who were born or have lived in Stoke Ferry over the centuries. There are most certainly many more stories just waiting to be told.

Dr. Henry Helsham (1767 - 1805), son of Henry Linhook Helsham.
After his death, The Hall was sold to James Bradfield

William English (1855 - 1927) with his wife and fourteen children.

The eldest son, also William (standing second from right), died in 1975 in his hundredth year

Riches' carpenter's yard (c. 1914). George Riches (on horseback) with his father, Mr. George Pymer Riches. Brother Frank (with bicycle) was a war casualty in Iraq in 1917 and is commemorated on Stoke Ferry War Memorial.

Jack Bayfield with his delivery motorbike, outside Bayfield's Butchers (1920s)

Empire Day 1909

The Stoke Ferry Territorials, preparing to go to war (August 1914)

The Bonnett family at The Forge. This business is still active today

Brown's Hairdresser and Tobacconist

English's motor cycle business and petrol station (1926). Sid Reeve (l) and Ernie English (r)

David Manning, Head Gamekeeper of the Micklefield Stoke Ferry Estate (c.1890)

*Dr. Henry Steele and his horse, Syntax (c.1910). Note the
fine example of a 'crinkle-crankle wall' behind*

*Dr. Anthony John Etheridge (1915 - 88).
Ear, Nose and Throat Physician and
international athlete (very nearly)*

*Sergeant James Walter Bent
(1917 - 41) – war casualty*

Stoke Ferry School pupils (c.1910) with Headmaster H. W. Clarke and Pupil Teacher Miss Letty Warnes

Last day at the old school and first at the new - Headmaster Chris Young with staff and pupils. Former Headmaster George Coates is back row, 3rd from left

Richard Harwin (1826–1912), benefactor of Stoke Ferry Wesleyan Chapel

Christopher (Kit) Hesketh-Harvey (right), now owner of All Saints Church, with his cabaret partner, James McConnel

The Fifth Part

In which is considered
the well-being of Stoke Ferry
in the modern age and the prospects
for its continued development
in the future

Chapter Eighteen

The Post-war World – a New Order

Previous chapters have described Stoke Ferry's golden age of prosperity during the eighteenth and nineteenth centuries, as well as the families who were instrumental in driving it. World War I (1914 - 18) brought changes that were so abrupt and dramatic that by the 1920s much of the past had been swept away.

Changes in Farming

Until 1914 farming was still carried on by 'horse and hand' as it had been for centuries. However, the country was far from self-sufficient, importing nearly two-thirds of essential agricultural products – 80% of wheat, 40% of meat and almost all sugar. During the early years of the war, food shortages lead to black market activity and profiteering, and distribution was badly disrupted. Increasingly, the German Navy succeeded in blockading imports using its U-boat fleet, particularly in the Atlantic. Despite all this, the government decided not to intervene and let market forces prevail, with the result that between July 1914 and July 1916 food prices rose by 61%.

It was not until the disastrous harvest of 1916 that the government realised that firm measures had to be taken to deal with the situation. By 1916, even potatoes were in short supply and outbreaks of scurvy were reported in some of the poor urban areas of the country. In December 1916, well over two years after the outbreak of war, the government appointed Lord Devonport as Food Controller. He was largely ineffective, prescribing self-constraint rather than rationing and doing little to increase production. In May the following year, he was replaced by Lord Rhondda and some rationing (particularly of sugar) was implemented.

Production remained the principal problem. Farms were short of labour and horses both of which had been recruited for the war effort. It was agreed that millions of acres had to be ploughed up if the civilian population was to be fed. However, there was a serious shortage of fertiliser and tractors to accomplish that enormous task.

By the end of the war the Department of Agriculture had enlisted 120,000 male workers (discharged soldiers, prisoners of war, schoolboys and volunteers) and 300,000 women. They had supplied 4,200 tractors, 10,000 horses and large quantities of ploughs and other implements. Three million extra acres had been ploughed in England but detailed figures are not available for the Stoke Ferry area. Nationally, vegetable allotments had trebled and the allotments once near Furlong Drove date from this time.

With price guarantees and government aid, farming enjoyed a short boom. When the war was over, many people, particularly demobilised soldiers, rushed to buy land at inflated prices but their success as farmers was short-lived. The wartime workforce had been dispersed and heavy war casualties had robbed villages of many of their young men. Seventeen died from Stoke Ferry alone. The use of tractors during the war had demonstrated the advantages of mechanisation, but that required capital investment which was not readily available.

Other countries, too, had increased their food production during the war, with the result that there was now a glut. In 1921 there was a steep drop in world grain prices and all agricultural guarantees were repealed. Farm labourers' wages dropped from 50 shillings a week during the war to 30 shillings a week. Wartime ploughed land was lost as farmers could not afford to sow it. In the 1920s farmers got as little as 5d a gallon for milk, 3½d a pound for wool and £5 a ton for oats[1]. Imported food was so cheap that it was impossible to compete.

Many people who had bought land in 1918 went bankrupt and many long-established farmers failed to weather the storm. It was impossible to sell land, so often it was just abandoned. Buildings became derelict, the land went back to weeds and workers left rural areas to try to find work in towns and cities. Locally the black lands of Wissington fen were particularly badly affected. The late John Waterfall used to tell how he struggled to hang on by selling his cattle one by one, until only a solitary milk-cow was left[2]. By this

---

1 In 2018 values, wages dropped from c£165 to c£64 per week; milk fetched 89p per gallon, wool 62p per pound and oats £212 per ton.

2 Yet, by the 1950s and '60s the Waterfalls had a thriving farm on Wissington Fen, sending daily lorry loads of celery to Covent Garden market.

time all his neighbours (many of them Scotsmen, who came to make their fortunes in Norfolk) had given up.

The End of the Old Order

It was against this background that the decline of the 'notable families' took place. For the Winfields[3] there was no trade at the Wharf, already badly hit by the railways. Etheridge's[4] business as merchants dwindled as farming slumped and bankruptcy ended their long period of success. Dr. Steele retired and moved away, although this was not influenced by the great depression.

It was in these circumstances that the Micklefield estate was dispersed, fetching very low prices for farmland[5]. Sam Wilson, a timber merchant, acquired The Manor House and large areas of woodland between Wretton Road and the river. He subsequently felled most of the trees and destroyed copses and coverts long preserved by the 'landed gentry' for game shooting. The result was a larger acreage of farmland, but rather less attractive surroundings.

Better days were to come but it was the new men who bought land cheaply in the slump, who were to benefit from the government's belated action to rescue farming. The Land Drainage Act (1930) and Credits Act (1928) helped to improve the land (particularly in the fen).

Other support to the farming industry occurred to the 1930s. The Agricultural Marketing Acts of 1931 and 1933 set up Marketing Boards for milk, potatoes, pigs bacon, wheat, hops, sugar and livestock.

Stoke Ferry farmers, now mostly owner-occupiers instead of estate tenants, were able to organise their operations on entirely new lines. The advent of motor transport and farm mechanisation allowed greater efficiency significantly reducing labour requirements.

Other changes of the 1920s and 1930s were the result of motor transport replacing horses. Wheelwrights and harness makers gradually went out of business and the blacksmith's role changed and diminished. The three Ward Brothers established a motor engineering business and by 1929 there were 'motor omnibuses' to Downham, King's Lynn, Norwich and Wisbech. Easier mobility meant that people could travel to nearby towns to shop, buying cheaper mass-produced goods. This rapidly threatened the livelihood of village tailors, dressmakers and shoemakers. Although they and other crafts

---

3 See Chapter 16.

4 See Chapter 14.

5 See Chapter 13.

people carried on for a number of years, few younger people came in to learn their skills and these small businesses gradually disappeared. At the same time, the number of village shops decreased with most of their premises being converted over the years to private houses.

So while the old structure and self-sufficiency of Stoke Ferry rapidly diminished in this post-war period, its dependence on agriculture and related processing industries continued to grow through most of the twentieth century. Four industries were of particular importance locally at various periods – malting, wool, grain processing and sugar manufacture.

Malting

Malting of barley is an industry dating back at least three centuries. The process entailed drying the barley on heated floors, steeping it in water for eight or nine days to encourage germination, and then manhandling it again into drying kilns. Finally, it was screened and the crisp sweet grains put in sacks for dispatch to breweries. The floors and kilns were heated by open-basket fires of coke and men worked in high temperatures regularly turning the grains with large wooden shovels.

It is known that barley was grown and processed in the Stoke Ferry area in the early eighteenth century. For example, the 1754 will of William Redmore, of Stradishall in Suffolk, surgeon and apothecary included:

Also I give and devise to Thomas Jarvis, Junr., my kinsman, watchmaker in London, and his heirs for ever, all my pieces of land with the Malting, Office and all appurtenances there-unto lying and being in Stoke Ferry in the County of Norfolk.

It is not known whether Thomas Jarvis Junr relinquished watch making in London for malting barley in Stoke Ferry, though it seems unlikely.

In the nineteenth century, there were a number of small maltings in the village at the Wharf and at Hegbin's farm, and these probably served the local brewery owned by the Winfields.

By contrast, the Maltings at Whittington was a major local employer over a period of at least 170 years. The earliest deeds for the property date from 1805 when it belonged to H. S. Partridge, the lord of the manor. It was acquired at that time by Thomas Salmon (merchant) and Roger Micklefield[6]. They in turn leased it to a consortium including Robert Partridge, Samuel Partridge, Anthony Etheridge, Samuel Fuller and Edmund Horrex[7]. The

---

6   Roger Micklefield 1773 – 1849.

7   Micklefield's brother-in-law.

property included *premises, freehold cottage, barn, staithe, fishery and lands* according to deeds.

By 1817 the maltings were owned by H. F. Day who sold it to Sir Basil Hobhouse, a banker, and sold to Whitbread & Co., the brewers, in 1832. They continued to be operated by Whitbread's until closure in 1975[8].

In 1845 White's History records:

Messrs Whitbread & Co, the great London brewers, have an extensive malt-house, with 5 cisterns capable of steeping 1700 bushels of barley at a time

As late as 1933, Kelly's Directory states:

Here (at Whittington) is an extensive malthouse belonging to Messrs Whitbread and Co. Limited, brewers of London

In the early period, barley was delivered and malt despatched from the firm's own staithe at Whittington. Later, horses and tumbrils were used between the maltings and Winfield's Wharf at Stoke Ferry bridge, and later to the railway station. Following the First World War, motor transport was increasingly used.

As the total population of Whittington was only 178 in 1845, 249 in 1888 and 222 in 1911, it can be assumed that the maltings provided employment for men from a wide area, including Stoke Ferry. These included workers in the maltings themselves and its associated transport requirements.

Favor Parker – Wool and Grain Processing

Stoke Ferry Mill stands at the heart of the village and has long been a source of controversy[9]. For much of the twentieth century the business operating the mill and associated facilities was known as Favor Parker and was the single largest employer in the village.

Favor Parker (1856-1927) was one of a large family whose father William Parker was a 'light farmer' of sheep, barley and rabbits in Mildenhall[10]. Following a severe drought in 1869 and 1870, William switched to smaller scale market gardening, growing asparagus and various root vegetables. Favor was the fifth of twelve children. As a young man, he emigrated to British Colombia with his brother Ebenezer, and served as an apprentice with a seed

---

8   The maltings premises were derelict for many years but are currently being converted to flats, with additional houses built in the yard.

9   See Chapter 19.

10 Information on family history and the development of the Favor Parker business taken from notes written by Gordon Parker in later life.

merchant there, before returning to Suffolk. Ebenezer stayed in Canada for the rest of his life, dying at Ruskin B.C. in 1925.

On his return, Favor established an auctioneer and estate agency business, as well as owning a range of agricultural machinery for hire. He also acquired land, so that by the first years of the twentieth century he was farming about 1000 acres. Favor also built up a Seed Merchant business, which Gordon Parker[11] joined on leaving school in 1909. When war broke out, Gordon, four of his brothers and their mother were evacuated to North America, returning to Suffolk after peace resumed.

In 1921, Gordon Parker decided to set up his own business and with his father's financial backing, acquired the Etheridge business in Stoke Ferry. Gordon was thirty at the time. The business was in a very poor state following thirty years of indifferent management and the impact of World War I. He immediately moved into 'The Cobbles' and took over the management of the business. In 1927, Favor Parker died and Gordon Parker bought the premises from his father's estate for £1,200[12].

The firm had been trading as wine, wool, seed and coal merchants. Gordon Parker immediately abandoned the wine trade, concentrating on wool and seeds.

The two decades after the First World War were grim times to try to revitalise a business. Some desperate smallholders simply abandoned their land and disappeared, leaving problems for lawyers trying to establish ownership in more prosperous days. At this low point of agricultural depression, the newly established Favor Parker business brought some hope to farmers and some employment to the village.

Gordon Parker's first focus was on revitalising the wool business. He recounts how he did this[13]:

> *At the end of the First World War I made many enquiries among the small farmers with whom I did business … to see how the supply of wool could be improved.*

---

11 Favor's second son and middle child of seven.

12 Favor Parker paid a mere £875 for the Etheridge business, equivalent to c. £40,000 in 2018 (see Chapter 14). Its value had risen to c. £70,000 in 1927.

13 Personal letter to Doris Coates, late 1970s.

I used to motorcycle to Bradford each Monday and Thursday[14] to trade in the Wool Mart and spent some time there learning the trade for English Wool in Yorkshire. There I sold my Norfolk wethers' and hoggets' wool, 90% of in grease and the remaining 10% washed.

I bought Cotswold wool from Davis Brown of Marham, who kept a large pedigree flock and had a ram sale annually…

My Suffolk wools I mostly sold to a firm called Ebenezer in Chichester who were large buyers of black-faced wools, with a big business to the spinners.

When the Wool Marketing Board was created (in 1950), I was not allowed to speculate in wool and do my own grading. Nor was I allowed to purchase at the wool-sales…but had to sell my purchases from the farmers direct to the Wool Marketing Boards for a small commission. This did not appeal to me…

I asked Ted Chapman, the farmer, wool-merchant and fellmonger at Fakenham if he would take over my wool connection which I had worked up considerably. No price was asked. I gave it to him on condition that he looked after my farmer-growers.

Gordon Parker finished his letter with: *I then moved to grain, mostly distilling barleys.*
In the early years, the seed business was an important element of the business which reflected the pattern of farming at that period. With few fertilisers available, land was still cropped on a rotation system: grain, roots, a green crop and a leguminous crop, and sometimes a fallow rotation. There was a wide demand for high-quality seeds which could successfully be used in this system. Favor Parker soon had a thriving seed trade in Great Britain and also in Europe where Norfolk seeds were highly regarded.

The firm was also a coal merchant and dealer in grain, particularly barley. At first, transport was by horse-drawn vehicles and the railway, but in 1929 Favor Parker bought its first motor lorry, speeding up deliveries and making the business more competitive. It acquired storage silos at Wells-next-the-Sea and a quay and leased grain warehouses at King's Lynn.

As the use of fertilisers increased in the inter-war period, the pattern of farming evolved. As a result, the seed business declined and barley became

---

14 A round trip of over 300 miles.

the company's main product. Norfolk produced top-class brewing barley and with scores of private breweries across the county there was a ready market. Individual brewers sought the type of barley that would create their desired distinctive flavour. Favor Parker thrived, and barley was brought in from ever-increasing distances.

This required the development of a significant distribution system including shipping, road transportation and storage. In his notes, Gordon Parker says:

> *In part, as a result of the difficulties created by labour on the dock at King's Lynn, when Felixstowe Dock and Railway Company was offered to me one night (in 1951), I had a look at it the next day and bought it lock, stock and barrel the following morning and converted the large barley maltings into a grain storehouse.*

By the late 1960s the company exported one-third of all brewing barley sent to Europe via the port of Felixstowe.

Further evolution occurred with the rationalisation of the brewing industry, with most of the small brewers being taken over by giant industrialised companies in the 1960s and '70s. This reduced the demand for Norfolk barley for beer prompting the development of a feedstuffs industry to continue providing an outlet for local farms. By the end of the 1970s this had become the primary business with its own mill and storage silos, with associated concerns producing pigs and poultry. Favor Parker became a Limited Company in 1962 and Gordon's son Michael joined the firm.

The Lynn News and Advertiser Industrial Review of 1979 stated:

> *The Company employs about 200 people at Stoke Ferry and pumps an annual £1 million[15] into the locality through wages. It also deals wherever possible with local businesses.*

> *Favor Parker turns out on average 4,000 tons of animal feed a week from Stoke Ferry and this has reached 5,600 at peak times. The firm operates a large grain warehouse at Stoke Ferry, the 14,000-ton capacity Furlong warehouse which enables the firm to stockpile raw materials when market prices are advantageous and to ensure that there is always an available supply of good quality raw materials.*

---

15 Equivalent to c £5.5m in 2018.

Raw materials such as soya flour from Brazil, Herring meal from Scandinavia and wheat from the Continent are imported through Wells where there is another 4,000-ton storage warehouse. There is also a 7,000-ton warehouse at Methwold and the company receives on average 3,000 tons a week of local grain to make animal feed…

From Stoke Ferry, Favor Parker services Norfolk, Suffolk, Essex, Cambridgeshire, Huntingdonshire and South Lincolnshire but also serves customers as far afield as Yorkshire and Kent…

Gordon Parker died in 1980 and Michael Parker took over as Managing Director. In the 1980s and '90s Favor Parker continued to expand the capacity of the mill in Stoke Ferry, so that by the early 1990s it had reached 10,000 tons per week. Due to automation, local employment numbers steadily declined from the 200 stated in the article above.

In 1996 Favor Parker was acquired by Grampian Foods, a Scottish company. Their focus was more on poultry-processing operations elsewhere than the mill and no substantial investment was made during their ownership.

In 2008 Grampian Foods sold the mill to a Dutch-based international consortium, Vion Foods. Five years later, in 2013, the company was sold on again, this time to 2Sisters, a West Midlands based food conglomerate and hived off into a new company known as 2Agriculture which remains the owners in 2018.

The Parker family had owned Favor Parker for seventy-five years and grown a highly successful business in the heart of Stoke Ferry. It provided considerable employment opportunities for local residents, both in the mill and driving its very large fleet of vehicles. Additionally, over many decades, it also provided a powerful stimulus for local agriculture in the area, giving an outlet for grain (and in earlier times wool and seed producers).

In the last twenty years, the business has had three separate owners, although it has not been core to any one of them. Levels of employment have declined as automation increased. Meanwhile, the mill and its associated traffic have operated at considerable environmental cost to Stoke Ferry, which will be considered in more detail in the following chapter.

Sugar Manufacturing

Sugar production from sugar cane is known to date back several millennia and can be traced to the Bengal area of India. More recently, sugar consumed in England from the seventeenth to the nineteenth centuries came from British colonies in the West Indies. This was produced by slaves before the practice was abolished in 1833 and under almost as harsh conditions afterwards. The wealth of many English families, including some from Norfolk, was built on the sugar trade and slave ownership.

As stated earlier, at the outbreak of the First World War, almost 100% of sugar was derived from cane, and imported. One sugar beet factory had started production in 1912 at Cantley near Yarmouth in Norfolk, but its production was a tiny proportion of consumption. After the war, the government, wanting to reduce this heavy dependency on imports, encouraged the planting of sugar beet and sugar refining in England. In the 1920s a further seventeen independent processing plants were built, including one at Wissington, near Stoke Ferry.

In 1936, British Sugar Corporation was established to consolidate sugar production based on sugar beet. The relatively small existing plant at Wissington, was initially only served by the river and the Wissington Light Railway[16]. The first road connection was built by Italian prisoners of war during the Second World War, and it was not until the 1990s that a purpose-built road, avoiding the villages of Stoke Ferry, Wretton, West Dereham and Wereham was built.

When it opened, Wissington factory produced about 600 tons of sugar per day. After total re-engineering in 1971, it took in around 9,000 tons of beet every day from a 30-mile radius, made 950 tons of white sugar and had storage capacity for 72,000 tons of white sugar in six massive silos.

Since then, the plant has continued to expand until it is now the largest sugar refinery in Europe. The annual 'campaign', typically from mid-September to the following Easter, sees thousands of lorry-loads of beet delivered to the factory from a 50-mile radius. Annual intake of beet in 2018 is 3 million tons (c. 24,000 tons daily during the campaign) and annual production of sugar a massive 400,000 tons (c. 3,000 tons per day).

The impact on farming in the region is obvious – whereas many farmers have to travel considerable distances to deliver beet to the factory, those from Stoke Ferry and surrounding villages have a mere two to three miles of

---

16 See Chapters 5 & 7.

transport time and costs. The impact on local residents, at any rate before the direct road was built, was that hundreds of lorries laden with beet rumbled through the village and past Stoke Ferry School for months on end, not infrequently dropping the occasional sugar beet on to the road or pavement. There were many near misses.

***

Thus it can be seen that, during the twentieth century and continuing to this day, Stoke Ferry's dependence on both farming and agriculturally based industry continues, the natural evolution of businesses first founded in the village nearly 200 years ago.

Chapter Nineteen

The Bypass and After

Since the first edition of this book was published in 1980, a number of important projects have had a significant impact on Stoke Ferry. These include the opening of the bypass; building the new school, chapel and community centre; developing the Parish Plan; and the ongoing controversy of Stoke Ferry Mill. Each of these in its time aroused passion and enthusiasm and involved a great deal of hard work from local individuals and organisations. How beneficial all this hard work and investment has been to Stoke Ferry will be reviewed later.

Building the Bypass – Lifting the Siege?

For centuries, traffic to and through Stoke Ferry was a major driver of its prosperity. The presence of the river, its bridge, as well as later the wharf and the nearby railway terminus encouraged or required road traffic. As earlier described, the town of Stoke Ferry a number of inns and hotels round The Hill, catering for travellers on the road between King's Lynn, Thetford and southwards to London as well as visitors to the weekly market. It was a thriving community and the road was key to its prosperity.

However, as the twentieth century progressed, the amount of traffic on what was by then the A134 grew decade by decade. The size and weight of commercial vehicles continued to get bigger, so that the winding village street, with houses close alongside the road through the centre of the village, became increasingly more dangerous. Like many towns and cities throughout the country, Stoke Ferry was in need of a bypass.

Although the need had been obvious for many years, Norfolk County Council took the view that there were even greater priorities for their roads' budget elsewhere in the county. Up until that time, miraculously, there had been no fatalities in Stoke Ferry, despite the state of the road. Sadly, that changed in 1978 and, perhaps coincidentally, the Stoke Ferry bypass reached the top of the list.

In the summer of 1980, the County Council issued a consultation document[1], describing the need as follows:

> *The A134 is an important cross-country route linking Suffolk and Essex (including the ports of Felixstowe, Harwich and Ipswich) with King's Lynn and the north via the A17. The average traffic flow through Stoke Ferry throughout the year is about 6,000 vehicles a day. Heavy goods vehicles form about 40% of the total traffic flow during the winter sugar beet season, and about 30% at other times.*
>
> *The A134 passes through the centre of Stoke Ferry, and its route is narrow and tortuous. The heavy traffic makes life in the town noisy and unpleasant and has contributed to the deterioration of property along the route. The traffic is a source of danger to both people and property.*
>
> *A recent study has shown that over 80% of all traffic on the A134 in Stoke Ferry does not need to be in the town. A bypass would remove this extraneous traffic.*

The Council proposed five alternative routes, two running north of the village and three to the south. They were each just over two miles in length and required between 22 and 27 acres of land. The proposals noted how many houses would be within 100 metres of the new road (between 13 and 42) and how many houses would be relieved of some noise (between 80 and 110). The cost ranged from £1.39m - £1.61m[2].

The first element of the debate was between the southern and the northern routes. In general terms, the southern routes were slightly more expensive and used more land. More importantly, however, they cut between Stoke Ferry and Wretton, and ran quite close to the site designated for the new school.

Of the northern routes, the one chosen, known as the Northern Outer Route, left the A134 at the bottom of the hill at Whittington and crossed a new bridge over the Wissey. Oxborough Road and Boughton Road were closed, with access to the route being via The Furlong. This was widened to

---

1 This document was followed by a public meeting and exhibition describing the proposed routes. Interestingly, the Council refer to Stoke Ferry as a 'town' throughout the document.

2 Equivalent to £6.7m - £7.8m in 2018.

allow easy access to the Stoke Ferry Mill, meaning that heavy goods vehicles were still running in and out of the village in significant numbers[3].

Work finally commenced on the bypass and was completed for an official opening by the local M.P., Sir Paul Hawkins, on 8th August 1985. The main contractors were May, Gurney and Co. Ltd., from Norwich. The final road was 2.1 miles long, and there was additional construction to side roads of about one mile. The final cost was £2.65m[4].

The brochure for the opening event gave a brief history of Stoke Ferry, under the headline *Lifting The Siege.* The writer stated:

> *Many of those attending today's opening ceremony will have horror stories to tell of the traffic through Stoke Ferry; stories of pedestrians knocked down, walls demolished, and buildings so scraped and blackened by traffic that the residents either abandoned them or shut up their front rooms to live only at the rear.*

> *(Soon)…Stoke Ferry, once under siege by (the A134) will be just another small Norfolk Town. But for the townsfolk the bypass will have been an instrument of relief and an opportunity to restore to Stoke Ferry something of the elegance and prosperity of earlier times.*

Is that how it transpired?

The New School, Chapel and Community Centre

As with the bypass, Stoke Ferry waited a very long time for its new school. It was mooted as far back as the 1950s but appeared no nearer to fruition when George Coates retired in 1973, although a piece of land had been designated. Eventually, by the early 1980s the Norfolk Education Committee decided that Stoke Ferry had reached the top of its priority list and authorised construction of a brand-new purpose-built school.

The Head at the time, Chris Young, appointed at the beginning of 1974, had for some time been developing the school's community links. A Parent Teacher Association (PTA) was established in 1974 and, with the blessing of the Parish Council, the school started the community magazine *The Village*

---

3   See following section on Stoke Ferry Mill.

4   Equivalent to £8.1m in 2018, a predictable overrun of about 15% on the estimate for this route.

Pump[5]. He also acquired a prefabricated building to use as a school hall and built an extension to house a small library resources room.

Inspired by experience of Village Colleges in Cambridgeshire which included facilities for the whole community, Chris Young set about trying to create something similar in Stoke Ferry. A Community Association was formed, including representatives of all village organisations, including the Methodist Church, asking them to put forward their ideas for the purpose, role and design of the new building. In 1986, a Blueprint was produced of what was being proposed.

Under the heading *Planning for Future Needs* it stated:

> *Forty years ago, the facilities we use at present might have been considered adequate. Now, in common with many other village communities, there is an urgent need to provide premises which will not only serve the present needs of all age groups… but on a site which offers possibilities for future expansion.*

The ideas in the prospectus and the subsequent design of the school and community premises owe a great deal to the inspiration and drive of Chris and the Community Association, together with significant fund-raising to accomplish it. Among the proposed community uses of the new building were the following:

Daytime Use

- Community room – available as an everyday centre for retirees, including social area, dining facilities – from the school canteen - chiropody, bathrooms for the disabled and so on
- Community Office for use by the District Nurse
- Kitchenette and coffee bar
- Library

After-school Use

- Available for any local organisation to hire using flexible space – in all capacity for up to ten activities at any time

---

5   No longer produced by the school, *The Village Pump* started as a cyclostyled print magazine covering the six villages of the Wissey Valley now printed digitally. Editorial content is published on the village website.

- Facilities could be used for receptions, dances, dinners and other larger functions[6]
- Sports hall
- Changing rooms and showers
- Stage for plays and shows
- Library
- Extensive storage facilities for local organisations
- Rooms available for Adult Education

In addition, the Methodist Chapel in Stoke Ferry would close (with the chapel buildings sold for conversion to houses) and a Methodist Sanctuary set up in the Community Centre. This could be extended in to the Community Room and Main Hall for large gatherings. The Sanctuary would also be available for other small groups, choirs, discussions, or as a place of quiet contemplation.

Outside there would be a large playing field for summer and winter sports and a running track. It was also envisaged that the playground could be used as a hard tennis court, floodlit football area or an outdoor roller-skating rink.

The whole centre had the great benefit of up to 40 parking spaces on-site, unlike any of the other existing facilities – church, chapel or Village Hall.

This was an expensive endeavour. In all the cost was calculated at £130,000[7]. Of this £25,000 would come from each of the Community Association, Norfolk County Council and West Norfolk District Council. The balance would be provided by Social Services / Local Health Authority (£21,000), Methodist Church (£18,000) and the Sports Council (£16,000)[8].

The Community Association set about raising their share by having a 'Founder Member' scheme, with each Founder agreeing to donate or covenant £20 per year for five years (which also allowed reclamation of tax). By this means a large part of the £25,000 was secured. This was supplemented by a range of traditional fund-raising activities and events – coffee mornings, raffles, plant parties, jumble sales, half-marathon events and sponsored daredevil activities such as parachute jumping[9].

---

6 In September 1988, George and Doris Coates held a reception in the Community Centre to celebrate their Golden Wedding Anniversary.

7 Equivalent to c £450k in 2018.

8 In the event the Methodist Church, Social Services and the Libraries and Recreations Committee contributed £26,500 each to the project.

9 Congratulations to Margaret Duhig!

The funds were duly raised and the building constructed, incorporating all of the wide-ranging and innovative proposals outlined in the prospectus. Summer Term 1987 was the last to take place in the old school, bringing an end to education on James Bradfield's original piece of land after 168 years. To commemorate, the pupils and staff held a costume re-enactment, including the use of a pony and trap as a reminder *of all who had gone forth from those humble buildings, enriched by Mr. Bradfield's grateful bequest*[10].

The School and the New Methodist Sanctuary were dedicated on 26th September 1987 by The Rt. Rev. Gordon Roe, M.A. D.Phil., Bishop of Huntingdon and Chairman of the Ely Diocesan Education Committee and by The Rev. Richard Jones, M.A., B.D., Chairman of the East Anglia District of the Methodist Church. This reflected the ongoing Anglican nature of the school, as well as the presence of the Methodist Sanctuary – a truly ecumenical occasion.

On 16th July the following year, the School, incorporating the Stoke Ferry and District Community Centre was officially opened by the local M.P., Gillian Shephard[11].

The Parish Plan – 2007

In 2007, the Parish Council undertook a detailed survey of residents' opinions to assist in the development of a Parish Plan[12]. The results were used to supplement the earlier Village Design Statement and were intended to influence local government bodies and potential developers by articulating inhabitants' aspirations for the future of Stoke Ferry.

Questions covered a wide range of topics and some of the key responses are given below –

- **Should the development of new housing be encouraged in Stoke Ferry?**
  55% positive response if it falls within the Village Development Statement (45% felt this should concentrate on affordable housing, 30% on family housing and 21% on single person dwellings).
  19% felt that there should be no new houses

---

10 Chris Young, last Head of James Bradfield's 1819 School and first of the new school 400 metres down the road.

11 Gillian Shephard had become the M.P. for South West Norfolk in June 1987 and was to go on to Cabinet level ministerial posts, including Secretary of State for Education between 1994 and 1997.

12 277 questionnaires were returned, 62% of the total.

- **Use of local business by villagers**

Post Office	96%	Takeaways	66%
Corner Shop	89%	Pub	47%
Hardware Shop	73%	Hairdresser	24%
Garage	66%		

- **Should village industry[13] be encouraged to improve?**
  Overwhelmingly positive answers to this section (in other words strongly negative feedback to the company). Percentage saying this was *Important* or *Very Important*:

Air Quality	93%
Dust	92%
Traffic	90%
Noise	88%
Appearance of buildings	88%

Other questions concerned local policing (regarded by up to 80% as 'Poor'), public transport (generally reasonably positive, except for the timetable!) and healthcare provision (overwhelmingly positive). In the main, people were more positive than not about the appearance of the village (although about a third of people said that it was 'poor'). There were also questions about facilities for young people, with the results suggesting that more should be done for children of all age groups.

As a result of this work, the committee produced a set of key planning guidelines and an action plan. While it was recognised that more houses were needed in the village, these should be a mixture of housing types including low-cost starter homes. Building designs should be in keeping with 'local design tradition' and brownfield sites (of which there were a number in the village) should be utilised. Local infrastructure needed to be maintained (keep the Post Office and the existing shops and amenities) and improved (expand the school, set up medical facilities, add at least one more shop, provide adequate parking and improve recreational facilities). Imaginatively, there was also a proposal to create a Village Green.

Another section of the plan looked at improving local employment opportunities, rather than the village becoming a dormitory for those working elsewhere (in local towns such as Downham Market and King's Lynn or even

---

13 Grampian Foods was the owner of Stoke Ferry Mill at that date.

commuting to London). The aim would be to provide accommodation for start-up businesses although the main concern was that any new light industry should not be 'intrusive'.

This was a comprehensive set of ideas, the result of a great deal of hard work by the Parish Council and praised by the local M.P. of the time, Christopher Fraser, who wrote:

> *I believe that this Village Appraisal will make a very important contribution to the development of Stoke Ferry at a difficult time for the rural economy... I support the consensus that controlled, mixed development on brownfield sites is the preferred way forward...*

How much of this ambitious Plan has been implemented in the last ten years? And what would the results be today if the survey was repeated?

The Ongoing Controversy of the Mill

Chapter 18 outlined the history of Favor Parker in Stoke Ferry and the positive contribution that the company made to the area, both in terms of direct and indirect employment and its support for local agriculture.

However, there is another side to the story that has been the subject of controversy for the past fifty years. In simple terms, Stoke Ferry Mill, now owned by 2Agriculture, is the source of considerable ongoing harm to the village. As seen in the Parish Plan questionnaire cited above, an average of 90% of respondents said that this was an *Important* or *Very Important* issue.

How has this come about?

In the 1960s, Gordon Parker, using land that he had acquired decades earlier behind the listed buildings[14] that the company owned, built the processing mill at the very centre of the village. The large numbers of trucks required to service it had to use the village's narrow main road for access. Planning regulations introduced shortly after the construction of the mill would certainly have prevented it on a number of grounds – not least that, in 1967, the historic centre of the village was designated a Conservation Area.

Ever since, there have been various unsuccessful attempts by residents to persuade Favor Parker and its successor companies to close or move the mill to a more suitable location. In fact, the mill was significantly expanded in the 1980s and again in the 1990s. Trucks still require access and now use The

---

14 The Hall was listed in 1951, Cobbles in 1959 and Bayfields listed in 1972.

Furlong for this, reducing the benefits that the bypass was intended to produce.

However, the mill is not without local support. In its early days, it was a large local employer with about 200 residents working there (this has reduced to a mere handful as mechanisation and automation have reduced the manpower required). Even now, the mill employs a fairly large number of office staff and drivers. Longer-term residents tend to be more tolerant of the nuisance than those who moved to the village more recently, with the commonly expressed view that 'newcomers' knew the mill was there when they came, so should not complain now. The company set up a local liaison committee to discuss specific issues, the existence of which is likely to increase focus internally to addressing potential problem areas.

Despite all this, it is evident to anyone visiting the village that the mill is an eyesore which creates dust and noise to an unacceptable level at the centre of a community. The traffic created by the business is potentially dangerous and certainly has a negative impact on The Furlong. The apparent neglect of the listed buildings is amplified by the ruin of The Duke's Head on Stoke Ferry Hill (once the social centre of Favor Parker) which has been 'on the market' for the last twenty years and is now in a dangerous condition.

The present owner is 2Agriculture, an Edinburgh-based company whose website states that:

2Agriculture supply top quality feeds formulated to deliver consistent, high quality, value performance from feed mills located across the UK

The company also states that it has exciting plans for the future.

What is clear, however, is that sooner or later, Stoke Ferry Mill will become surplus to requirements for its present or future owners and be closed. At that time, this could be due to a number of factors – economies of scale, change in markets, a need for costly renovation or changing environmental regulations. One thing seems certain, however: it will close on its own terms and in its own time, not because of pressure from local residents, which it has comfortably withstood for the last fifty years.

***

So, how beneficial have these developments been to the Stoke Ferry? The simple answer is that, on the whole, the outcomes have been disappointing.

The bypass was successful in diverting all through traffic around the village. Together with the purpose-built road to the Wissington Sugar Factory, this has relieved the village of very large numbers of HGVs which have become larger and heavier[15] in the period since. Unfortunately, as mentioned above, the requirement for large HGVs to access Stoke Ferry Mill means that they still have to travel in and out of the centre of the village, albeit on a single route only.

The new school is thriving, and in 2019 celebrates the 200th anniversary of its founding by James Bradfield. Now known as All Saints Academy, it has around 100 pupils from Stoke Ferry and nearby villages and shares a Head with Shouldham School. Little Oaks pre-school was opened on the site in 1996 and moved into its own mobile classrooms in 2002.

Not so the Chapel and the Community Centre. Activity levels at the Community Centre never lived up to original expectations, while the Village Hall continued to provide a lower-cost alternative venue for many events. Adult education attracted very few participants and was discontinued after a year or so. Badminton sessions, dance classes and a youth club continued for a number of years but now only one group uses the community room on a regular basis. The District Nurse no longer has an office there, and the other facilities, having become disused, have been taken over by the school. The Methodist Sanctuary attracted a smaller and smaller congregation and was closed in 2015.

The Parish Plan was creative and inspirational. However, few of its recommendations have come to pass, and it is assumed that the Borough Council have merely filed it. The Station brownfield site is still awaiting development, few new starter homes have been built, there is still no medical centre in the village and few employment opportunities have been created by light industry. There is still no Village Green. While the number of houses has increased, there has been no investment to improve the infrastructure to support the growth[16].

Stoke Ferry Mill still dominates the heart of the village, with all the detrimental features listed above.

There is no active Church or Chapel, only one pub (and that more often than not closed) and no doctor's surgery. In practice Stoke Ferry never fully established itself as the town it was Chartered to be; now more than ever, it gives a strong impression of a *village*[17] in decline.

However, are there reasons to be hopeful about its future? The final chapter of this book looks at the positives.

---

15 The weight limit was increased from 40 to 44 tonnes in 2009.

16 For example, repeated attempts to set up a medical centre have not attracted Borough Council support.

17 It is a very long time since Stoke Ferry was referred to as a *town* and, as discussed in the introduction, it has few of the attributes usually associated with towns.

Chapter Twenty

Opportunity for Renaissance

Casual visitors to Stoke Ferry, or those who have not been to the village in many years could be forgiven for initially forming an unfavourable opinion of the place. Once a thriving market town with an annual fair, a number of busy hotels, an active church and chapel as well as large, successful businesses, much of the village now looks run down and neglected.

However, beneath the first impression there are reasons to be hopeful, even optimistic, about its future. Indeed, Stoke Ferry could be ready for a renaissance over the next decade.

Stoke Ferry Today

The population is growing. A number of small housing developments have been built over the last few years in several areas of the village. By 2017, there were 394 houses in total, an increase of over 30% since the turn of the twenty-first century. In the 2001 census, the population of Stoke Ferry was 896; by 2011 it had reached 1,020 and has continued to grow in the years since. People are moving in, most probably reducing the average age of the population.

The local economy, too, is doing well. The traditional employers may be declining, but there are more than 50 small businesses based in the village, many of them dependent on the very good broadband available. While many people commute for work to nearby towns or take the train to Cambridge or London, a large number spend their working lives in the village itself.

Unlike many rural communities, Stoke Ferry still has a Post Office – seen as vital to the community in the 2007 Plan. There is a long-established village shop (The Corner Shop on the corner of Oxborough Road). Thomas B.

Bonnett's (established in 1909 and still in the same family) was once the village forge and is now a specialist hardware and ornamental ironwork store. E.W. English and Son is a petrol station and car service centre, descendent of a petrol pump and bicycle repair shop set up on Lynn Road in the 1920s. The village boasts two takeaways, a hairdresser and a dog grooming parlour.

As described earlier, in 2019 All Saints Academy is celebrating the bicentenary of its foundation by James Bradfield with commemorative events.

Stoke Ferry has a playing field and football club which plays in a local league; there is a youth club and a Ladies Group.

There are three separate venues – the Village Hall, All Saints Church and All Saints Academy - capable of holding meetings, events, concerts, art exhibitions and some sports activities.

Politically, the current and former M.P.s[1] for the South West Norfolk constituency have actively supported Stoke Ferry events and are well-known senior politicians on the national stage.

The village also has a number of natural assets, as described in the Parish Plan:

> *Stoke Ferry has a wealth of natural amenities, including a common, a huge diversity of agricultural land, footpaths and bridleways. The River Wissey flows through (the village) and is fully navigable to small craft, including canal barges, a number of which are permanently moored near the village.*

The Village Pump is a highly regarded parish magazine covering the Wissey valley, which has been in print for over 35 years and the main content is now also available on the village website.

And Stoke Ferry is the home of The Strollers, a Rock 'n Roll band to rival The Stones – in longevity, if not in world-wide fame.

These are a number of the reasons to be hopeful about the future.

Stoke Ferry Tomorrow

So, what could trigger a true renaissance? The most significant change in the next few years is likely to be the inevitable closure of Stoke Ferry mill[2]. What happens next will define the village for decades to come.

---

1 Gillian Shephard, now Baroness Shephard of Northwold, was MP from 1987 to 2005 and sits in the House of Lords. Elizabeth ('Liz') Truss has been MP since 2010 and in September 2018 was Chief Secretary to the Treasury.

2 See Chapter 19. In September 2018 2Agriculture announced plans for closure in the coming years, providing 'suitable' planning permission is forthcoming for the sites of The Mill and the grain store on Furlong Road.

Stoke Ferry must prepare for this long hoped-for event and have a ready plan to restore and revitalise the area around the mill, which will undoubtedly be a costly venture.

What could be achieved using the site of the mill and the historic buildings on its estate?

- The Hall could become a museum, documenting and commemorating all of Stoke Ferry's rich history, as described in this book.
- The Cobbles, Bayfields and The Crown could be restored and converted to a small hotel, restaurant and maybe a craft centre.
- The Duke's Head and Parish Hall could become a small business centre with shared facilities and meeting rooms aimed at start-ups, particularly technology-based companies of all types.
- Other facilities on the mill site or the grain store site on The Furlong (or a purpose-built building) could be developed as small workshops for craft-based and specialist engineering companies or as artists' studios.
- There could be a farm-shop, artisan bakery or even a medical centre.
- The dream of a Village Green could be realised.
- On the remaining space a number of starter homes could be built, aimed solely at assisting local residents to stay in the village.
- Car parking space can be made available for all of these ventures.

The derelict old station site – awaiting development for decades – is large enough to contain something more inspirational than just another housing development.

What else could contribute to the renaissance?

The Stoke Ferry Festival of Sport and the Arts has a prestigious ring to it. As described above, the village already has three usable indoor venues, as well as a playing field and a river. These could facilitate a range of activities including:

Sporting Events

- Stoke Ferry triathlon
- Adult and children's sports day
- Water-based events such as swimming, kayaking, canoeing
- 5-a side football tournaments

- Netball matches
- Beach volleyball (if a beach can be created in Horse Guards Parade for the Olympics....)

Arts Events

- Music events – from The Strollers to String Quartets
- Art exhibitions
- Pottery, art or sculpture master-classes
- Literary events – visiting authors
- Creative writing classes

These are grand ideas, and there could be many more. They raise the obvious questions - is this what people want? where will the money come from? and who will lead the way?

During Stoke Ferry's illustrious history, the Harveys, Helshams, Micklefields, Winfields and Etheridges all made significant contributions to the wealth and well-being of the village. Most important of all was James Bradfield who brought education to the poor more than half a century before universal education was even on the political agenda.

Now, 200 years after the founding of Stoke Ferry School, who is going to provide the leadership and drive to bring about Stoke Ferry's revival and renaissance?

The opportunities are enormous. Another great campaign beckons. Perhaps it needs a slogan? With no apologies to anything similar elsewhere, I would propose:

Make
Stoke Ferry
Great Again

By Order of the Executors of the late A. E. R. MICKLEFIELD, Esq.

> ## STOKE FERRY and WRETTON
> ....NORFOLK.................

Particulars and Conditions of Sale of the
———— *Valuable Freehold* ————
Sporting and Agricultural Estate

— KNOWN AS THE —

Stoke Ferry & Wretton Estate

EXTENDING TO ABOUT

1457 ACRES.

Comprising in one Lot that portion of the Estate lying mainly between the Great Eastern Railway and the River Wissey, well known for the EXCELLENT SHOOTING and FISHING it affords, with TWO CONVENIENT FARM HOUSES and PREMISES, and about **648** ACRES OF ARABLE, PASTURE and WOOD LANDS, mostly with vacant possession. The remainder is divided into THREE HIGHLY PRODUCTIVE SMALL FARMS, THREE CAPITAL SMALL HOLDINGS, several lots of ACCOMMODATION ARABLE and PASTURE LANDS, EIGHT COTTAGES, TWO FAMILY RESIDENCES (*one with vacant possession*), FOUR VALUABLE SHOPS, in all **40** LOTS,

— WHICH —

Messrs. CRUSO & WILKIN

Will offer for Sale by Auction,
At the *TOWN HALL, DOWNHAM MARKET,*
On *FRIDAY 24th JUNE, 1921, at 2.30 o'clock in the Afternoon punctually.*

Further particulars may be obtained from the Auctioneers, King's Lynn ; or of

DONALD F. JACKSON,
VENDORS' SOLICITOR,
BANK CHAMBERS, KING'S LYNN.

Sale Notice for the auction of the Micklefield Estate in June 1921

Workers outside Whittington Maltings (c.1900)

Whittington Maltings under redevelopment as residential property today

From horses to horsepower

Darkins' cattle wagon, bought from the R.F.C. after WWI (c.1920)

Favor Parker's first lorry, carrying wool fleeces (1920s)

First village bus, introduced by the Darkins family (c.1920)

Catering for the motorist: English's motorbike repairs (above) and petrol station (below)

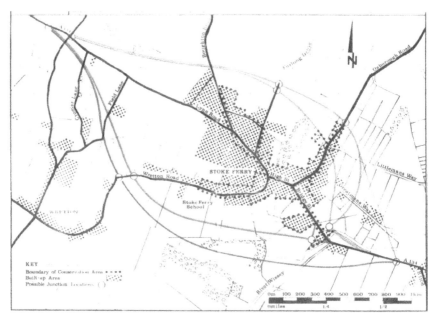

Proposed routes for the Bypass, 1980

Under construction

*Official Opening by Sir
Paul Hawkins, M.P. for
South West Norfolk
8th August 1985*

Stoke Ferry Mill, at the heart of the village

Neglected property belonging to Stoke Ferry Mill The former Duke's Head (above)
Bayfields - listed property (below left)
Cobbles - listed property (below right)

A village of delights, clockwise from top:
Listed telephone box
Park House
Peaceful River Wissey
New development at The Moorings
Lions at Trafalgar House

Important businesses

The Post Office

*Sea Star Fish Bar
Kebab and Pizza*

*Thomas B. Bonnett, agricultural engineers,
bespoke ironwork and retail shop*

Acknowledgements

This book was inspired by *Stoke Ferry – the Story of a Norfolk Village*, written by my mother, Doris Coates in 1980 and which included numerous pen and ink drawings by my father, George Coates, as well as some of his photographs. They had moved to Stoke Ferry (with me, aged 7) in 1953 for George to take up the post of Headmaster and spent the rest of their lives in the village. Doris died in 1998, George in 2002 and they are buried in the cemetery on Furlong Drove.

The task of researching and producing a book has changed beyond their imagination since it was first published. I inherited boxes of notes, letters and typed drafts of the original book, as well as many of the pictures that were used. My first and most important thanks and acknowledgement is, therefore, to Doris for the many years of patient research, correspondence and writing that went into creating *Stoke Ferry*.

I set out to reprint the original, perhaps including an additional chapter on the post-1980 period, but quickly discovered that there was much more to say. *A Farthing for the Ferryman* is the result. I have used much of Doris's research and some of her original writing, but essentially this is a very different book. Part 1 elaborates the pre-history and early history of Stoke Ferry and the region, while Part 2 describes its developing transport infrastructure. Part 3 puts into context how Stoke Ferry became a thriving commercial centre in the eighteenth and nineteenth centuries and in Part 4 I have undertaken further in-depth ancestry research on the notable families and individuals who have lived there, correcting some understandable errors in the original. In Part 5 I have written about the village since 1980 and its future prospects.

I would also like to acknowledge the help and support that I have received from many people in Stoke Ferry and beyond in preparing this new edition:

- George Coates, my late father, for his drawings and photographs
- Vicki Coates, my daughter, for her cover picture
- Anna Jackson, my daughter, for her ideas on structure, design and illustrations
- Louise Coates, my wife, for her endless support and encouragement, including many hours spent proof-reading and improving my original drafts as well as sourcing pictures
- Janet Taylor, for the loan of old postcards of Stoke Ferry, many of which I have used in the book. These were collected by her late husband, John Stocking, a contemporary of mine at Stoke Ferry School and in the Scouts
- Helaine Wyeth, for prompting me to undertake this work, and setting up a range of contacts and discussions for me
- Carol Nicholas-Letch, for allowing me to review the church records for Stoke Ferry
- Dr. Julia Poole of Wolfson College, Cambridge for providing me with extensive records and analysis of the Harvey family
- J. J. Heath-Caldwell, for further insights into the Harveys and for allowing me to use the picture of Dr. Henry Helsham
- Mary and Julian Cox, and their grandson Teddy Parker for information on Sergeant James Bent and use of his picture
- Kit Hesketh-Harvey for his enthusiastic support and permission to use his picture
- Beverley Phillips, for her information and insight into The Hall and the Favor Parker business and its successors
- Chris Young for his detailed reminiscences of Stoke Ferry School
- Dr. Patsy Dallas for reviewing my history and infrastructure chapters and providing valuable feedback and insights
- Arthur Fletcher of *Stoke Ferry Restored* for use of pictures from the site
- Pictures of Seahenge and Grime's Graves courtesy of Historic England
- All pictures not otherwise acknowledged above are from Adobe Stock, the author's personal collection or are in the public domain

I also had discussions with a large number of other current or past residents of the village, all of whom gave me valuable information and insights. These include Margery Bayfield, Marie Taylor, Sue Marler, William Buckenham, Jenny Elsey, Jane Cowieson, Katherine Howe and Eleanor Grimsey. Mally

Reeve provided a summary of the history of the village hall and Stephen Parker sent notes on his grandfather, Gordon Parker.

Thanks too to the contributors to Doris Coates's original work, especially F.T. Bush with whom Doris had an extensive correspondence. Many people wrote to her after the book was published, and these are referenced in the text where I have quoted from their letters.

Especial thanks to Ray Thomson for his encouragement and support throughout this project and to *The Village Pump* for their generous donation to the publication costs.

Doris and George Coates, with their blind collie 'Lady' c. 1959

Richard Coates grew up in Stoke Ferry and attended school there in the 1950s, before moving to Downham Grammar School and Jesus College, Oxford. After graduating, he spent his career in various aspects of human resource management in the UK, Netherlands and the Middle East.

Writer of business articles, industry reports and co-author (with daughter, Vicki) of three children's books, this is his first full-length publication. He recently edited his mother Doris Coates's Derbyshire-based books Tuppeny Rice and Treacle and Tunes on a Penny Whistle, republished by The Harpsden Press.

Richard now lives in Bath with his wife, Louise, and spends his time travelling and writing. He is also a partner in a community theatre in Dubai.

9 781999 823627